Narrative and the Triune Reality

Narrative and the Triune Reality

Examining Robert W. Jenson's Doctrine of the
Trinity with Reference to Eberhard Jüngel

by
Wai Luen Kwok

☛PICKWICK *Publications* • Eugene, Oregon

NARRATIVE AND THE TRIUNE REALITY
Examining Robert W. Jenson's Doctrine of the Trinity with Reference
to Eberhard Jüngel

Copyright © 2022 Wai Luen Kwok. All rights reserved. Except for brief quotations in critical publications or reviews, no part of this book may be reproduced in any manner without prior written permission from the publisher. Write: Permissions, Wipf and Stock Publishers, 199 W. 8th Ave., Suite 3, Eugene, OR 97401.

Pickwick Publications
An Imprint of Wipf and Stock Publishers
199 W. 8th Ave., Suite 3
Eugene, OR 97401

www.wipfandstock.com

PAPERBACK ISBN: 978-1-7252-5257-8
HARDCOVER ISBN: 978-1-7252-5258-5
EBOOK ISBN: 978-1-7252-5259-2

Cataloguing-in-Publication data:

Names: Kwok, Wai Luen, author.

Title: Narrative and the triune reality : examining Robert W. Jenson's doctrine of the trinity with reference to Eberhard Jüngel / by Wai Luen Kwok.

Description: Eugene, OR: Pickwick Publications, 2022 | Includes bibliographical references and index.

Identifiers: ISBN 978-1-7252-5257-8 (paperback) | ISBN 978-1-7252-5258-5 (hardcover) | ISBN 978-1-7252-5259-2 (ebook)

Subjects: LCSH: Jenson, Robert W. | Jüngel, Eberhard | Trinity | Christian Theology | Narrative theology | God—History of doctrines—20th century

Classification: BX8080.J44 K86 2022 (print) | BX8080.J44 (ebook)

05/10/22

Scripture quotations are from New Revised Standard Version Bible, copyright © 1989 National Council of the Churches of Christ in the United States of America. Used by permission. All rights reserved worldwide.

Contents

Preface | vii
Acknowledgements | x
List of Abbreviations | xi

Introduction | 1
    1. Jenson on the Problem of Contemporary Theology: The Meaninglessness of God   3
    2. Jenson's Narrative Trinitarian Theology, Reality, and Revisionary Metaphysics: Finding Meaning from Triune Reality in Temporality   8
    3. The Consistency of Jenson's Theology and the Importance of Theology of Language in Assessing Jenson   11
    4. Jenson's Narrative Trinitarian Theology and Related Intellectual Background   13
    5. Discussion on Jenson's Doctrine of the Trinity   36
    6. Chapter Outlines   37

Chapter 1: Jenson on Narrative and the Trinity: Biblical Narrative as Triune Story of Promise | 39
    1. Proper Names, Biblical Narrative, and the Trinity   39
    2. The Gospel and the Identification of the Trinity   41
    3. The Biblical Narrative in Both Testaments and the Identification of the Trinity   50
    4. Trinity, The Story of Promise, and Dramatic Coherence   56
    5. Summary   58

Chapter 2: How Does Jenson Advance Barth's Doctrine of the Trinity? | 59
    1. Enlightenment, Liberal Theology, Barth, and Jenson   60
    2. Jenson's Reading of Barth   66
    3. How does Jenson advance Barth's Doctrine of Trinity?   75

Chapter 3: Jenson's Theology of Language and Narrative Trinitarianism | 82

1. The Unintelligibility of Language about God and the Traditional Timeless Metaphysics 83
2. The Unintelligibility of Language about God, the Problem of Verifiability, and the Problem of Historicism 101
3. The Relation of Narrative, History, and Metaphysics: Jenson's Theology of Language and Ultra-realism 112

Chapter 4: Divine Temporal Infinity, Triune Persons, and the Problem of One and Three in Jenson's Trinitarianism | 117

1. Nicaea and Constantinople: "Of One Being with the Father" 118
2. The Cappadocians's Trinitarianism: μία οὐσία τρεῖς ὑποστάσεις 119
3. Jenson's Trinitarian Proposal and Revisionary Metaphysics: Analysis and Criticism 135

Chapter 5: God's Being Is in His Becoming: Evaluating Jenson's Doctrine of the Trinity with Reference to Eberhard Jüngel | 159

1. God's Being is in Becoming and the Knowledge of God 160
2. Knowledge of God and God's Being-as-object 165
3. God's Being is in His Becoming, Correspondence, and Analogy of Relation 175
4. Summary 188

Chapter 6: Theology of Possibility and Theology of Actuality: Two Approaches to the Contemporary Theological Problem of God's Death. A Further Evaluation of Jenson's Doctrine of the Trinity with Reference to Eberhard Jüngel | 190

1. The Death of God as Theological *Aporia* in Jüngel's Theology 191
2. The Doctrine of the Trinity as Jüngel's Solution for Contemporary Theological *Aporia* 204
3. Theological Response to "The Death of God": Jüngel's Possibility of God and Jenson's Actuality of God's Promise 233
4. Summary 247

Conclusion | 249

Select Bibliography | 251

Subject Index | 259

Preface

ROBERT W. JENSON CAN be considered to be one of the most important theologians in the late twentieth century. His academic career over decades generated an impressive volume of works. Though Jenson's oeuvre has diverse foci, they show that he has a consistent theological agenda throughout his writing. I divide Jenson's intellectual enterprise into three stages: (1) *Alpha and Omega, God after God, Religion against Itself,* and *The Knowledge of Things Hoped For* are the studies that lay down Jenson's perspective on theological language, the relationship of the doctrine of God and the western metaphysics, and his dissent from theologies after the nineteenth century (e.g., neo-Protestantism, liberalism, process theology, and existential theology). We may treat them as "prolegomena" of Jenson's theology. (2) *Story and Promise* is an important starting point of Jenson's own account of how to construct a theology without western metaphysics. In this book, the concept of God as a God of unsurpassed promise (an infinite God) emerges. (3) *Triune Identity, Christian Dogmatics, Visible Words, American Theologian,* and *Systematic Theology* are the works that aim to form a "holistic" account of the whole enterprise of Christian theology. They articulate the idea that originated in *Story and Promise* through a comprehensive reflection of historical, philosophical, and metaphysical aspects of the theology. In a personal email exchange with Jenson, he confirmed to me that, "Your periodization looks fine to me."

Therefore, I will treat Jenson's theology as a consistent whole. I argue that the core of his doctrine of the Trinity is a revisionary metaphysics. It asserts that the Trinity is identified *by and with* the biblical narrative. It is his answer to the problem of the death of God. This research argues that the biblical narrative is crucial to Jenson's doctrine of the Trinity because it denotes God's temporal reality. Biblical narrative is a story of God's promise. It *really* depicts the triune *reality*. I argue that Jenson attempts to establish the meaningfulness of theology through this integration of *language*, *reality*, and *time*. But it eventually makes God's story identical to the totality of historical reality. Because Jenson prioritizes metaphysics over linguistic communication, theological language may become God's monologue. I argue that because Jenson puts much emphasis on the temporality of being, he cannot satisfactorily articulate both the identity and the distinction of the immanent and economic Trinity. His doctrine of the Trinity is paradoxically in a risk of becoming modalist. He also fails to express the proper relation and distinction of Creator and created.

I suggest that we may revise Jenson's doctrine of the Trinity if we balance the temporality of being (i.e., as word-*event*) with the linguistic communicative dimension of being (i.e., as *word*-event). I argue that Eberhard Jüngel's assertion of God's word-event as God's coming to humanity and analogy of relation is helpful to this task. The metaphorical nature of theological language explicates how God and man interact in the linguistic-temporal-space. This interaction depicts the relation and distinction of God and humanity. Finally, I argue that Jüngel's theology is a theology of possibility while Jenson's a theology of actuality. It can enrich and strengthen Jenson's doctrine of the Trinity to meet the challenge of the death or meaninglessness of God.

The present book is originated from my doctoral dissertation at King's College London. When Prof. Jenson was invited to deliver a series of lectures at China Graduate School of Theology in 2003, as a junior research officer, I had been asked to be an escort of Prof. Jenson in Hong Kong. I am fascinated by his wisdom and theological depth through personal contact and dialogue. The experience affirmed that I am researching and engaging with one of the greatest theologians in the Twentieth Century. When I have graduated from King's, he encouraged me to get the dissertation published. But, after I have come back to Hong Kong, I was fully occupied by the rapid growing mainland China ministry and set the whole publication project aside for years. I hope that it is not too late to share my analysis as a monograph.

I am most grateful to the late Prof. Colin Gunton, Dr. Stephen Holmes, Prof. Oliver Davies, and Dr. Paul Janz for supervising my research with enthusiasm and critical care. My profound thanks to the late Prof. John Webster and Dr. Susannah Ticciati for examining my project and endorsing my analysis. I am deeply grateful for Prof. Paul Fiddes's suggestion of publishing it with Wipf and Stock. I wish also to thank Rev. Wilfred Ho for his discussions and support throughout my research. I am indebted to Dr. Douglas Knight for his comments and correction of my English. I would like to acknowledge the Langham Foundation, Alliance

Bible Seminary, King's College Theological Trust, Mrs. Tat-chi Kung, and the brothers and sisters of Tsing Yi Alliance Church for their financial and spiritual support. I am especially grateful to my family for their continuous support and love for me.

Acknowledgements

Parts of the Chapters 1, 2, 5, and 6 have been appeared in two articles of mine:

1. "The Narrative and the Triune Reality in the Theology of Robert Jenson: A Post-Karl Barth's Development." *Yearbook of Chinese Theology* 5 (2019) 3–27.

2. "Word, Event and Communion: Trinity in Robert Jenson and Eberhard Jüngel's Thought as Seen in Their Interpretation of Barth." *Sino-Christian Studies: An International Journal of Bible, Theology & Philosophy* 14 (2012) 27–58.

Abbreviations

Works by Jenson

A&O	*Alpha and Omega: A Study in the Theology of Karl Barth*
AT	*America's Theologian: A Recommendation of Jonathan Edwards*
GAG	*God after God: The God of the Past and the God of the Future, Seen in the Work of Karl Barth*
KTHF	*The Knowledge of Things Hoped For*
OTH	*On Thinking the Human: Resolutions of Difficult Notions*
RAI	*A Religion against Itself*
S&P	*Story and Promise: A Brief Theology of the Gospel about Jesus*
ST1	*Systematic Theology, vol. 1: The Triune God*
ST2	*Systematic Theology, vol. 2: The Works of God*
TI	*The Triune Identity: God according to the Gospel*
UG	*Unbaptized God: The Basic Flaw in Ecumenical Theology*
VW	*Visible Words: The Interpretation and Practice of Christian Sacraments*
"The Logic"	"The Logic of the Doctrine of the Trinity"
"Triune God"	"The Triune God"

Other

CD	Barth, *Church Dogmatics*
GBB	Jüngel, *God's Being is in Becoming: The Trinitarian Being of God in the Theology of Karl Barth*
GMW	Jüngel, *God as the Mystery of the World: On the Foundation of the Theology of the Crucified One in the Dispute between Theism and Atheism*
KD	Barth, *Die Kirchliche Dogmatik*.

Introduction

KARL BARTH BELIEVED THAT the doctrine of the Trinity is the distinguishing way that Christians know, believe in, and talk about God.[1] However, since the Reformation the doctrine has become more of an embarrassment to Christians than a source of pride. In *The Conflict of the Faculties*, Immanuel Kant claimed that: "The doctrine of the Trinity, taken literally, has no practical relevance at all, even if we think we understand it; and it is even more clearly irrelevant if we realize that it transcends all our concepts. Whether we are to worship three or ten persons in the Deity makes no difference."[2] Schleiermacher also taught that the Christian faith would be the same with or without the "transcendental fact" of Trinity.[3] Claude Welch lamented that the Trinity was a "second-rank doctrine" in *The Trinity in Contemporary Theology* in the 1950s.[4] In the 1980s, Moltmann wrote that still "[m]any people view the theological doctrine of the Trinity as a speculation for the theological specialists, which has nothing to do with real life. That is why modern Protestants like to content themselves with the young Melancthon's maxim: 'We adore the mysteries of the Godhead. That is better than to investigate them.'"[5] Though Cunningham notices there is a "renaissance" of trinitarian theology in the twentieth century, he admits that the doctrine "remains esoteric and irrelevant" for many people. In his view, these difficulties stem from the "cryptic formulas" of the doctrine, and the lack of significance of trinitarian reflection for day-to-day Christian lives.[6]

---

1. Barth, *CD* 1/1:301.
2. In Kant, *Religion and Rational Theology*, 264.
3. Schleiermacher, *The Christian Faith*, 741.
4. Welch, *The Trinity in Contemporary Theology*, 45, 48.
5. Moltmann, *The Trinity and the Kingdom of God*, 1.
6. Cunningham, *These Three are One*, ix.

This research investigates the doctrine of the Trinity in the work of Robert W. Jenson. Jenson defends the doctrine of the Trinity as the proper means of relating divine narrative and reality, and offers "proposals for its reform and further development."[7] Jenson's effort can be regarded as part of, what Christoph Schwöbel believes, a general "renaissance" and "revival" of the doctrine of the Trinity. This is not merely a restoration of past teaching but intends to solve contemporary theological problems by exploring possibilities that have been neglected in the history of doctrine.[8] It is a "renaissance" that attempts to make the doctrine no longer "esoteric and irrelevant."

Jenson places very great emphasis on the temporality of God's being. It is my thesis that Jenson overburdens the concept of the temporality of God. I will argue that Jenson cannot simultaneously hold all the following three assertions, as he intends: (1) the immanent/economic distinction of the Trinity—the transcendence and freedom of God; (2) the identity of immanent and economic Trinity—economic Trinity *is* immanent Trinity and vice versa; (3) the relatedness and distinction between Creator and creatures—the communion of God and human. The work argues that Jenson overemphasizes God's temporality because he believes it is a solution to the contemporary problem of the meaninglessness of God-talk.

Jenson argues that his doctrine of the Trinity is a *narrative* Trinitarianism. This work argues that if we balance Jenson's concern for temporality of being (word-*event*) with the linguistic and hermeneutical dimensions of being (*word*-event), some of the difficulties faced by Jenson's doctrine of the Trinity can be overcome. This work will suggest that the justification for revising Jenson's trinitarian theology can be found in Eberhard Jüngel. Jüngel's conception of God's word as God's coming, along with his understanding of analogy, and his theology of possibility offer the correction that Jenson's trinitarian theology needs.

In this introduction, I will clarify the concepts and background that this research depends on. First, I will show that the meaninglessness of the triune God is the problem to which Jenson's narrative Trinitarianism responds and that he identifies traditional timeless metaphysics as the origin of the problem of the meaninglessness of God. Secondly, I will delineate the defining characteristics of Jenson's narrative Trinitarianism, which he terms revisionary metaphysics. Thirdly, I will clarify why his writings can be considered as a consistent whole, and why assessing his trinitarian theology through the concept of word-event is significant. Fourthly, I will discuss the

---

7. Jenson, *TI*, xii.
8. Schwöbel, "Introduction," 12.

problem of the meaninglessness of speaking about God, and the concepts of word and event within a wider intellectual background. Fifthly, a brief review of current research on Jenson will be offered. Finally, I will set out the sequence of the chapters of this book.

1. Jenson on the Problem of Contemporary Theology: The Meaninglessness of God

Robert W. Jenson is regarded by Wolfhart Pannenberg as "one of the most original and knowledgeable theologians of our time."[9] John Webster acclaims his *Systematic Theology* as "the most striking and ecumenically potent English-language statement of Christian theology of the last fifty years."[10] Right from the beginning of his theological career, Jenson realized that contemporary Christian faith is threatened by a loss of credibility. In this secular modern society, the Christian religion "survives only as a performance which is in fact irrelevant to most of the rest of what we think and do. Yet it must pretend to be the guide and motivation of all that we think and do. It survives, necessarily, only as a pretense."[11] This is the situation in which modern society talks of a secular or nonreligious gospel, and of "the death of God."[12] Jenson's entire career has been marked by a concern for the credibility of Christian theology in this situation. "Very early in my theological reflection I was struck with the secularizing impact of the gospel." He believes that the consequence of this "secularizing impact" is "nihilism"—the triumph of "nothingness," a world with "hope for nothing."[13] In Jenson's view, the "current vocabulary refers to the period under this threat as postmodern."[14]

1.1 The Root of the Problem: Positing God as the Timeless Being of Classical Theism

In *Alpha and Omega*, the published version of his doctoral dissertation, Jenson describes the statement "Christianity is an historical religion" as the "cliché" of modern theology. This cliché points to the central problem

---

9. Pannenberg, "A Trinitarian Synthesis," 49. Jenson's theological life can be found in Braaten, "Robert William Jenson," 1–9.
10. Webster, "Systematic Theology after Barth," 258.
11. Jenson, *RAI*, 21. See also, Jenson, *GAG*, 6.
12. Jenson, *RAI*, 11.
13. Jenson, *ST1*, ix, 220.
14. Jenson, *ST1*, ix.

of modern theology: "how Jesus Christ, a past event, can be the decisive reality in our present life?"[15] In Jenson's view, the relation of Jesus Christ to our present life has become the modern theological problem because of the demise of classical theology.[16] Traditional or classical theology and premodern culture presumed that Goodness, Beauty, and Truth, were timeless realities. They were the "bedrock" of reality and provided the norms and meaning of human life. They were the perfection and immortality that the premodern human tried to attain. The history of Jesus Christ was thus "the place where man, who lives in time, might be united with nonhistorical timeless realities for which he already sought."[17] In this schema, the history of Jesus Christ as a past event is related to our present life because it serves as the point through which we can gain access to timeless ultimate realities and our own perfection. But the modern human no longer lives in such a schema. Now, modern theology has no recourse to sources of meaning beyond time and cannot assume timeless realities are the ultimate ground of existence. It must deal with the question of how we may find our meaning in Jesus Christ if "Christianity is an historical religion." Jenson does not deal with the "cliché" by reaffirming a timeless and transcendental divine reality. He urges that "we must look, not to the timeless, but to history" for the final nature of reality.[18] It is this concern that motivates Jenson to find his answer in the doctrine of the Trinity.[19]

1.2 Trinitarianism as an Answer to the Contemporary Theological Challenge

It is Jenson's contention that only a revival of trinitarian faith can help the Christian church meet the challenge.[20] He tells us that in our situation the question "who is God?" is primary, because the question "is there any god at all?" is now a religious and intellectual triviality. The relevance and significance of the Christian faith, which can counter the threat of nihilism, can

---

15. Jenson, *A&O*, 13.

16. In this early work, Jenson states that "This vague term lumps patristic, medieval, and Protestant scholastic theology together." Jenson, *A&O*, 13. In some of his work, he refers to the classical theology as traditional theology or inherited theology. For examples, see Jenson, *TI*, 132; Jenson, *AT*, 6; Jenson, "The Kingdom of America's God," 54; Jenson, "The Logic," 249.

17. Jenson, *A&O*, 14.

18. Jenson, *A&O*, 17.

19. For a helpful and initial sketch of the continuity of Jenson's thought, see Yeago, "Catholicity, Nihilism, and the God of the Gospel," 18–23.

20. Jenson, *TI*, 186.

only be found when we specify who or which God we are talking about, and whether that God is "a threat or a promise, a solution or a conundrum."[21] Christians's answer to this question must be trinitarian. The answer must point to the "Father," "Jesus," and the "Spirit." He insists that "In a religiously plural age . . . [t]hose who suppose Christianity to be true, and therefore wish to answer so, must in our time relearn the answer's depths and subtleties; that is, they must relearn—and carry further—Trinitarian piety and thought."[22] Since trinitarian theology has been the concern of his entire career, this research will set out the coherence of his theological system.

Jenson's approach to the issue of the relevance of Christian faith in contemporary society is interesting precisely because it is trinitarian. Since the Enlightenment, the doctrine of Trinity has been marginal to modern theological reflection. He is well aware of this. In one of his early works, *God after God*, he states:

> The doctrine of the Trinity is . . . one of our most clearly moribund inheritances from the past, moribund to the point where bishops can go about denying it without so much as needing first to inform themselves about what it says. In the piety even of most traditional churches and believers, it is safe to say that the triune character of God plays no role at all.[23]

But Jenson insists that this doctrine is crucial. Trinitarian theology is the reflection internal to the church's labor on her mission of speaking the gospel.[24] The gospel can be summarized in the single sentence: "The God of Israel has raised his servant Jesus from the dead."[25] Therefore, "The whole task of theology can be described as the unpacking of this sentence in various ways."[26]

1.3 Gospel Narrative, Triune Reality, and "Vicissitudes" of the Trinitarian Doctrine of God

Jenson believes the gospel induces Christians to identify their God through a narrative that uses the tense-structure of ordinary language. In this

---

21. Jenson, *TI*, xi.
22. Jenson, *TI*, xi–xii.
23. Jenson, *GAG*, 96.
24. Jenson, *ST1*, 11.
25. Jenson, *ST1*, 4; also in Jenson, *TI*, 21; Jenson, "Triune God," 99.
26. Jenson, *TI*, 21.

narrative, we can identify the gospel's God as a triune God. He[27] bears the proper name of "Father, Son, and Spirit."[28] But the God of gospel is not immune to time. He is identified *by* and *with* the gospel narrative. The gospel narrative obliges us to accept that we encounter God in time.[29]

Jenson contends that the problem of current trinitarian reflection is the result of the "vicissitudes" the doctrine has experienced since Augustine: it is not the doctrine itself that is problematic.[30] For western theology, there is another force pulling theological reflection away from the gospel narrative. This force is Greek philosophy. Jenson finds the Western heritage of Greek theology and philosophy moves in a direction different from the gospel narrative.[31] Greek theology or philosophy posits a timeless divine being, the past, present, and future of which are the same.[32] This position leads to two beliefs: (1) Timeless and temporal realities are different kinds of being. They are defined by mutual negation, and all meaning and value are located in timeless being.[33] (2) The Deity is conceived as impassible while creatures are passible. We are in time, and God is not, and so all creatures are threatened by loss of meaning. Thus, "the religion of late antiquity was a frenzied search for mediators, for beings of a third ontological kind *between* time and Timelessness, to bridge the gap."[34]

Hence, when the gospel came to the Hellenic World, an unavoidable confrontation between the faith and the Olympian religion occurred. Jenson does not think Christianity should avoid this confrontation, as the gospel is to be proclaimed to all, Greeks included. The gospel had to be brought to the Hellenic world and is the proper answer to Hellenism's chief religious problem, the distance of God.[35] Jenson shows how the initial confrontation between Christianity and Hellenism took place within Hellenism—the "christianizing of Hellenism." The pastors and teachers of the early church who witnessed this confrontation of Greek "Deity" and the God of Israel were Hellenists who had to find how to be Christian and to follow the God

---

27. Jenson insists on using "masculine" gender pronouns to identify God the Father. So, in this research I follow his practice. Ref. to Jenson, "The Father," 95–109; Jenson, *TI*, 13–16; Jenson, "Triune God," 94–95.

28. Jenson, *TI*, 9–13; also in Jenson, "Triune God," 92–94.

29. Jenson, *ST1*, 59–60; Jenson, "A Call to Faithfulness," 91.

30. Jenson, *TI*, 131; Jenson, "Triune God," 149.

31. Jenson, *TI*, 57; Jenson, "Triune God," 115. We should also note that, for Jenson, Greek philosophy indeed is a theology. Jenson, "The Logic," 245; Jenson, *ST1*, 20.

32. Jenson, *TI*, 25; Jenson, "Triune God," 102.

33. Jenson, *TI*, 60; Jenson, "Triune God," 117.

34. Jenson, *TI*, 60–61; Jenson, "Triune God," 117.

35. Jenson, *TI*, 61.

of the gospel.³⁶ The trinitarian discourse of "one substance in three persons" and "of one being with the Father" was the outcome of this confrontation. Jenson reminds us that the meaning of this formula is the result of both the internal conceptuality of biblical proclamation and its confrontation with Hellenic religion and reflection.³⁷

In Jenson's view, the Cappadocian fathers did a remarkable work in articulating the trinitarian formula as one *ousia* and three *hypostases*. He argues that the Cappadocians made good use of Hellenistic terminology to express the biblical teaching of the triune God, without allowing this biblical teaching to be subverted by Hellenism.³⁸ However, the Hellenic interpretation of God was never fully overcome. For all his extraordinary achievement, it was Augustine who made divine timelessness axiomatic for subsequent Western theology.³⁹ Jenson complains that from Augustine until very recently, the Western-Christian doctrine is an alliance of Greek philosophy and Christian gospel.⁴⁰ The Christian God is thus conceived along the lines of Greek metaphysics. It is this alliance, Jenson believes, that makes the doctrine of the Trinity abstract and remote from the religious practice of believers. "From Augustine on, the doctrine of the Trinity has tended to become increasingly a 'revealed Mystery.'"⁴¹

In the Enlightenment this alliance of Western philosophy and Christian theology breaks apart.⁴² This means that Christian theology must find new terms in which to give an account of itself. Jenson terms this development in philosophy the "death of metaphysics." Analytical philosophy and Nietzsche's anti-metaphysical metaphysics question the meaningfulness of talk of metaphysical entities. From another direction, the dialectical theology of Karl Barth, Rudolf Bultmann, and Friedrich Gogarten assaulted the classic synthesis's last incarnation, in which the metaphysical God could be understood as our subjectivity's point of unity with itself.⁴³ Thus the Augustinian synthesis of Christian gospel and Greek philosophy has collapsed. The result is the contemporary conviction that the God in which theology and philosophy once believed is now *dead*.

---

36. Jenson, *TI*, 62; Jenson, *GAG*, 19.
37. Jenson, *TI*, 57.
38. Jenson, *TI*, 103–14; Jenson, "Triune God," 135–40.
39. Jenson, *TI*, 116–31; Jenson, "Triune God," 141–47.
40. Jenson, "The Logic," 245.
41. Jenson, *TI*, 131; Jenson, "Triune God," 149.
42. Jenson, "The Logic," 248.
43. Jenson, "The Logic," 248. This so-called classic synthesis's last incarnation refers to liberal theology since Schleiermacher.

2. Jenson's Narrative Trinitarian Theology, Reality, and Revisionary Metaphysics: Finding Meaning from Triune Reality in Temporality

In reply to this challenge, Jenson tells us that there are three ways to attempt a solution. (1) To carry on the tradition of metaphysical theology, now freed from any obligation to take notice of the gospel. Jenson lists Robert Neville and Wilhelm Weischedel as its examples. (2) To promote a non-metaphysical theology that makes no ontological assertions. Theology is then only analysis of the empirical event of Jesus. Paul van Buren and Dorothee Sölle are examples of this approach. (3) To promote a revisionary metaphysics. The third is the alternative that interests Jenson.[44] In Jenson's view,

> [The efforts of revisionary metaphysics are] vigorous attempts to pick up where the Cappadocians left off, directly and innovatively to pursue the metaphysical enterprise, intentionally as explication of the gospel's talk about God and on the explicit assumption that traditional metaphysical doctrines, as the theology of another religion, have no inherent authority.[45]

For Jenson's revisionary metaphysics, the first step "is to free trinitarian doctrine from captivity to antecedent interpretation of deity as timelessness."[46] The critical move to free the church from this kind of captivity is to assert that God must be "identified *by* and *with* the particular *plotted sequence of events* that make the narrative of Israel and her Christ."[47] Thus the key to identifying the Christian God as triune God is the biblical narrative. In Jenson's words, "the phrase 'Father, Son, and Holy Spirit' is simultaneously a very compressed telling of the total narrative by which Scripture identifies God."[48] The biblical narrative that reveals the triune God is thoroughly temporal: "The specificity of the triune God is not that he is three, but that he occupies each pole of time as a *persona dramatis*; precisely this characterizes Israel's story of God."[49] Thus, Christians identify the triune God by and with biblical narrative and this means they identify him by a specific temporal-spatial framework. Because Western Trinitarianism presents the "immanent" and "economic" Trinity as "two distinct sets of trinitarian relations," the doctrine of Trinity finally "loses

---

44. Jenson, "The Logic," 248.
45. Jenson, "The Logic," 249. See also Jenson, "Response," 230.
46. Jenson, *TI*, 138; Jenson, "Triune God," 154.
47. Jenson, *ST1*, 60. Italics mine.
48. Jenson, *ST1*, 46.
49. Jenson, *ST1*, 89.

its original history-of-salvation meaning, and indeed threatens to lose all meaning of any kind."[50]

Jenson's discussion reminds us that his attempt at a "revival" or "revitalization" of the doctrine of the Trinity is not limited to the application of "trinitarian facts" to daily Christian life. *For Jenson, the identifying narrative inevitably becomes a reflection of divine reality too*: "The revelation to Israel and the church . . . claims to be not a pointer to deity but God's personal self-introduction: 'I am the Lord your God.' God is not only identified by Exodus and Resurrection; he is identified with them."[51] This is the reason Jenson terms his account of divine reality "revisionary metaphysics."[52] In this way, it is a kind of *realism*.[53]

Why does Jenson refer to his project as a metaphysical quest, albeit "revisionary," in the era of the "death of metaphysics"? He tells us that because the logical positivists took the physical sciences as the paradigm of descriptive legitimacy, they regarded facts that are unverifiable as bogus and misleading.[54] They labeled such facts, in their terms, communicated in the so-called "material mode"[55] of discourse, "metaphysical." Jenson insists that theology must also be what the positivists derided as "metaphysics," because it claims to know elements of reality not directly available to the empirical sciences or their modes of cognition.[56] But he rejects the positivists's view of metaphysics. He contends that later analysts, led by Wittgenstein, "became aware that there are many language acts besides describing, that there are many games with words besides the one played by scientists . . . They found the positivists' catch-all category of other-than-descriptive entirely

---

50. Jenson, *TI*, 125.
51. Jenson, *ST1*, 60.
52. Jenson, "The Logic," 248–49; Jenson, "Response," 230.
53. For a definition of realism, I follow Andrew Moore: "When Christian faith is subjected to philosophical scrutiny, typical realist claims are that (1) God exists independently of our awareness of him and of our will, but that (2) despite this, we can know him, and that (3) human language is not an inadequate or inappropriate medium for truthful speech about God." Moore, *Realism and Christian Faith*, 1–2.
54. Jenson, *ST1*, 19.
55. According to Rudolf Carnap, sentences of "the material mode of speech" are "pseudo-object sentences." They "are formulated as though they refer (either partially or exclusively) to objects, while in reality they refer to syntactical forms, and, specifically, to the forms of the designations of those objects with which they appear to deal." See Carnap, *The Logical Syntax of Language*, 285. Jenson gives a "classical" example of "material mode of speech": "every event has a cause." Jenson, *ST1*, 19.
56. Jenson, *ST1*, 20.

too undifferentiated."⁵⁷ Therefore, *the realist claim of Jenson's doctrine of the Trinity induces him to term it metaphysics.*

Jenson recognizes that theology is metaphysics for two other reasons: theology is a universal hermeneutics and grammar. According to him, these are both metaphysics in their own sense.⁵⁸

For Jenson, theology is an act of interpretation. Christians receive the gospel through a chain of witnesses. Each generation reflects how to continue the proclamation of the gospel and Christian life that they received from the generation before them. In Jenson's summation, "Thinking located at such a place in life, where past hearing turns to new speaking, is what twentieth-century usage has called 'hermeneutics.'"⁵⁹ This kind of hermeneutics is *universal* for theology. It must apply to, and provide an interpretation for, every aspect of life. When this is done, theology becomes metaphysics.

Because theology is hermeneutics, Jenson believes that it is a "second order discourse." For Christians, this "second order discourse" is their grammar. Statements of creed and doctrine express the rules of Christian discourse. They are the grammatical rules of Christian life and thus of the Christian community. Subsequently theology can also be described as the attempts of theologians to identify these rules. *For Jenson, this Christian "grammar" is no intra-linguistic game. He insists that the authors and teachers of doctrine believe the Christian "grammar" is about an extra-linguistic entity.*⁶⁰ This makes it a "material mode" of discourse so this universal hermeneutics cannot avoid the label of metaphysics. Theology is also a universal grammar. Jenson traces the term "grammar" back to find that Aristotle labeled his own attempts to discern a universal grammar *The Metaphysics*.⁶¹

Jenson's Trinitarianism is *metaphysical* because it insists that theology not only *really refers to* but also *identifies with* divine reality. God's *reality* is God's *word-event*. Jenson asserts that, as the knowledge of God, theology is possible because God speaks. God's speech is no empty word. When he speaks, creatures are created and his promise is actualized. His word does things. For this reason, we can say that God's word is an event: "All events and all words are 'word-events'; there is no event that does not speak and no meaning that does not occur."⁶² *The object of enquiry for revisionary metaphysics is the word-event of God.*

57. Jenson, *KTHF*, 14.
58. Jenson, *ST1*, 20–21.
59. Jenson, *ST1*, 14.
60. Jenson, *ST1*, 18.
61. Jenson, *ST1*, 21.
62. Jenson, *ST2*, 160.

God's word-event, as the trinitarian metaphysics, is *revisionary* because its realist claim is not based on timeless eternity or logical positivism, but on a communal hermeneutics. Jenson's narrative Trinitarianism is a sophisticated attempt to articulate divine *reality* by God's narrative. As our analysis proceeds, we will find that at its core it is thoroughly idealist.[63] I will argue that because Jenson places so much emphasis on the temporality of being, his Trinitarianism finally collapses into a process of dialectics within a "supreme" consciousness. I will argue that if God's triune reality is a word-event, this implies that he should emphasize both the ontological claim and the linguistic-communicative function of God's word. *The fundamental problem of Jenson's theology is that the linguistic-communicative dimension of God's word-event is eclipsed by his narrative trinitarian metaphysics.*

To summarize: Jenson's trinitarian or revisionary metaphysics is his proposed answer to the contemporary theological challenge of the death of God. It is a *revisionary* account of divine *reality*.[64] It attempts to conceive human life, the economic Trinity and the immanent Trinity as united. He argues that with this metaphysics we can *meaningfully* and *really* speak of the Christian God in the contemporary world. There are four defining characteristics of Jenson's revisionary metaphysical-narrative Trinitarianism. It: (1) has a valid claim to the knowledge of God through biblical narrative; (2) avoids assuming a dichotomy of the timelessly eternal and temporal and contingent, or between spirit and material; (3) is hermeneutical but universally regulative; (4) is God's word-event. These characteristics show that both word and event are important components of Jenson's doctrine of the Trinity. In this work, I will argue that Jenson fails to hold the balance as his proposal proceeds.

3. The Consistency of Jenson's Theology and the Importance of Theology of Language in Assessing Jenson

Before we go further, one may note that in analyzing the work of someone who has been writing as long as Jenson has, one must exercise some caution in mixing earlier and later writings together. I argue that Jenson's theology can be considered as a consistent whole. David Yeago suggests that Jenson's writings show "an impressive continuity of theme and purpose, a persistent

---

63. Here, one should not think realism and idealism as irreconcilable with each other. As William P. Alston puts it: "And idealists, so called, do not deny any reality to the physical world, abstract entities, space and time, and the like. They only insist that these items are somehow mental." "Absolute idealist metaphysics is in no tension with a realist conception of truth." See Alston, *A Realist Conception of Truth*, 75, 79.

64. Jenson, "The Logic," 248–49; Jenson, "Response," 230.

exploration of certain fundamental convictions over thirty years."[65] Jenson, in his reply, said that "David Yeago's interpretation of my theology . . . is precisely and penetratingly correct."[66] Yeago states that this continuity can be found in Jenson's "search for 'a truly Christian doctrine of God,' a doctrine of God which would consist in 'a description of Jesus Christ.'"[67] In a recent memoir, Jenson points out that his fundamental and long-term conviction, which he shares with Pannenberg, is that: "if there is one God and he is triune, reality must be historical, history must be a whole with an outcome, and revelation must be God's inner-historical anticipation of that outcome."[68] From Yeago's and Jenson's account, we find sufficient justification to analyze the coherence of Jenson's theology as a whole in terms of the revisionary metaphysics that narrative Trinitarianism provides.

Next we have to establish the significance of assessing Jenson's trinitarian theology through theology of language (i.e., through a dialectic relation of word and event). He emphasizes that the Triune God is identified by and with *narrative*. One may argue that his concern is more on God's *drama* than the problem of language. This question can be answered in two steps. Firstly, one must not see drama and language as mutually exclusive categories, in which one may think drama is about dynamic acts while language static texts. Conversely, as Kevin Vanhoozer suggests, God's drama is experienced and performed by Christian community in a canonical linguistic way.[69] Likewise, Jenson makes no dichotomy between language and event in his theology. He insists both dimensions should come together: "Christians can live only in a *dramatic and linguistic* space determined by the coordinates of the triune name."[70]

Secondly, in Jenson's theology, God's drama or history is identified by and with narrative. Narrative, which Jenson uses as short term for Scripture in Jenson's thought, is a fundamentally *linguistic* phenomenon. One may say that after *The Knowledge of Things Hoped For*, Jenson does not explicitly address the importance of theological language. But Jenson nonetheless regards language as the basis of his trinitarian theology. God is identified by and with narrative in Jenson's later work, as much as in his early work. Narrative provides us with the proper names and identifying descriptions.

---

65. Yeago, "Catholicity," 18.
66. Jenson, "Thanks to Yeago," 22.
67. Yeago, "Catholicity," 18.
68. Jenson, "A Theological Autobiography to Date," 49.
69. Vanhoozer, *The Drama of Doctrine*.
70. Jenson, *ST1*, 93–94. Italics mine.

Jenson claims that these means of identification are "linguistic means." He emphasizes that they are "*a necessity of religion.*"[71]

I suggest that for the earlier Jenson, theology of language is a problem. It cannot meet, but rather intensifies, the challenge of the meaninglessness of God. But language is still the theological resource for the later Jenson, and the basis of his theological construction. Through his *linguistic* means, he can articulate God's drama or story of promise successfully. Language occupies a very important role in Jenson's later theology.

In short, we are fully justified in studying Jenson's trinitarian theology through a theology of language that emphasizes the dialectic relation of word and event.

4. Jenson's Narrative Trinitarian Theology and Related Intellectual Background

That Jenson revitalized the doctrine of the Trinity with narrative and time is not an accident. We should study his proposal through a broader intellectual background. In this section, I argue that the problem of the meaninglessness of the doctrine of the Trinity began with the demise of metaphysical realism since the Enlightenment. The Enlightenment initiated new developments in philosophy and biblical studies. Because of these challenges, the doctrine is considered meaningless.

The most important contemporary theological resource for Jenson's proposal to meet the Enlightenment's challenges is Barth's theology. Barth suggests that the doctrine of the Trinity is possible and meaningful because God is a self-revealing God. God's self-revelation is not something other than God. It is God himself. It is the coming of God's word. The doctrine of the Trinity is an account of God's self-revelation as a word-event. Jenson follows Barth in thinking of God as self-revealing and revelation as a word-event. The relation of word and event in Barth's doctrine of the Trinity leaves some open space for later theologians to develop their trinitarian theologies in very different directions. Jenson takes one of the options. His choice determines the characteristics and limitations of his revisionary metaphysics.

In this book, I interpret Jenson's revisionary metaphysics using the concept of word-event. As "word-event" is Gerhard Ebeling's phrase, an introduction of Ebeling's understanding can give us a wider theological background of the nature and characteristics of the concept. Narrative and identity are two other important concepts of Jenson's doctrine of the Trinity. Because Paul Ricoeur also identifies the dynamic relation of time and

---

71. Jenson, *TI*, 3. Italics mine.

narrative identity as a possible alternative for the problem of timeless metaphysics, I will introduce Ricoeur's interpretation of narrative and identity briefly. It helps us to establish some critical issues for our analysis of Jenson's theology. Finally, because I intend to bring Jüngel into dialogue with Jenson, I will offer a brief discussion of how Jenson and Jüngel differ in their understanding of Lutheran theology.

4.1 The Demise of the Doctrine of the Trinity since the Enlightenment: A Broken Relationship between Word and Reality

Samuel Powell suggests that word, self/personhood, and history are the concepts that capture all the permutations of German trinitarian theology since the sixteenth century. They relate to each other in various ways in different trinitarian reflections.[72] I will use Powell's concepts to show how the broken relationship of word and reality leads to the demise of the doctrine of the Trinity.

4.1.1 The demise of metaphysics: Kant

Moltmann lists two groups of people that expressed objections and tacit reservations towards the doctrine of the Trinity. Kant and Schleiermacher are the representatives of these groups respectively.[73] One may note that Schleiermacher's theological agenda was set by the Enlightenment. As Braaten and Jenson point out, "Schleiermacher did not defend traditional interpretations of God; he assumed that the Enlightenment had undone them . . . He accepted that religion could be defended neither as a metaphysical sort of knowledge nor, as the proponents of 'natural' religion often thought."[74] Thus, our discussion should start with Kant. Barth recognizes him as "a stumbling-block or rock of offence . . . a prophet whom almost everyone even among those who wanted to go forward with him had first to re-interpret before they could do anything with him."[75]

In the eighteenth century, Christian philosophers such as Christian Wolff, still tried to articulate God as a "timeless" or "simple" transcendental reality. It is real while it transcends the empirical world. God is a transcendental being with three "persons." The relationship between these

---

72. Powell, *The Trinity in German Thought*, 11.
73. Moltmann, *The Trinity and the Kingdom of God*, 2–9.
74. Braaten and Jenson, "Introduction," 4.
75. Barth, *Protestant Theology*, 252.

three persons comes from their "eternal" unbegottenness, begottenness, and procession. While God is transcendental, his existence is demonstrated through certain proofs. God's eternal persons and being (self), revelation (word), and salvation history (history) are thus interconnected. The connection is the basis of transcendental knowledge of God.

Kant divides all proofs for God's existence into three basic types: ontological, cosmological, and physico-theological. He finds all these proofs, which attempt "to construct a theology through purely speculative reason, by means of a transcendental procedure, are without result."[76] Knowing *a prior* entity or knowledge by pure reason is impossible because it cannot be affirmed or denied.[77] Between the phenomenal and noumenal realm there is an epistemological gap. The gap between phenomena and noumena is also a gap between timeless eternity and experiential space and time. That we can perceive are "mere appearances" in mind: "It is, therefore, not merely possible or probable, but indubitably certain, that space and time, as the necessary conditions of all outer and inner experience, are merely subjective conditions of all our intuition, and that in relation to these conditions all objects are therefore mere appearances."[78] Because the doctrine of the Trinity tries to present "what God is in himself," Kant finds that it makes the Christian faith unintelligible—"unsuited to man's powers of comprehension."[79]

Kant suggests that though God is unknowable through theoretical reason, God can be brought into foreground with one of the three postulates of practical reason, i.e., the freedom of will, the existence of God, and the immortality of the soul. Pure human reason cannot prove the existence of God but within practical reason the existence of God is presupposed. In *Opus Postumum*, Kant teaches that God is the morally practical reason legislating for itself.[80] God is not a transcendental being but the subjective moral self: God is not "a being which exists independent of my thought—but the idea (one's own creation, thought-object, *ens rationis*) of a reason which constitutes itself into a thought-object . . . There is not and cannot be a question as to whether such an object exists."[81] "There is a God. There is a being in me, which is different from me and which stands in an efficient causal relation (*nexus effectivus*) toward myself (*agit, facit, operatur*); itself free (that is, not being dependent upon the laws of nature in space and time) it judges me

76. Kant, *Critique of Pure Reason*, 529.
77. Kant, *Critique of Pure Reason*, 529–31.
78. Kant, *Critique of Pure Reason*, 86.
79. Kant, *Religion within the Limits of Reason Alone*, 133.
80. Kant, *Opus Postumum*, 202, 205.
81. Kant, *Opus Postumum*, 231.

inwardly (justifies or condemns); and I, man, am this being myself—it is not some substance outside me."[82]

Therefore, in subjective sense, religion is "the recognition of all duties as divine commands."[83] Kant's Jesus is exactly the ideal model of moral perfection and the founder of a moral community in this sense. Thus, the Christian God can be our appropriate object to believe because the "doctrine of Christianity . . . gives at this point a concept of the highest good (the kingdom of God) which is alone sufficient to the strictest demand of practical reason."[84]

Because the persons of God make no difference to Christian practical life, Kant believes that it is futile to talk about the doctrine of the Trinity. The source of moral theology is the morally practical reason that operates in our free-will instead of the biblical narrative. The ontological questions of God's person and being are of no importance in proving God's existence and developing one's moral self. The biblical narrative is an account of Jesus as a moral exemplar. It cannot be perceived as a depiction of the triune reality that penetrates the noumenal realm.

As a result, Kant's challenge calls Christian speculative metaphysics into question. It challenges that there can be no valid relationship between the word (the Scripture and the religious discourse in the phenomenal world), and the transcendental selfhood/personhood of God. Jenson mentions that the "modern" theological prolegomena is "epistemologically pretentious."[85] The problem of God-talk in the contemporary world exactly comes from the fact that the "timeless" transcendental is no longer the bedrock of Christian ontology and life.[86] Kant's Enlightenment project shakes the legitimacy of metaphysical transcendental and denies the meaning derived from them.

4.1.2 *God as Spirit: Hegel*

Hegel questions Kant's critique of pure reason for its epistemological dualism of phenomena and the thing-in-itself (noumena). In Hegel's opinion, Kant separated the human, the world, and God as cognitive subject, and objects of subject's cognition. The thought of an object is posited by the thinking subject, while the object is something external to the thought.

---

82. Kant, *Opus Postumum*, 229–30.

83. Kant, *Religion within the Limits of Reason Alone*, 142.

84. Kant, *Critique of Practical Reason*, 230–31. Cited from Berkhof, *Two Hundred Years of Theology*, 8.

85. Jenson, *ST1*, 6.

86. Jenson, *A&O*, 13–16. See also, Jenson, *GAG*, 51–53; Jenson, *RAI*, 27–30.

Because God, a transcendental being, cannot be grasped by sense as another phenomenon, he is unintelligible.[87] Hegel contends that this position is subjective and dualistic. He suggests that we can overcome this dualism when we realize that finite subjects are the necessary self-expression, or rational necessity, of the cosmic thought or consciousness, i.e., *Geist* or Spirit. We are the necessary vehicles of this thought. We are not just finite subjects, but the vehicles of a thought which is more than just ours—the thought of the universe as a whole. The world is the point where the cosmic thought becomes conscious.[88] As Charles Taylor summarizes, "the opposition is overcome in the fact that our knowledge of the world turns ultimately into *Geist's* self-knowledge."[89]

According to Hegel, the triune God is *Geist* or Spirit.[90] God—the absolute self-expressive subject—is thoroughly trinitarian. Also, he reveals himself to us in our experience in trinitarian mode. God reveals himself through his self-particularization—its negation and differentiation—in the universe.[91] It operates in three moments. The first moment is the moment of God-in-himself—universality. God, as a self-knowing subject, knows himself through self-particularization that articulates himself to himself in thought—the eternal idea.[92] This differentiation does not divide God into different beings. Hegel explains that, "What God thus distinguishes from himself does not take on the shape of an other-being, but rather what is thus distinguished is immediately only that from which it has been distinguished."[93] God can be unity-in-difference because God is "love"—an "intuition of oneself in another."[94] "Love" unites one with his love while requiring one to "give up one's personality." Because of love, the trinitarian persons are real self-differentiation in the thought of God.[95] From God's "process of thinking himself, God in eternity, the idea in and for itself," one can find "God as triune."[96] The second moment is God's self-expression in

---

87. Hegel, *Hegel's Science of Logic*, 1:55. See also, Hegel, *Hegel's Logic*, 67–68.

88. For Hegel's whole thesis, see Hegel, *Hegel's Phenomenology of Spirit*.

89. Taylor, *Hegel*, 117.

90. Hegel, *Lectures on the Philosophy of Religion*, 3:67–68. For more detail discussion, see Calton, *Hegel's Metaphysics of God*, 39–60.

91. Hegel, *Hegel's Philosophy of Mind*, 163.

92. Hegel, *Hegel's Phenomenology of Spirit*, 465–67; Hegel, *Lectures on the Philosophy of Religion*, 3:78.

93. Hegel, *Lectures on the Philosophy of Religion*, 3:284n93.

94. Hegel, *Lectures on the Philosophy of Religion*, 3:78, 83.

95. Hegel, *Lectures on the Philosophy of Religion*, 3:25. Schlitt, "The Whole Truth," 179.

96. Hegel, *Lectures on the Philosophy of Religion*, 3:77.

the particularity of the World. It embraces three subordinated moments: creation, opposition of good and evil, and incarnation of Jesus Christ.[97] The third moment is the reconciliation of God with the world or the moment of individuality. In this moment, the world is reconciled with God in the spiritual community.[98] These three moments constitute the absolute Spirit—the term that Hegel uses for the ultimate reality. Schlitt summarizes that Hegel's doctrine of the Trinity is a construction of "'immanent' Trinity in the form of absolute logic as thinkable (*begreifbar*) inner pulsation constituting the divine Subject and the 'economic' Trinity as the reconciled otherness of nature and finite Spirit in absolute Spirit."[99]

In short, Hegel, contrary to Kant, believes that God is revelatory and eminently knowable.[100] On the one hand, we can say that Hegel tries to relegate the brokenness between word (revelation), history, and self in Kant's thought. God selfhood is known or revealed through God's self-knowing or self-expression movements in the history. On the other hand, though Hegel thinks he has captured the core spirit of the Bible in the light of his idealist convictions, Barth rightly points out that the objectivity of God and God's word was not firmly established. Revelation and God can easily become a mere imagination of the knowing subject. It results that "God and Man can never confront one another in a relationship which is actual and indissoluble."[101] Its consequence is that everything is absorbed into the self: "Either the human is swallowed up in the divine as an all-devouring absorbing god; or the divine is interiorized by the human, and the human declares itself as the one, true, and holy absolute of history."[102] Hegel had offered an inspiring trinitarian proposal to counter the loss of transcendentalism. Its thrust is a complete amalgamation of word or knowledge and reality. Unfortunately, it may become a monism of the self.

Hegel's influence declined rapidly after his death and Schleiermacher and Ritschl dominated the theological arena of the eighteenth and nineteenth centuries.

---

97. Hegel, *Hegel's Phenomenology of Spirit*, 467–76.

98. Hegel, *Hegel's Phenomenology of Spirit*, 476–78. There are other important accounts on the moments of self-expressive consciousness: Hegel, *Lectures on the Philosophy of Religion*, 3:187, 271–73.

99. Schlitt, *Hegel's Trinitarian Claim*, 72.

100. Hegel, *Hegel's Philosophy of Mind*, 298–99.

101. Barth, *Protestant Theology*, 419.

102. Desmond, *Hegel's God*, 201.

4.2.2 *God's word-event as God's veiling and unveiling and the different interpretations of the relation of word and event in Barth's theology*

Though Barth's doctrine of the Trinity reconnects the relation between word and God's event or reality, it does not mean human beings can know God's reality exhaustively. Rather, Barth emphasizes God's revelation—God's word-event—is a *mystery*.[146] God remains hidden in the midst of his revealedness. Because God's word-event comes to us through a unity of the divine content and the worldly form, God's revelation is always both God's veiling and unveiling:

> [I]t is a matter of hearing the full and true Word of God, the unveiling of God in His veiling or the veiling of God in His unveiling. The secular form without the divine content is not the Word of God and the divine content without the secular form is also not the Word of God. We can neither stop at the secular form as such nor can we fly off beyond this and try to enjoy the divine content alone.[147]

Because of God's veiling and unveiling, Barth rejects that both realistic theology (which stops at the secular form of God's word) and idealistic theology (which extends beyond the secular form and claims to have the divine content) can be good theology.[148] Therefore, on the one hand, Barth's doctrine of revelation reconnects the broken relation between word and reality or being and knowing. On the other hand, Barth's rejection of realism and idealism indicates that his doctrine of revelation needs to be worked under a new epistemological paradigm. The *mystery* of God's word-event opens the possibility for theologians to interpret the relation of word and event, or word and reality in Barth's thought in different ways. Essentially, there are three models.

First, one may use the event to integrate the word. This model emphasizes the eventfulness of God's revelation in Barth's thought. It highlights that God's revelation is the event of Jesus Christ which unfolds God's eternal decision—God decides to reveal *himself* in a worldly form. Because God takes up a worldly form as *his second mode of being*, God's revelation as Jesus Christ is God's *act of being*. Thus, this event can overcome the inadequacy of the human word. Charles Waldrop terms this model the Alexandrian interpretation of Barth. He summarizes that in this model, Jesus Christ by definition "is the act of revelation in which all the moments which witness to that

---

146. Barth, *CD* 1/1:165, 168.
147. Barth, *CD* 1/1:175.
148. Barth, *CD* 1/1:175.

revelation have their being."¹⁴⁹ Jesus Christ, as both human and God, bears the *mystery* of revelation. But the Alexandrian Interpretation has its own drawbacks. The most important criticism is that it does not provide sufficient distinctions between God and creatures. Waldrop points out that, because the necessary distinction between God and men collapsed, the reality and value of the present human life cannot be secured. Also, the independence of the existence of humanity is threatened.[150]

Secondly, one may emphasize the apartness. Richard Roberts observes that Barth's whole theological scheme can only be preserved if the unity of God's word and act is sustained.[151] God's revelation should be his word-event. He criticizes Barth for unfortunately failing to unite human words and reality with God's word-event: "Wherever the content of revelation and its time draws close to the reality common to humanity, ambiguity results because the 'reality' of revelation must both affirm and deny, recreate and annihilate at the same moment."[152] Therefore, Barth shows "the disrelation of Christian theological categories and the reality of which they speak from our own culture."[153]

Graham Ward, though he discerns the same phenomenon as Roberts does, argues that it is not an ambiguity, but a powerful account of *the paradox of language* which is similar to Jacques Derrida's *différance*.[154] Barth's doctrine of revelation indicates that the central problem of theology "is the ineradicable otherness which haunts discourse and yet the impossibility of transcending metaphoricity and positing a real presence."[155] It shows the problematic nature of signs and significance, in which, God "erases his presence and endlessly defers his truth."[156] For Ward, the thrust of Barth's doctrine of revelation is on *a law of textuality*, "in which God's passing resonates in a language which has learnt how not to say."[157] Theology is always a necessary but impossible task.[158]

Thirdly, one may interpret the dialectic and tension between veiling and unveiling as an outcome of communication and participation. In this

---

149. Waldrop, *Karl Barth's Christology*, 167.
150. Waldrop, *Karl Barth's Christology*, 176–77.
151. Roberts, "Barth's Doctrine of Time," 105–7.
152. Roberts, "Barth's Doctrine of Time," 144.
153. Roberts, "Barth's Doctrine of Time," 146.
154. Ward, *Barth*, 30, 34.
155. Ward, *Barth*, 247.
156. Ward, *Barth*, 248.
157. Ward, *Barth*, 251.
158. Ward, *Barth*, 256.

model, God's revelation is not essentially the significance of signs. It is a word-event of *relation* or *correspondence*. It is a *dynamic*—on-going—*communicative act* or *language event*:[159] "God is in His act the One who seeks and creates fellowship with us."[160] This relation is not something new for God. It is God's eternal decision and God's own life: "As and before God seeks and creates fellowship with us, He wills and completes this fellowship in Himself. In Himself He does not will to exist for Himself, to exist alone. On the contrary, He is Father, Son, and Holy Spirit and therefore alive in His unique being with and for and in another."[161]

In this model, God's revelation keeps the distinction of God and creature on the one hand, and holds the togetherness of God's word-event and the created language and reality on the other.[162] Because God's word-event is *dynamic communicative* and *relational*, the mystery of the revelation does not mean agnosticism. Rather, it means creativity and open-endedness of the meaning grasped in our *relation* with God. According to Trevor Hart,

> God is known. But in the knowing, God remains mysterious. The mystery is never fathomed but indwelt in the relation of faith. Revelation, therefore, is not a matter of the replication or "imaging" of the divine on a this-worldly scale, but rather of the opening-up of this-worldly phenomena and human minds/wills/hearts to a level of self-transcendence in which God is corresponded to in an appropriate creaturely manner and thereby "known" in relation.[163]

The above three models show that we can understand how Barth's theology of word-event meets the challenge of the meaninglessness of God-talk differently. They also indicate that there is space for different theological moves on this problem. In this research, I argue that Jenson's doctrine of the Trinity, which employs Barth's conceptuality of word-event, is developed in the manner of the first model. It also faces the problem of an inadequate distinction of God and creature as Waldrop suggested.

---

159. Torrance, *Persons in Communion*, 205–7. See also, McCormack, *Karl Barth's*, 16–17, 159–60.

160. Barth, *CD* 2/1:276.

161. Barth, *CD* 2/1:275.

162. McCormack, *Karl Barth's*, 129–30.

163. Hart, "Revelation," 47.

4.3 Word-Event: Ebeling

In this research, one of the central conceptualities is "word-event" (*Wortgeschehen*). It is Gerhard Ebeling's phrase. Ebeling is concerned that the Word of God "means nothing," or becomes "a mythical expression" in the contemporary world.[164] Theological language is meaningless, because contemporary thought thinks the Word of God cannot enter language, and thus is no more than an alleged word. But for Ebeling the Word of God has entered language. It enters language as a word-event. It is meaningful because it brings *effects*. It is an act that changes things. "The power of words as an event is that they can touch and change our very life . . . So we do not get at the nature of words by asking what they contain, but by asking what they effect, what they set going, what future they disclose."[165]

We should note that, as a student of Rudolf Bultmann, Ebeling's word-event carries a strong sense of the present-tense character. God's word-event and its effects *happen* in Christian proclamation. Word-event thus mainly refers to proclamation: "Whatever precise theological definition may be given to the *concept of the Word of God*, at all events it points us to something that happens, *viz.*, to the movement which leads from the text of holy Scripture to the sermon ('sermon' of course taken in the pregnant sense of proclamation in general). As a first definition of the concept of the Word of God the reference to this movement from text to proclamation may suffice."[166] Word-event is the experience of the biblical text speaking to us in a way we did not expect. It can "illumine that which is dark." It "makes man true and so for the first time real."[167] In this way, we can say Ebeling's thought and Jenson's trinitarian proposal, in which the problem of the meaninglessness of God and the concept of word-event play an important role, share a similar concern. We can even say Ebeling's thought may be one of the intellectual origins for Jenson's theology.

Secondly, Ebeling seeks to avoid "pious words which have no bearing on reality."[168] He believes that the reality of God and the word-event belong together:[169] "God meets us as the Word."[170] At the same time, the word-event shows "the reality of man" "in its true light."[171] Theology does

---

164. Ebeling, *The Nature of Faith*, 182–83.
165. Ebeling, *The Nature of Faith*, 186–87.
166. Ebeling, *Word and Faith*, 311. Italics Ebeling's.
167. Ebeling, *Theology and Proclamation*, 28–29.
168. Ebeling, *God and Word*, 5.
169. Ebeling, *Word and Faith*, 324–25.
170. Ebeling, *The Nature of Faith*, 86.
171. Ebeling, *Theology and Proclamation*, 28.

not only speak of the reality of divine revelation. It also speaks "of the world, of history, of man, and thus of all the things which everyone encounters as reality and whose reality no one calls in question."[172] Even, it is wrong to think that the reality of divine revelation is "another reality of our own," and the task of theology is to look for "connections between the two as an afterthought."[173] "God, man, and the world cannot be spoken of in theology separately and on their own, but only as a single coherent reality."[174] Ebeling suggests that there is only a single reality, because our reality is revealed to us by God's word-event: "The world, as the reality which concerns us, in whatever language it has hitherto been expressed, is the call and question of God to us, even though we do not understand."[175] In this sense, the word-event carries ontological weight and shapes reality. Accordingly, "man's task is not merely to ask *about* language, or even to let language speak *about* a given subject-matter. The subject-matter of language *itself* comes to speech *through* language."[176] A close relation of God's word-event, meaning, and the reality is thus established. One should note that for Ebeling reality as such is linguistic in nature. "We *live* on the reality that *is disclosed to us by language*."[177] However, Jenson argues that reality is *God's history*.

Thirdly, God's word-event, for Ebeling, is basically "the spoken word."[178] It is an event of one person addressing another: "The Word as an event is always something said from one to another . . . God comes to the one addressed and is with him, and the one addressed is with God."[179] Therefore, the word-event is a communication.[180] In this sense, the word-event is not only eventful, meaningful, and ontological, but also communicative. I will argue that the weakness of Jenson's narrative Trinitarianism is that the linguistic-communicative dimension of word-event is suppressed by the temporal-eventful dimension.

---

172. Ebeling, *Word and Faith*, 197.
173. Ebeling, *The Nature of Faith*, 16.
174. Ebeling, *Word and Faith*, 200.
175. Ebeling, *The Nature of Faith*, 190.
176. Thiselton, *The Two Horizons*, 342. Italics Thiselton's.
177. Ebeling, *The Nature of Faith*, 188. Italics mine.
178. Ebeling, *Word and Faith*, 325.
179. Ebeling, *The Nature of Faith*, 189.
180. Ebeling, *The Nature of Faith*, 87–88.

4.4 Narrative and Identity: Ricoeur

If Jenson's theology can be characterized by narrative, identity, and temporality, Ricoeur's insight on these themes is very helpful to this research. In his massive *Time and Narrative*, Ricoeur explores the complex interconnection between time, narrative, and human experience. He argues that human experience of time is aporetical. Time, according to Augustine, is *distentio animi* (the distention of the soul). We experience the future, the present, and the past as expectation, attention, and memory. But, all three directions of time are still three kinds of "present" in our mind. Also, there is a gap between our mind and objective reality. Thus, human subjective experience of time is discordant.

Ricoeur believes that only narrative can reply to the aporias: "Speculation on time is an inconclusive rumination to which narrative activity alone can respond."[181] We always experience temporality through narrative: "time becomes human time to the extent that it is organized after the manner of a narrative."[182] With the aid of Aristotle's *Poetics*, Ricoeur suggests that narrative helps us to hold the tension between our continuously discordant experience, and our struggle for a concordant life meaning together.[183] He borrows from Aristotle the two notions of "plot" (μῦθος) and "imitation" (μίμησις).[184] The plot of a narrative "'grasps together' and integrates into one whole and complete story multiple and scattered events, thereby schematizing the intelligible signification attached to the narrative taken as a whole."[185] It is "the privileged means by which we re-configure our confused, unformed, and at the limit mute temporal experience."[186] In this way, narrative organizes our confusing experience of time into meaningful wholes.

At the same time, Ricoeur emphasizes that the plot "is the *mimésis* of an action."[187] Imitation is a creative work. It is not a lifeless copy of an action: "Imitating or representing is a mimetic activity inasmuch as it produces something, namely, the organization of events by emplotment."[188] Narrative is thus a poetic strategy for constructing a meaningful experience of time. It is both historical and mimetic.

---

181. Ricoeur, *Time and Narrative*, 1:6.
182. Ricoeur, *Time and Narrative*, 1:3.
183. Ricoeur, *Time and Narrative*, 1:52, 72.
184. Ricoeur, *Time and Narrative*, 1:31.
185. Ricoeur, *Time and Narrative*, 1:x.
186. Ricoeur, *Time and Narrative*, 1:xi.
187. Ricoeur, *Time and Narrative*, 1:xi.
188. Ricoeur, *Time and Narrative*, 1:34.

Ricoeur then suggests that history and fiction—the two major modes of narrative discourse—cannot be dichotomized as real and unreal, or fact and imagination. History, for Ricoeur, is like fiction in relying on the power of the imagination to construct the course of the past events. Historians write history under the rubric of "singular causal imputation." They try to give a single and unified account of the past events.[189] Ricoeur points out that though they are under the constraint of the past, the imagination is required in order to construct such a causal explanation. He quotes Max Weber: "In order to penetrate the real causal inter-relationships, *we construct unreal ones*."[190] In this sense, a singular imputation of a history and an emplotment of a fiction are similar. It shows that history can only refer to the reality *indirectly* as fiction does:

> Not that the past is unreal, but past reality is, in the strict sense of the word, unverifiable. Insofar as it no longer exists, the discourse of history can seek to grasp it only *indirectly*. It is here that the relationship with fiction shows itself as crucial.[191]

History cannot directly refer to the past. It describes the past reality by "standing-for" or "taking-the-place-of" that "reality." It tells "the facts *as they really* happened."[192] From the function of "standing for," Ricoeur finds that fiction is able to speak of reality as history by its power of revealing and transforming.[193] Because of the revealing power, fiction is paradoxically imaginative and real: "The more imagination deviates from that which is called reality in ordinary language and vision, the more it approaches the heart of the reality which is no longer the world of manipulable objects, but the world into which we have been thrown by birth."[194] Because of the transforming power, fiction "remakes" reality, it "has the power to 'remake' reality and, within the framework of narrative fiction in particular, to remake real praxis to the extent that the text intentionally aims at a horizon of new reality which we may call a world."[195]

In short, Ricoeur identifies "an interpenetration of history and fiction, stemming from the criss-crossing processes of a fictionalization of history

---

189. Ricoeur, *Time and Narrative*, 1:182–85.
190. Ricoeur, *Time and Narrative*, 1:183.
191. Ricoeur, "On Interpretation," 181.
192. Ricoeur, *Time and Narrative*, 3:155.
193. Ricoeur, *Time and Narrative*, 3:158.
194. Ricoeur, "The Function of Fiction in Shaping Reality," 139.
195. Ricoeur, "On Interpretation," 185.

and a historization of fiction."[196] Both history and fiction speak of our reality. Narrative reveals and transforms our reality in time, and organizes our temporal experience in a meaningful way. Nonetheless, the reality opened by narrative is not that of positivism. It is a reality of possible. Vanhoozer nicely summarizes Ricoeur's project as follows:

> Insofar as these past values are different from the present ones, the historian opens up the real towards the possible . . . Fiction too is about possible ways of human being in the world. Because of its freedom from the constraints of history, however, fiction is able to take us to the "heart" of the real.[197]

Ricoeur's thought of reality as possible is in sharp contrast to Jenson's. I will show that Jenson does not want to loosen the referential relation of narrative to God's reality exactly because he worries this move may lead to the meaninglessness of speaking about God. I will argue that the problem of Jenson's theology is the absence of a theology of possibility.

Ricoeur also suggests that we find our personal identity in and through narrative. (Or, we may borrow Jenson's terms to say *by and with narrative*.) He distinguishes two major meanings of identity: *idem* and *ipse*, or substantial and narrative. An *idem* identity understands oneself as "being the same" or "unchanging" in time; while an *ipse* identity as "self-constancy," "character," or keeping "promise."[198] But our historicity forbids us from establishing our identity as an *idem* identity. We only can find a unity of self from an *ipse* identity without the dismissal of diversity of different temporal states and reality of otherness.[199]

Though narrative identity helps us to understand ourselves in a meaningful way, it cannot be a meta-narrative that totalizes our experience. Diversity, heterogeneity, and otherness are still in our narrative identity. According to Ricoeur, narrative identity is "an open-ended, incomplete, imperfect mediation, namely, the network of interweaving perspectives of the expectation of the future, the reception of the past, and the experience of the present, with no *Aufhebung* into a totality where reason in history and its reality would coincide."[200] It is not an identity of *a story* but *stories*. "Just as it is possible to compose several plots on the subject of the same

---

196. Ricoeur, *Time and Narrative*, 3:246.
197. Vanhoozer, *Biblical Narrative*, 102.
198. Ricoeur, *Time and Narrative*, 3:246; Ricoeur, *Oneself as Another*, 2–3, 118–19.
199. Ricoeur, *Time and Narrative*, 3:246.
200. Ricoeur, *Time and Narrative*, 3:207.

incidents ... so it is always possible to weave different, even opposed, plots about our lives."[201]

In this research, I will show that Jenson's narrative theology understands God's identity in a manner similar to Ricoeur's narrative identity. However, Jenson suggests God's narrative identity is a grand narrative of history and reality. I will argue that it cannot give creatures a proper otherness in God's reality.

4.5 Jenson, Jüngel, and Lutheran Theology

In this work, I have chosen Jüngel to be the partner in dialogue with Jenson. As both of them are notable Lutheran theologians, a brief discussion on the differences of their understanding of Lutheran theology is beneficial to our analysis. In his *Systematic Theology*, Jenson states that his understanding of Lutheran theology is far away from the standard scholarly reception of Luther:

> The following may not much resemble what readers expect from Luther. His texts in fact contain what will here be cited from them, but standard Luther exegesis, conducted mostly by liberal Protestants or philosophical existentialists, has tried to explain these systematics away as too metaphysical and therefore tending to Catholicism. Luther is praised, indeed, as theology's great deliverer from ontological thinking. The contrary has now been demonstrated in detail from the texts, by a sustained cooperative research project at the University of Helsinki, sometimes referred to as "the Mannermaa school" of Luther research ... The received scholarly understanding of Luther must now be taken as in large part discredited.[202]

---

201. Ricoeur, *Time and Narrative*, 3:248.

202. Jenson, *ST2*, 293n17. Mark C. Mattes finds that Jenson has a shift in his understanding of Lutheran theology of justification: "justification is no longer primarily seen in forensic terms but rather in ontological terms." Mattes assesses this move in a very critical way: "Why did Jenson disavow confessional Lutheranism? The confessionalism that he, early in his career, represented wanted to package itself as mainline Protestantism. However, this mainline Protestantism that he then helped to create was too accommodating to the wider culture ... Ironically, the content of Jenson's views of God remained mainline Protestant—as mediated through Hegel." See Mattes, *The Role of Justification in Contemporary Theology*, 118, 142–43. Though Mattes finds that Jenson's understanding of Lutheran theology is changed during his theological career, it does not mean that Jenson has a drastic change in his doctrine of God. If Mattes identifies Jenson's later doctrine of God as Hegalian, we must also recognize that this Hegelian tone has already existed in Jenson's earlier works. For a much quoted example, in *KTHF*, Jenson states that "Hegel's only real fault was that he confused himself with

The main difference between the "standard" Lutheran theology and "the Mannermaa school" or the "Finnish school," which Jenson agrees with, is that the latter takes the ontology in Luther's thought very seriously, while the former gives no place to this ontology in their interpretation of Luther. Jenson, as with the Finnish school, believes that God's event of justification causes a real-ontic relation between Christ and Christians: "Thus when God in Christ forms us by his word to the virtues displayed in it, he forms us to himself, he indeed becomes the metaphysical forms of believer's humanity, the defining shape that makes these entities human. We must here adduce the guiding slogan of Luther's *Commentary on Galatians: In ipsa fide Christus adest*, 'In faith as such Christ is present.'"[203] In short, the evangelical event of justification is not merely a forensic imputation. It is effective and real, for the Christian is united with Christ.

According to Jenson, Luther's teaching, "By faith the human person becomes God," should be understood as "a mode of deification." Believers are "swallowed up" in the divine Son.[204] Jenson even believes that the person "within my personhood is God the Son."[205] He explains that for, the Christians, the *totus Christus*—the risen Christ including and included in his community[206]—"becomes the subject by whose liveliness I am what I am. And that is to say, Christ himself becomes the subject by whose liveliness I am what I am. In the Spirit, the Christ who is *what* I am is the Christ who is *who* I am."[207] In other words, Christ, Christians, and the church are in an ontological relationship in which Christians and the church receive their being from Christ.

Jenson's narrative Trinitarianism emphasizes that God is identified by and with the biblical narrative. God is not only identified *by* but also *with* the narrative. This identification also indicates a real ontic-bond between biblical narrative and God's reality. One may expect Jenson's interpretation of Lutheran theology is a resource for Jenson to make his ontological claims in his revisionary metaphysics.

Mattes has concisely summarized that how Jüngel is indebted to Luther:

---

the last judge; but that is quite a fault." See Jenson, *KTHF*, 233n327. One may say that Jenson's change in Lutheran theology fuels his metaphysical agenda.

203. Jenson, *ST2*, 296.
204. Jenson, *ST2*, 296–97.
205. Jenson, *ST2*, 299.
206. Jenson, *ST1*, 81.
207. Jenson, *ST2*, 299. Italics Jenson's.

> With Luther, he takes justification by grace alone through faith alone to be the heart of theology . . . With Luther, he claims that we are fundamentally human in our passivity, our reception of God's gifts in both creation and renewal. With Luther, he believes that the old being cannot be reformed, but only annihilated . . . With Luther, he believes that Christ is primarily sacrament (*sacramentum*), and only secondarily example (*exemplum*). With Luther . . . he is skeptical of all human ethical attempts to create an earthly utopia to supplement faith. With Luther, he understands the inevitability of the will to bind itself to an idol in the face of its impotence.[208]

However, for this research it is important that Jüngel understands Luther's theology of justifying Word in a very different way from Jenson. For Jenson, Christ and Christians are united through the justifying Word. This word is effective. In justification, Christ is *present*. He swallows up the justified sinners in him. He places the effective aspect of justification over the forensic aspect. For Jüngel, both forensic and effective dimensions are emphasized. Also, the effect of justification is not "a mode of deification" but "a refinement of the definition of the external reference of justified sinners": "What renews the inner person is the external Word, which addresses us from outside ourselves and grants us God's righteousness. If any discussion of the gracious renewal of the inner person (*renovatio interioris hominis*) is to be acceptable to Protestant theology, it must never be seen as complementary, as an alternative or as completing the extrinsetist view of justification. It can only be seen as a refinement of the definition of the external reference of justified sinners."[209] Jüngel thinks that justification rebuilds the relation between God and humanity. In sin, human beings are relationless. Justification causes the Christians become in relation with God: "the justifying Word remakes our human existence anew, by relating us to Jesus Christ and there bringing us to ourselves, outside ourselves."[210] In short, relation between God and humanity, and not deification, is the thrust of Jüngel's interpretation of Lutheran doctrine of justification. In this research, I will show that this relation makes Jenson and Jüngel construct their narrative Trinitarianism differently.

---

208. Mattes, *The Role of Justification*, 50–51.
209. Jüngel, *Justification*, 212.
210. Jüngel, *Justification*, 213.

5. Discussion on Jenson's Doctrine of the Trinity

As Webster observes, reception of Jenson's theology is still in its early stages.[211] But Jenson's emphasis on God's temporality has been quickly identified by his admirers and critics. Some celebrate Jenson's Trinitarianism as a provocative metaphysical reflection on God's infinity and temporality. It revitalizes the trinitarian piety and theology in a new direction.[212] Wolfhart Pannenberg appreciates that "Jenson secures the potential for integrating his trinitarian doctrine with the history of salvation."[213]

On the contrary, some worry Jenson's theology of God's temporality threatens God's independence from creatures in creation and redemption. If time is more primary than God himself, God is not transcendental or free.[214] Paul Molnar accuses Jenson of seeming "to blur the distinction between events in God and events in history,"[215] and make God's eternal being "dependent on a historical or a series of historical events."[216] Jenson is to blame for making God "a dependent deity" of time.[217] Hunsinger thinks Jenson's theology is a kind of "dialectical historicism with a teleological contour."[218] He asks whether it does not suppose "God's metaphysical dependence on the world."[219] Though Molnar and Hunsinger rightly identify Jenson's overemphasis on God's temporality, they seem to suggest a simple return to the timeless concept of God.[220] One may suspect whether it is an appropriate theological move in an era of the demise of metaphysical transcendentalism. In this research, I will propose a revision rather than a refutation of Jenson's theology. I find that narrative is the theological resource for this revision. The communicative dimension of narrative can help us to concretize the otherness between God and creatures in Jenson's theology.

211. Webster, "Systematic Theology after Barth," 258.

212. For examples, LaCugna, Review of *The Triune Identity*, 135–36; Shea, Review of *The Triune Identity*, 178–79; Yeago, "Catholicity," 18–22; Douglas Knight, "Jenson on Time," 71; Cary, Review of *Systematic Theology*, 133–35; Mattes, "An Analysis and Assessment," 463.

213. Pannenberg, "A Trinitarian Synthesis," 49.

214. See Farrow's and Di Noia's questions in Farrow et al., "Robert Jenson's *Systematic Theology*," 92–93, 103; Ive, "Robert W. Jenson's Theology of History," 157; Ochs, "A Jewish Reading," 427.

215. Molnar, *Divine Freedom*, 70.

216. Molnar, *Divine Freedom*, 74.

217. Molnar, *Divine Freedom*, 72.

218. Hunsinger, "Robert Jenson's *Systematic Theology*," 175.

219. Hunsinger, "Robert Jenson's *Systematic Theology*," 176–79.

220. Molnar, *Divine Freedom*, 80; Hunsinger, "Robert Jenson's *Systematic Theology*," 200.

Narrative is another important facet of Jenson's theological project. Various theologians identify the importance of narrative in Jenson's theology. But the discussion is mainly on Jenson's vivid description of God's drama.[221] Some theologians have initially pointed out the close relation of narrative and the triune identity in Jenson's theology.[222] However, how the conceptualities of narrative and identity work out Jenson's theology of God's triune reality is still a topic that has been little investigated.

Mark C. Mattes praises Jenson's narrative approach to theology saying that it makes him "far more a 'post-modern' thinker than Pannenberg."[223] Though Jenson uses narrative and not propositions to develop his theology of God's reality, I will show that the ultra-realist character of his narrative theology reveals that Jenson is still a thinker of modernity rather than post-modernity. Francis Watson points out that Jenson's narrative theology implies God is a communicative agent and Jesus as God's Word indicates that God opens his intradivine converse to human participation.[224] But I will argue that Jenson's metaphysical agenda hampers the communicative character of narrative. I believe that a dialogue with Jüngel's theology may strengthen the communicative dimension of Jenson's theology.

6. Chapter Outlines

This work is structured as follows: In the next chapter, I will give an account of Jenson's narrative Trinitarianism. This will set the stage for this work. I show that, for Jenson, biblical narrative is a story of God's promise and a drama of the triune God. It *really* depicts the triune *reality* as God is identified *by* and *with* it.

In chapter 2, I will argue that Jenson's interpretation of Barth indicates that Jenson attributes the utmost importance to his schema of time and eternity. I argue that Jenson's critique of Barth's doctrine of analogy of faith shows that Jenson does not give sufficient attention to the communicative and dynamic dimension of the God-man relation.

In chapter 3, I will make my case for Jenson's over-reliance of temporality from another direction, that of his theology of language. I argue that Jenson proposes to establish the meaningfulness of theological language through

---

221. For examples, Buckley, "Intimacy," 14–17; Seitz, "Handing over the Name," 23–41.

222. For examples, Buckley, "Intimacy," 12; Cary, Review of *Systematic Theology*, 133–34; Albright, "The Story of the Triune God," 36–54; Grenz, *Rediscovering the Triune God*, 106–16.

223. Mattes, "An Analysis and Assessment," 485.

224. Watson, "America's Theologian," 216–17.

a close relationship between *language*, *reality*, and *time*. The eventual outcome of his proposal is that God's word absorbs all other realities into it, so that theological language is in danger of becoming a monologue of God.

I argue in chapter 4 that Jenson's adaptation of the Cappadocians's Trinitarianism is generally well-founded. His proposal here is to understand God as temporally infinite. I argue that because Jenson interprets the persons of God almost entirely in terms of temporality, he cannot properly handle the relation of the immanent and economic Trinity, the transcendence and freedom of God, and the relatedness and distinction between Creator and creatures—the communion of God and human. It is not the temporal interpretation of the reality of God that creates a problem, but I argue that the single demonstration of time is not adequate for the articulation of reality.

In chapter 5, I will introduce Eberhard Jüngel as a partner in dialogue. Through their interpretation of Barth, I will argue that Jüngel's assertion of God's word-event as correspondence and analogy of relation brings out the varied meanings of the term "word." It explicates how God and man interact linguistically within time and space. We must consider this linguistic and communicative dimension in order to articulate the relatedness and distinction of triune and human reality. I argue that Jüngel's insights can help us to find the better expression of the proper relatedness and distinction between Creator and creatures in the communion of God and humans that Jenson's Trinitarianism requires.

In chapter 6, I will argue that Jüngel is motivated by concerns similar to Jenson. Both are aiming to reply to the problem of the death of God. To this end Jüngel offers us a linguistic ontology. This suggests that it is the concept of *address* that gives theology the *possibility* of speaking of God, and allows the authenticity of the event in which God is encountered. In comparing Jenson and Jüngel, I show that Jenson puts the emphasis on the actuality of God's promise, while Jüngel places it on the possibility of God's coming to humans. Jüngel's theology of possibility articulates the eventfulness of the Trinity and provides the proper relation and distinction of God and humans. It also provides a means of securing both the identity and the distinction of the immanent and economic Trinity. These corrections and clarifications from the work of Jüngel provide the conceptual reinforcement that Jenson's theological project requires.

Chapter 1

Jenson on Narrative and the Trinity

Biblical Narrative as Triune Story of Promise

THIS CHAPTER EXAMINES THE relation of triune reality and biblical narrative in Jenson's trinitarian theology. I will argue that Jenson understands biblical narrative as the story of God's promise. This story is the drama of the triune God. It *really* depicts, and it really is, the triune *reality* as God is identified *by* and *with* it.

1. Proper Names, Biblical Narrative, and the Trinity

Jenson believes that trinitarian discourse represents the determination of the Christian church to identify the God who has claimed her.[1] We must trace the beginning of this identification back to Israel's identification of God, because "It is the God of Israel whom Jesus called Father and to whom the disciples wanted to pray."[2] It should be noted that both Israel and Christianity identify their God through proper names and descriptive narratives.

The basis of Israel's identification of God is the experience of deliverance from Egypt and migration to Canaan. Jenson contends that Israel's confession in Deuteronomy 26:5–9[3] provides the proper name (JHWH) and identifying description of God (the narrative of the Exodus events) that are determinative of Israel's religious life.[4] This proper name and narrative

---

1. Jenson, *TI*, 4.

2. Jenson, *ST1*, 42.

3. "A wandering Aramean was my father; and he went down into Egypt . . . And the Egyptians treated us harshly and afflicted us . . . Then we cried to JHWH . . . and JHWH brought us out to Egypt with a mighty hand . . . and he brought us into this place and gave us this land." Cf., Jenson, *ST1*, 43.

4. Jenson, *ST1*, 43–44; Jenson, *TI*, 5–7; Jenson, "Triune God," 89–90.

description come together to make this identification.[5] We should notice that this double identification does not come from Israel's projection of God. It is the self-introduction of the God who permits Israel to call on him by the name he gives.[6] Jenson believes that the biblical God can be identified by this narrative, and at the same time, identifies himself with this narrative. The narrative and revelatory events are not clues about God or our own projection of God. The narrative that comes with this proper name is God's personal self-introduction—God identifies himself with this narrative.[7]

According to Jenson, the New Testament provides a new identifying description for this same God. The Apostles identify the God of Israel as he who raised Jesus our Lord from the Dead.[8] Thus, the identification by the death and resurrection neither replaces nor is a simple addition to the identification by Exodus—the God who raised Jesus is the same God who freed Israel from Egypt. The resurrection is verification of that earlier liberation.[9] The exile is catastrophe or national death for Israel. Hope in the God of Israel is a hope of a victory over this death.[10] The resurrection of Jesus verifies the hope of Israel in its God, and without it this hope cannot be sustained.

This new description enables the emergence of new kinds of naming.[11] "Jesus" is the first kind of naming that the apostolic church uses to speak of God. In Jenson's opinion, "Jesus" was the way that the various groups of primal church invoked God.[12]

The triune name "Father, Son, and Holy Spirit" is another kind of naming which appears in the New Testament. Jenson suggests that "Father, Son, and Holy Spirit" occupies the place in the church occupied by JHWH in Israel.[13] Why does the triune name become the church's name for God? Jenson believes that this is because the triune name contains the content and logic of this God's identifying descriptions that embody the church's primal

---

5. Jenson cites Exod 3:13–16; 6:2–7; 19:4; 20:2; 34:5–6; Isa 43:3–25; Ezek 16:62; 20:5–26, as scriptural supports. Jenson, *ST1*, 44; Jenson, *TI*, 3, 5–7; Jenson, "Triune God," 88–90.

6. Jenson, *ST1*, 43–44.

7. Jenson, *ST1*, 59–60.

8. Jenson cites Rom 4:24; 8:11; 1 Cor 15:15; 2 Cor 1:9; Gal 1:1; Col 2:12; 1 Pet 1:21. Jenson, *ST1* 42; Jenson, *TI*, 8; Jenson, "Triune God," 91; Jenson, *S&P*, 6.

9. Jenson, *ST1*, 44; Jenson, *TI*, 39; Jenson, *VW*, 42–43.

10. Jenson, *ST1*, 66; Jenson, *TI*, 38–39.

11. Jenson, *TI*, 8; Jenson, "Triune God," 91; Jenson, *ST1*, 44; Jenson, "A Call to Faithfulness," 92.

12. Jenson cites Luke 24:47; Acts 4:17–18; 8:12; 9:15. Jenson, *TI*, 9; Jenson, "Triune God," 91; Jenson, *ST1*, 45.

13. Jenson, *TI*, 10; Jenson, "Triune God," 92.

experience of God in a single phrase.[14] Though Jenson admits that the earliest formulating process and history of this naming are obscure, he thinks its logic is clear. He expounds the logic of triune name:

> In it [the triune name] "Son" is a title for Jesus, who "made himself the Son of God" simply by addressing God as "my Father." Conversely, God is here called "Father" not generally, but specifically as the Father of this, next to be mentioned, Son; thus "Father" does not here appear as a predicate of God, whether straightforward or metaphoric, but as a term of address within a narrative construction that displays a relation internal to the logic of the construction. And the Spirit is the enabling future of the community so established, among themselves and with us. By these inner relations the phrase uniquely identifies the particular God of the gospel, recounting at once the *personae* and the basic plot of the scriptural story.[15]

The triune name, Father, Son, and Spirit, simultaneously recounts the *personae* of God and the plot of the scriptural story. Next I will set out the logic of his exposition of the biblical narrative.

2. The Gospel and the Identification of the Trinity

2.1 The Gospel and Jesus as God the Son

In Jenson's view, the new identifying description of God in the New Testament ("God is who raised Jesus our Lord from the Dead.") and its related "new kinds of naming" ("Jesus," and "Father, Son, and Holy Spirit") are developed around the life and work of the particular person of Jesus. If we want to identify the gospel's God, we must identify Jesus. Because we cannot identify God without identifying Jesus at the same time, he contends that we may initially state that God "is" Jesus. If God "is" Jesus, we cannot avoid speaking of this God by and with the narrative of Jesus — gospel. The temporal sequences and details of this narration are essential to God's being.[16] Jenson even states that "God, we may therefore identify, is *what happens* with Jesus."[17] We should note that at this point Jenson defines the

---

14. Jenson, *TI*, 21; Jenson, "Triune God," 91; Jenson, *ST1*, 46.

15. Jenson, *ST1*, 45. For a similar account, see Jenson, "Triune God," 93.

16. Jenson also expresses the point negatively: "we cannot rightly talk of this God in any way which would make the temporal sequences, the stuff of narration, unessential to his being." See Jenson, *TI*, 22; Jenson, "Triune God," 100; Jenson, "Three Identities," 2.

17. Jenson, "Three Identities," 2. Italics mine.

being of God as event. If we conceive *being* as a substance with the various attributes familiar to the classical western philosophical mind, we may miss Jenson's point. In his words, "We will do new metaphysics as our grasp of God's being as an event, rather than as an analogue to a—a personal—thing. God—we will learn to say—does not exist, he happens. He does not exemplify attributes, he does them."[18]

Jenson goes on to say that we do not know about God in advance and then decide to identify God by reference to Jesus. It is what happens with Jesus that obliges us to use the word "God."[19] This assertion may seem to be self-defeating. Even if we find that the life and work of Jesus in his narrative encourages us to identify him as God, we still want to know what God is, and why the label "God" is appropriate before we apply it to him. If we use this label, does this not imply that we know something about God and then "decide" to apply it to Jesus's case?

Jenson's position can be defended if we understand how he articulates the relationship between the self-identity of God and the concept of "god" which is common to different religions. Jenson asserts that Israel's concept of God does not come from projection, but from the claim that the God of Israel makes for himself: "The God of Israel claims . . . to have and introduce a specific and integral personal identity prior to our projections."[20] Thus, the reason for us to identify God by and with Jesus's narrative is not that the narrative matches our projection or speculation of God. It is because the narrative matches the pattern of God's self-claim and then it obliges us to do so: "The Lord, in full antecedent individual identity, is the God of Israel not because of a fit between his characteristics and Israel's values but by historically contingent events—the rescue from Egypt and, retrospectively, the call of Abraham."[21]

Jenson does not refuse to recognize that "god" is a common phenomenon within human society. He states that "the word 'God' has a common function across the religious spectrum."[22] He provides an analysis of the

---

18. Jenson, "The Futurist Option in Speaking of God," 22.

19. Jenson, *TI*, 22; Jenson, "Triune God," 100; Jenson, "Three Identities," 2.

20. Jenson, *ST1*, 53. Italics Jenson's. A detail discussion of this point, see Jenson, "The God Question," 47–48.

21. Jenson, *ST1*, 52. So, in Jenson's response to Francis Watson, he states that the biblical God is never a matter of "generalizing." We rather *identify* the God by and with biblical narrative. See Jenson, "Response," 228.

22. Jenson, *ST1*, 54.

features that religions have in common.[23] He says that "religion is the cultivation of some *eternity*; *gods* are eternities of a certain sort."[24]

Jenson does not refuse to accept a common concept of "god" concept or values associated with "god" in human society. He simply insists that we identify the God of Israel by and with what happens with Jesus.

In view of all this we have to answer three questions: Who was Jesus? What does "is risen" mean? What difference does it make?[25]

The question "who was Jesus" invites us to follow what Jesus did and said and what came of it, and so to investigate the details of the identifying descriptions of the New Testament narrative.[26] Jesus the Nazarene was a wandering preacher and rabbi who proclaimed the coming of the "Kingdom of God." His message can be summarized as "The time is fulfilled, and the kingdom of God has come near; repent, and believe in the good news."[27] The idea of the "Kingdom" in Jesus's proclamation is not something new. Jesus took over the teaching of the prophets that the Kingdom is the world that God rules and in which his will is done.[28] It is striking that Jesus made his proclamation of the Kingdom unconditional.[29]

In the announcements of the prophets and Pharisees, there is a space of time between the present proclamation and the future fulfillment. The fulfillment will happen only when the law-like "if . . ." clauses or the required conditions are achieved. But Jesus took away "the space of time between the moment of their hearing him and the future he promised."[30] Jesus proclaimed the Kingdom as future, but this future is not separated from the present by any temporal distance. Through his proclamation of the God's coming Kingdom, he established God's *rule* over those who heard him. The Kingdom is therefore here now.[31] Jenson illustrates this point with two examples. (1) To the poor, the publicans, and the sinners, Jesus did not merely proclaim that in God's future they would be new men, but already treated them as these new men.[32] In Jenson's own words, Jesus "enacted God's future

---

23. Jenson, *ST1*, 54–56.
24. Jenson, *ST1*, 54. Italics Jenson's. Also, in Jenson, *UG*, 119.
25. Jenson, *S&P*, 32.
26. Jenson, *S&P*, 33.
27. Jenson, *S&P*, 35; Jenson, *ST1*, 176; Jenson, "A Call to Faithfulness," 93.
28. Jenson, *S&P*, 35–36; Jenson, *ST1*, 176.
29. Jenson, *S&P*, 38.
30. Jenson, *S&P*, 37. A "prototype" of this viewpoint, see Jenson, *GAG*, 17.
31. Jenson, *S&P*, 176–77.
32. Jenson, *S&P*, 38–39. There is a similar account in Jenson, *GAG*, 18.

for them as their present with him."³³ (2) Jesus performed miracles which were the *acted-out* signs of the immediacy of the Kingdom for all alienations of human life were overcome.³⁴ So Jenson claims that the "kingdom was present with Jesus *as* promise, as word and meaningful action; and as the unconditional promise which abolished all space of controllable time between itself and its fulfillment."³⁵

Moreover, the unconditionality of Jesus's promise was shown in his death. Jenson points out that Jesus died for others. The result of this radical mission of Jesus was inevitably death. That Jesus took up this mission means he accepted this. Jesus's contemporaries feared the freedom brought by his proclamation of the fulfillment of the Kingdom and so they killed him. Jenson believes that Jesus's death shows that he was completely the unconditional speaker of God's promise to his contemporaries. Though they rejected the promise and killed him, he accepted this death without withdrawing his promise.³⁶ Jesus is therefore "the one who lived wholly in the hope he had to bring his fellows, giving himself to that hope even to death."³⁷

Jenson points out that, according to the New Testament, the word "love" captures what humanly happened to the historical Jesus. By his definition, love means an unconditional self-giving and an acceptance of death. Jesus loved with an unconditional love because he died for the fellows that he loved.³⁸ We should note that Jenson regards love as a kind of promise. To love is a promise to promise unconditionally.³⁹ He gives an illustration for this point: "If I love, I promise to my beloved not this or that, but my future self . . . to promise *myself* is to try to give up this reservation. Therefore to love is to accept death."⁴⁰ Thus Jesus's unconditional promise of the kingdom is the explication of his love.

Jenson also notes that Jesus forgave sin and perfected the law. These could only be said and done by God's immediate authority. Jesus also called God "Father" in the same immediate manner. Jesus presented himself as the Son of God "in a way unprecedented by an individual."⁴¹ Jenson argues that the priests and lawyers understood the issue posed by Jesus's

33. Jenson, *ST1*, 177.
34. Jenson, *S&P*, 39.
35. Jenson, *S&P*, 41.
36. Jenson, *S&P*, 41.
37. Jenson, *S&P*, 43–44.
38. Jenson, *TI*, 22; Jenson, "Triune God," 100; Jenson, "Three Identities," 3.
39. Jenson, *S&P*, 55.
40. Jenson, *S&P*, 55. Italics Jenson's.
41. Jenson, *ST1*, 177.

self-presentation: Jesus was either indeed the Messiah and a unique Son, or a blasphemer.[42]

Now we have to tackle two final questions: What does "is risen" mean? And what difference does it make? Jenson points out that the account of Jesus's promise and love cannot stop at the point of his death. There must be *resurrection* to accomplish his promise and love. Jenson even contends that "in an account of Jesus that leaves out the Resurrection, no one now hears the Gospel."[43] Jesus gave his companions a promise of the future kingdom. He called them to give up clinging to the past and to live by hope for the future. Had not Jesus been raised, he could not fulfill his promise of futurity, for he himself would have become merely "the past"—a dead man. If Jesus is dead, those who follow him would be imitating of a figure of the past, which would become self-defeating.[44] If Jesus was not raised from the dead, his love would have been in vain. A "successful love would be an acceptance of death which nevertheless did not result in the lover's absence from the beloved, but in his presence."[45] So if Jesus is not risen, he is absent from his beloved and his love is no more. Finally, we can add one final point that Jenson does not explicitly state: if Jesus is not risen, his *self-presentation* is false. Then his exercise of God's authority as would have been merely a religious desire rather than a *real* promise. Some, such as Rudolf Bultmann, insist that Jesus's *kerygma* has existential significance regardless of Jesus's resurrection. But Jenson believes it is "doubtful that Bultmann's history-dissolving concept of eschatology is adequate . . . how the eschatological proclamation can be understood, if it is supposed to be talk about history which, however, narrates no history."[46]

Jenson contends that because of Jesus's resurrection, his unconditional love and promise is actualized. As we have seen, Jenson believes that death imposes an ultimate or final condition that would bring Jesus's love and promise to an end. But if Jesus died and lives, there is no limit to hamper the fulfillment of his love and promise; nothing can separate him from his future any more.[47] If Jesus lives, he can act freely.[48] If Jesus died and lives, life opens unconditionally to him and nothing may interrupt the

42. Jenson, *ST1*, 178.

43. Jenson, *KTHF*, 195.

44. Jenson, *S&P*, 44; Jenson, *GAG*, 18.

45. Jenson, *TI*, 23; Jenson, *S&P*, 56; Jenson, "Triune God," 100. A similar account is in Jenson, *ST1*, 199.

46. See Jenson, *KTHF*, 173–75. There is a similar discussion in Jenson, *ST1*, 166–71. Jenson's objection to Bultmann shows his interest in realism.

47. Jenson, *S&P*, 48; Jenson, *WV*, 43.

48. Jenson, *ST1*, 198.

fulfillment of his unconditional promise of the Kingdom. Neither space for preparation, postponement, failure, death, nor law can intervene between the promise and the fulfillment of the Kingdom. Alienation is *no longer a possibility*.[49] If the resurrection of the unconditional lover has happened, the limit of love—death—is behind him. Jesus's unconditional love has triumphed, and its triumph means Jesus's love can and must embrace all people and the whole circumstances of their lives.[50] If death is behind Jesus, the fulfillment of the unconditional promise and this all-embracing love is the "last future" or "conclusion" of the enterprise of humanity. Because "nothing can any more limit his hopeful self-giving; it will necessarily encompass all men and all man's history."[51]

If Jesus died and lives, God's promise of the Kingdom is fulfilled unconditionally. According to Jenson, the God of Israel is a God of promise. The final demonstration of the truthfulness of this promise, and of the God who makes it, can be given only if history ends in God's fulfillment. But what God was able to promise unconditionally, and how he could do so, remained uncertain right through the Old Testament.[52] An unconditional promise means the acceptance of death, while a *successful* unconditional promise must mean a triumph over death. Unless the God of Israel died and lives, we cannot be certain of the real identity of this promising God. Jesus proclaimed the promise of the Old Testament and presented himself as the Son of God, so in his death and resurrection, the identity of this God of promise became clear. "The news of Jesus's death and resurrection is a claim on behalf of a God unequivocally identified as a God of *unconditional promise*."[53] Through Jesus's resurrection, we identify the triumph of his Father—the God of Israel.[54] Jenson's conclusion is that the God of Israel is identified by and with Jesus's death and resurrection.

Apart from asserting that the God of unconditional promise had been identified by and with Jesus's death and resurrection, Jenson contends that *"God" is an appropriate word for the reality identifiable as what happened with Jesus—his life, death, and resurrection.*[55] Jenson asserts that the difference between a living person and a dead person is that the one who is alive

---

49. Jenson, S&P, 48.
50. Jenson, TI, 23. Also in Jenson, "Triune God," 100; Jenson, "Three Identities," 3.
51. Jenson, S&P, 44.
52. Jenson, S&P, 60.
53. Jenson, S&P, 60. In ST1, Jenson refers to Luther's explanation of the unconditionality of promise. See Jenson, ST1, 181.
54. Jenson, ST1, 48.
55. Jenson, TI, 23; Jenson, "Triune God," 101; Jenson, "Three Identities," 3.

can surprise us.[56] As Jesus has died and now lives, he is the *One* who we can definitely know as an unconditional lover of all human beings, fulfilling the promise of Kingdom unconditionally in our present, and opening up a future in which we may anticipate still further surprises from his love. He is the one who, being remembered and looked forward to, is able to comprehend time in his embrace.[57] Jenson points out that "God is always some sort of eternity, some sort of embrace around time, within which time's sequences can be coherent."[58] This is the reason why, by the definition Jenson has given, Jesus is appropriately called "God."

2.2 The Gospel and the Identification of Father and Spirit

In our discussion we have seen that Jenson demonstrates how the God of Israel is identified by Jesus's death and resurrection, and have arrived at the argument for identifying Jesus as God. From the gospel summary that God is he "who raised Jesus our Lord from the Dead," Jenson argues that we have to make two further identifications of God. From this one gospel summary comes the identifications of God the Spirit and God the Father.

We have seen that in Jenson account, Jesus's resurrection is the event by which God is identified. But this resurrection event is an event that comes after Jesus's life as presented in the gospel narrative—after his death.[59] The life of the risen Jesus is not a mere continuation of the one that ended on the cross.[60] In this point, Jenson follows Thomas Aquinas's verdict: "One sort of resurrection would be resurrection only from actual death, so that someone began again to live after having died. Another sort would be that someone was freed not only from death but even from . . . the possibility of dying. Only this latter is true and authentic resurrection."[61] Jesus's crucifixion is the mark of completion of the life Jesus lived in Palestine. His resurrection, by which God is identified, is "the event in which Jesus is future to himself and to us."[62] For this futurity, we may identify God in the gospel summary for a second time: "God is what will come of Jesus and us, together . . . In the Bible

---

56. Jenson, *S&P*, 42–44; Jenson, *ST1*, 198.

57. Jenson, *TI*, 23; Jenson, "Triune God," 101; Jenson, "Three Identities," 3; Jenson, *S&P*, 112. For how Jenson gets this definition, see Jenson, *ST1*, 54–56.

58. Jenson, *TI*, 23; Jenson, "Triune God," 101; Jenson, "Three Identities," 3.

59. Jenson, *S&P*, 114; Jenson, *TI*, 23; Jenson, "Triune God," 101; Jenson, "Three Identities," 3.

60. Jenson, *ST1*, 200.

61. Aquinas, *Summa Theologiae*, 3.53.3; cf. Jenson, *ST1*, 200.

62. Jenson, *S&P*, 114; Jenson, *TI*, 23; Jenson, "Triune God," 101; Jenson, "Three Identities," 3.

generally, the 'Spirit' is God as the power of the future to overturn what already is, and just so fulfill it... The Spirit is the power of the Eschaton now to be at once Goal and Negation of what is."[63]

We should note how Jenson's case for the Trinity is supported by his choice of words. He describes the event of resurrection as "*the event in which Jesus is future to* himself," in order to make it an event that is distinguishable from "Jesus." He goes on to emphasize that this future is the event "in which *Jesus is* future to *himself*" so that this "futurity" does not become totally external to Jesus. There are two reasons why Jenson offers this form of expression: (1) To avoid his proposal becoming either a kind of tritheism or modalism. If he does not describe the future event as "the event in which *Jesus is* future to *himself*," Father, Son, and Spirit may be understood as three gods of past, present, and future respectively. If he does not describe the future as "*the event* in which Jesus *is future to* himself," we could suspect that this futurity is just another mode of God or another kind of manifestation of God in a temporal sequence. (2) This is a mark of the distinctiveness of Jenson's Pneumatology. He asserts that "God is Spirit," while insisting that the "paradigmatic uses of 'spirit' are and must remain those in phrases with the pattern 'the spirit of...' Spirit is precisely the person or group as not immediately identical with itself; the genitive phrase marks the nonidentity."[64] The elasticity of the personhood of God's three persons and their relation in temporality are key components of this trinitarian theology. They stretch his account to its limit and later we will ask whether they do in fact become tritheistic or modalistic.

Finally, Jenson asserts that we may identify God for a third time from this same summary of the gospel "God is who raised Jesus our Lord from the Dead." In this sentence, "Jesus" is an object and God is identified as the one who raised Jesus. Moreover, because the embrace of God's love as revealed in the Resurrection event is unconditional, it follows that it is the universal destiny of all things. God who raised Jesus is therefore also the *will* to grant all things Jesus's love as their destiny, and is the antecedent of Jesus's life, and of our own life and destiny. God is identified as he who *accomplishes* Jesus's resurrection, as well as a *given* Transcendence, prior, to all that Jesus is and does. Jesus addresses this Transcendence as "Father" in the New Testament. Thus "Father" is the Transcendence *given to* Jesus's work and sufferings. "Father" is also the Transcendence in contrast with Jesus's life, and the Transcendence that Jesus is responsible to and addresses

---

63. Jenson, *TI*, 23–24; Jenson, "Triune God," 101; Jenson, "Three Identities," 3–4.
64. Jenson, "The Holy Spirit," 105–7.

in trust.[65] Therefore God must be identified as "Father," who is "a given active transcendence to all that Jesus is and does."[66]

Thus, simply through analysis of this gospel summary "God is who raised Jesus our Lord from the Dead," Jenson shows that God is identified as Father, Son, and Spirit by and with the gospel event. He goes on to demonstrate a relationship between this triple identification of God and time. Time has three arrows[67]—past, present, and future. As the gospel event is an event in time and which embraces time, and as identification is a form of indication or pointing, we have to use all three arrows in order to point to the gospel God.[68]

Our study has set out the basic structure of Jenson's trinitarian theology. For Jenson, the God of gospel is firstly identified by and with the narrative of Jesus. Then through the temporal nature of the gospel narrative, we learn the importance of time for identifying the triune God. First, Jesus's life, proclamation of the Kingdom, death, and resurrection mark God as an unconditional lover who embraces all things in the whole span of time and transcends all the limitations of time. God is the God of love who embraces the time with a realized unconditional open future. Secondly, the temporal relation, intrinsic to the gospel narrative, indicates that the gospel's God is also His own given and futurity—Father and Spirit. So, the temporality of the gospel narrative indicates the truth of the Trinity. From it we find that God unites past, present, and future "from within time."[69] In Jenson's view, this makes temporality the crucial characteristic of the triune God. The means by which we may access this triune God is Jesus. God can only be rightly understood and identified with Jesus through the gospel narrative: "the Bible tells precisely a story about God; in that it tells its story in such fashion that we cannot transcend the story in some way to find the 'real' God, without declaring the story to be merely false."[70] In Jenson's own summary of his scheme:

---

65. Jenson, S&P, 114; Jenson, TI, 24; Jenson, "Triune God," 101; Jenson, "Three Identities," 4.

66. Jenson, TI, 24; Jenson, "Triune God," 101; Jenson, "Three Identities," 4.

67. In later works Jenson prefers "the poles of time" for his understanding of time as past, present and future. E.g., Jenson, ST1, 89, 218; Jenson, "Does God Have Time?," 191, 194.

68. Jenson, S&P, 114; Jenson, TI, 24; Jenson, "Triune God," 101; Jenson, "Three Identities," 4.

69. Jenson, "The Triunity of Truth," 92.

70. Jenson, "What is the Point of Trinitarian Theology?," 38. A similar account is in Jenson, "Does God Have Time?," 192.

[W]hat we are trying to analyze is the way in which the gospel identifies an event in time as itself the embrace around time. First, God is identified as Jesus: when we try to pick God out, to point at him, we have nothing whatever to point to but the man Jesus. Second, God is identified as one to whom Jesus is related, as to the authority and origin of his destiny: God is the one Jesus called "Father." Third, God is identified as the futurity of this relation, as what comes of Jesus's self-giving to "the Father."[71]

3. The Biblical Narrative in Both Testaments and the Identification of the Trinity

We have seen that Jenson constructs his trinitarian proposal from the narrative of the New Testament. He regards the gospel narrative as the fulfillment of the Old Testament, and the two narratives together as the whole story of the God of Israel. We must therefore examine the identification of the triune God with the biblical narrative of both Testaments.

3.1 The Appropriateness of the Biblical Narrative as Defining Genre for the Bible and the Trinitarianism for the Old Testament

It is often asserted that the doctrine of the Trinity is foreign to the Hebrew Bible.[72] Jenson regards this belief as simply false. On the contrary, the Trinitarianism of the gospel is the Christian explication of the fulfillment of the promise in the Hebrew Bible.[73] He claims that the entire New Testament shows apostolic dependence on the Old Testament. The authors of the New Testament interpret Jesus's life, death, and resurrection through the Old Testament and vice versa.[74] The Christian church finds the fulfillment of the promise of the God of Israel in the narrative of Exodus and Gospel: The gospel-proclamation—God is who raised Jesus our Lord from the Dead—comes in the form of narrative. The present four gospel books are long versions of this narrative gospel-proclamation. The New Testament's non-narrative genres are commentary on this gospel-proclamation. Because "it

---

71. Jenson, *S&P*, 115.

72. Again, the most notable example of this thought is Rudolf Bultmann and his school. For Jenson's discussion on this issue, see Jenson, *ST1*, 58n95.

73. Jenson, *TI*, 34; Jenson, "Triune God," 103; Jenson, *ST1*, 63; Jenson, "The Bible and the Trinity," 329–30.

74. Jenson, *ST1*, 30; Jenson, "Simplistic Thoughts," 184.

is the God of Israel whom Jesus called Father and to whom the disciples wanted to pray";[75] the narratives of the gospel and the Exodus are read as one story of promise rather than two unrelated pieces of work. The church therefore reads the Torah of the Hebrew Bible as narrative of the Exodus and Israel's recital of her experience and confession. It treats the Prophets and the Writings as commentaries on the narrative of the Exodus.[76] Finally, because the Spirit is identified as the enabling future of the Son and the Father; as we are to participate in that future, the relationship between the doctrine of the Trinity and the narrative of the both Testaments is clearly demonstrated.[77] The doctrine of the Trinity is the outcome of the Christian reading, by which Christians discover that within this narrative of two Testaments the future is opened also to them.

Jenson believes that the Christian church should declare that "the" biblical narrative runs through all the Scriptures. It runs through all historical discontinuities and Scripture's non-narrative genres. The church and Israel *confess* that one chief *agent*—God—*acts* through all these different books and genres. The purpose of assembling these various books as the Bible is to identify its agent.[78] Thus to make the narrative the defining genre is not to deny that there are other genres but to highlight the fact that the Christian faith confesses that its God is identified by the unity of this Scripture. One should note that the authenticity is not guaranteed by historical research but *God's agency*.

In sum, according to Jenson, biblical narratives were recognized as the story of God and his people by the early church. So, from this discussion of the appropriateness of the Trinity to the Old Testament and of narrative as the genre of Scripture, we can move on to examine Jenson's identification of the biblical narrative and the triune God.

---

75. Jenson, *ST1*, 42.

76. Jenson, *ST1*, 57–58. Jenson is well aware that "[i]t is regularly noted that the Bible is not a book but a library, that it contains many sorts of documents, and that the use of Scripture as norm must take account of this variety." See Jenson, "Simplistic Thoughts," 183. In this point—"narrative is Scripture's encompassing genre"—Jenson aligns himself with Hans Frei. Indeed, he states that the "currency of this phrase itself in recent theology is the work of Hans Frei, *The Eclipse of Biblical Narrative*." Jenson, "Simplistic Thoughts," 57n92. See Frei, *The Eclipse of Biblical Narrative*, 12–13.

77. Jenson, *ST1*, 45; Jenson, "Triune God," 93.

78. Jenson, *ST1*, 58–59; Jenson, "The Religious Power of Scripture," 91; Jenson, "Hermeneutics and the Life of the Church," 99.

3.2 The Old Testament Narrative as Triune Story of Promise

As we have seen, Jenson contends that Gospel represents a promise. Because it is a promise, it has to be made. Jenson believes that the history of Israel, through Jesus, is the event of the making of this gospel-promise. We can identify the content of this gospel-promise by telling Israel's history and in particular the history of the one Israelite—Jesus.[79] The content of the gospel-promise is God himself: "I have proposed a slogan for what the gospel promises: the triumph of Jesus's love."[80] This *"triumph will be the reality of God."*[81] This means that we can trace the origins of the doctrine of the Trinity in Israel's story of promise.

Jenson believes that the story of Israel begins with the narrative of Exodus. All Israel's theology can be derived from the identification of God by the narrative of Exodus.[82] Exodus was the single event that made Israel a people. According to Jenson, in "Egypt they had been no people: they had had no laws, no autonomy, and above all no place in which to be and become a civilization of their own. In Egypt they had had no identity."[83] JHWH rescued them from Egypt, gave them an identity as his people, and granted them laws to sustain that identity. The most important point about the Exodus event is that the narrative shows the God of Israel is the God of his acts—the one who rescued Israel and made a covenant with Israel is JHWH himself.[84] "If God is . . . *the one who* rescued Israel from Egypt, the main characteristics of this God are immediately evident."[85] Two of these characteristics are that: (1) JHWH "is not on the side of established order," and (2) JHWH's "will is not identical with natural necessity—that is, his will is indeed what we mean by 'will.'" We will come to a third characteristic shortly.[86]

---

79. Jenson, *S&P*, 13.

80. Jenson, *S&P*, 62.

81. Jenson, *S&P*, 60. Thus we can understand why Jenson says: "it is by telling Israel's history and in particular the history of the one Israelite, that the gospel-identifies what, or rather *who*, is promised." Jenson, *S&P*, 13.

82. Jenson, *TI*, 34; Jenson, "Triune God", 103.

83. Jenson, *S&P*, 14.

84. Jenson, *ST1*, 44; Jenson, *S&P*, 15.

85. Jenson, *TI*, 34; Jenson, "Triune God," 103. Italics Jenson's.

86. Jenson, *TI*, 35; Jenson, "Triune God," 104. Jenson then interprets God's will as God's consciousness. Through the concept of consciousness, he links temporal events and God's inner life to form his account of triune reality.

From these two points Jenson wants to show that God is a God of freedom. In his view, the eternity or guarantee of salvation of other ancient deities is "the Persistence of the beginning," "The Certainty of Return," or "the Guarantee of Continuance."[87] JHWH is not on the side of established order though; the founding of Israel is a rescue from "oppression under the archetypically standing order" of Egypt. Significantly, after rescuing Israel from this established order, JHWH leads the people into the insecurity of the desert. JHWH's eternity or salvation is no static defense against possible future changes but an embrace of all future possibilities. JHWH *poses* the future. Jenson suggests that after the "dialectical theology" of Barth and Bultmann in 1920s, declaring that God is "the *Eschatos*" should "need no further justification."[88] In Jenson's words, "God, said Barth, is 'the eternally future.' God, said Bultmann, is 'the insecurity of the future.'"[89]

Jenson observes that throughout her history, Israel desired to become an established order "like all nations" (1 Sam 8:4-5) and strove more for security than for God. However, God himself was the great opponent of such security: the prophets regularly denounced such attempts (1 Sam 8:7-9) and even proclaimed that the destruction of Israel's *status quo* was a new act of God.[90] Jenson states that "God . . . can be understood as so free as to be free even from his own past acts, to be God precisely by his freedom to initiate radical change, rather than by his ability to resist and protect from it."[91]

The God of Israel is a God of freedom. All his deeds come from his own will and choice. His will is not identical with natural necessity. In their myths ancient peoples asserted that they were founded by their gods at the beginning of time. The events narrated in these myths were also events of natural necessity that set time in motion.[92] "Therein lay assurance: nothing

---

87. Jenson, *TI*, 35; Jenson, "Triune God," 103.

88. Jenson, *ST1*, 67n16.

89. Jenson, "The Futurist Option," 18. However, we should note that Jenson has pointed out the inadequacy of the dialectical theology in the same article. He thinks that "All its reflection remained under the spell of timelessness; the eschaton was not proclaimed as a time, but as the immanent crisis of every time, having no extension in time, no before and after, and so no narratable content of its own . . . [God] is abstract futurity . . . About *this* 'Power of future' there is nothing to say." Jenson, "The Futurist Option," 19. Italics Jenson's.

90. Jenson, *ST1*, 67, 69; Jenson, *TI*, 35; Jenson, "Triune God," 103-4; Jenson, *S&P*, 23.

91. Jenson, *S&P*, 23-24. One should note that in later chapters I argue that Jenson's position is not valid if we consider his narrative Trinitarianism along with his "revisionary metaphysics."

92. Jenson, *TI*, 35-36; Jenson, "Triune God," 104; Jenson, *S&P*, 16-17.

can overthrow the people's basis, since outside it there is nothing."[93] By contrast the founding of the Israel was not identical with creation's beginnings or with a natural necessity. The founding event of Israel—the Exodus—happened only once, *in* time rather than outside time. Though Israel like other ancient religions attributed the general creation to her own God, the creation of the world and the creation of Israel were two acts of JHWH, not one. Jenson points out that Israel understood that created reality did not include her by necessity: she existed as a *choice* of God.[94]

Jenson has showed us that God's freedom is shown by his deeds *in time*. The God of Israel is not like the gods of other mythic religions. He does not need timeless persistence to guarantee his sovereignty. He can act freely in time *by his own will*. God's freedom is his transcendence.

After demonstrating that God is a God of freedom, Jenson points out a third characteristic of the God of Israel: God is a God of promise. Israel knew itself to be God's people not by necessity, but by God's word and promise. The God who created Israel and is worshiped by her is a God of promise. The time before the founding of Israel's nationhood at the Exodus is the period of the fathers, Abraham, Isaac, and Jacob, in which JHWH made these ancestors the promise of the land and nation of Israel. Thus, the story of the "preexistent" Israel is a story of promise.[95] In the narrative of Exodus, the rescue from Egypt was followed by a long journey of wandering in the desert, so that "salvation for Israel is given by promise of what is not yet, of the future that is now real only in the word that opens it."[96]

Though the establishment of Israel's kingdom seems not to fit this theology of promise, Jenson argues that we cannot simply regard the Davidic covenant as a distortion of the Exodus covenant or Israel's truth faith. Though the establishment of the temple could lead Israel to identify God as their past remembrance or present *status quo*, Jenson contends that we should note that the moral content of both covenants is the same: "Righteousness and justice are the foundation of your throne; steadfast love and faithfulness go before you" (Ps 89:14). The Davidic covenant prevented Israel's faith in JHWH from becoming intangible and remote. The temple's ceremony and ritual which borrowed from the Canaanites reinforces the non-verbal aspect of God's words. The Davidic covenant, the dynasty, and the temple show that God's will and promise was invested in the changing of

---

93. Jenson, "Triune God," 104; Jenson, *TI*, 35.
94. Jenson, *TI*, 36; Jenson, "Triune God," 104; Jenson, *ST1*, 67.
95. Jenson, *TI*, 36; Jenson, "Triune God," 104; Jenson, *ST1*, 68; Jenson, *S&P*, 17–18.
96. Jenson, *TI*, 36; Jenson, "Triune God," 104.

Israel's context and so in the reality of this world.[97] Jenson asserts that "Jahve acted through men, and Moses was dead; but the king could be a living and responsible incarnation of God's presence among his people."[98]

Because of these representations of God's commitment, we can say that "righteousness and justice and love must in this world be objects of faith, things hoped for and not seen."[99] Jenson thus contends that the *temporally* actual palace and temple reminded Israel that their objects of faith were spoken as an *eschatological* promise, not ascribed to the palace and temple themselves. Therefore, the Davidic covenant be seen positively function as a continuation of the Exodus covenant and continuation of God's promise, for they "came together after all."[100]

Ironically, according to Jenson, the main event after the founding of Israel's state was its undoing. The Exile of 587 BC took away all secure national existence or *status quo* that Israel could rely on.[101] Jenson finds that the prophets in the exilic period proclaimed that God will do something new. They called Israel "to live by hope rather than by possessions, by what was promised rather than by what already was, by hearing rather than by sight."[102] Thus the motif of the God of promise re-appears in this period. But the prophetic line came to an end in bitter alienation, as prophets could not see the fulfillment of the promises. Jenson contends that only a triumph over death can sustain the validity of the God's promise to Israel: "All hopes are invested in someone, and the only thing certain about that someone is that he will die. Such hopes as those evoked by the prophets . . . must either overcome death or be made implausible by it."[103]

Thus, it is clear that, for Jenson, Jesus's death and resurrection is the distinctive act and characteristic of JHWH the God of Israel, who is the God of promise. Only Jesus's death and resurrection can verify and sustain the promise of God. *We can identify the God of Israel from the Exodus to the resurrection of Jesus as the God who is free, who acts in time, and who has made and kept his promise. We confess that the two Testaments narrate one story of promise, by which we identify the triune God.*

97. Jenson, S&P, 18–19; Jenson, ST1, 69.
98. Jenson, S&P, 19.
99. Jenson, ST1, 69.
100. Jenson, ST1, 69.
101. Jenson, TI, 37.
102. Jenson, S&P, 25.
103. Jenson, S&P, 26.

4. Trinity, The Story of Promise, and Dramatic Coherence

As we have seen, Jenson asserts that the biblical God can really be identified by, and with, the narrative in the Old and New Testaments of the Bible. This narrative is a story of promise. God is the one who sets out, and acts in, this story. Jenson believes that God's self-identity[104] is *constituted* by dramatic coherence. According to Jenson, the "classic definition of this sort of coherence is provided by Aristotle, who noticed that a good story is one in which events occur 'unexpectedly but on account of each other,' so that before each decisive event we cannot predict it, but afterwards see it was just what had to happen."[105] In other words, despite there being discontinuities and crises in Israel's story, Israel and the Christian church can sort out the coherence of the story and identify the God of Israel dramatically. The crises in the story of promise have their resolutions eventually and dramatically. Jenson says that this coherence was not the result of a synthesis of the religious and conceptual deposit that available to Israel and Christians at that time. It came rather from their conviction that their God had been and would be the central character of their own lives and suffering, however apparently discontinuous.[106] From the concept of dramatic coherence and its relationship to God's identity, Jenson makes three assertions that support his trinitarian proposal.

First, he claims that there should be a closure if the dramatic coherence of a narrative is to constitute identity. The narrated individuality is uncertain if the story continues. Jenson argues that the creatures in created time cannot reliably understand a personal identity unless the individual concerned comes to their own temporal closure—death. If God is to be reliably identifiable by human beings, he must also have a closure in created time. Because the biblical narrative is a story of promise within dramatic coherence, there must be God's resurrection too. This dictates that death and resurrection is the only appropriate move for a God willing to be known by human beings.[107] If this contention is accepted, the gospel narrative ("God is who raised Jesus

---

104. In *ST1*, Jenson uses "identity" and "hypostatic being" interchangeably (p. 64), but says that he prefers "identity" to "hypostasis." See Jenson, *TI*, 105–11; Jenson, "Triune God," 138; Jenson, *ST1*, 106. "Identity" is a core concept for Jenson's trinitarian proposal. It will be investigated fully in chapter 4. But for our discussion of dramatic coherence, one definition Jenson offers is that "divine identity is a *persona dramatis dei* who can repeatedly be picked out by a name or identifying description or by pronouns, always by relation to the other two." Jenson, *ST1*, 106.

105. Jenson, *ST1*, 64.

106. Jenson, *ST1*, 64.

107. Jenson, *ST1*, 65–66.

our Lord from the Dead.") is the proper means of expounding the biblical doctrine of the Trinity in its dramatic coherence.

Secondly, Jenson contents that a story is constituted by the outcome of the narrated events. These narrated events are that story's future possibilities. If our beginning in a story was the same as our end, we would have no story at all, because the future's possibilities are wholly neutralized in advance.[108] In the openness and futurity of the narrative in dramatic coherence, Jenson believes that we may understand that, in his story with Israel, Israel's God is not a God without eternal change or who remains the same as when he began the story. On the contrary, he is a God of freedom. In freedom, he chooses Israel and keeps his promise to them. Regardless of the betrayal of his people, God is faithful to them and keeps his promise unconditionally, even to death. Not even death can end or hold up God's promise, for the Son has overcome death. The fulfillment of this story of promise is not a return to its beginning but the fulfillment of God's unconditional love in the eternal future. In this future, though there will be changes and new experience, nothing will fall away from God's unconditional love. So, we can say that the characteristic of the narrative in dramatic coherence demonstrates the rationale for Jenson's rejection of the Greek philosophical concept of God's eternity as persistence, along with his refusal to construct a trinitarian theology in terms of being as substance. As he puts it, "Since the Lord's self-identity is constituted in dramatic coherence, it is established not from the beginning but from the end, not at birth but at death, not in *persistence* but in *anticipation*."[109]

Thirdly, Jenson uses the concept of the agents of the story to illustrate why God cannot be a monadic agent. Like any story, the biblical narrative has more than one agent. In God's story, we can speculate that the plurality of agents is "constituted only by external relations between God and persons who are simply other than God, so that God is himself but one monadic agent of the history."[110] But Jenson argues that because "God's identity is told by his story with creatures, this cannot be the case."[111] God cannot be a single monadic agent, because otherwise, his "identity would then be determined extrinsically by creatures or it would at some depth be after all immune to the gospel events."[112] If God's identity were determined extrinsically by creatures, he could be no absolutely free and sovereign

---

108. Jenson, "Second Thoughts," 340; Jenson, *ST1*, 66.
109. Jenson, *ST1*, 66. Italics Jenson's.
110. Jenson, *ST1*, 75.
111. Jenson, *ST1*, 75.
112. Jenson, *ST1*, 75.

God. Since such a speculation contradicts the account of God's events in Exodus and the Resurrection, God cannot be monadic in this sense. If we still wanted to understand God's identity as monadic, our next choice would be to regard it as, at some deep level, immune to the events of the gospel. But Jenson contends that God is truly identified by and with the gospel and narrative. He rejects this alternative too, and instead concludes that we must "reckon with and seek to identify a plurality of what can only be called *dramatis dei personae*, 'characters of the drama of God.'"[113] These *personae* are Father, Son, and Spirit of the Trinity.

5. Summary

We have seen that Jenson's narrative account of the Trinity and claim of a *dramatic* coherence of God's identity are based on his conviction that God's being and act are identified by and with the narrative of Scripture. We can say that dramatic coherence is a reading strategy that enables us to identify the God who, despite all discontinuities, acts in coherence in the biblical narrative. Israel and Christians employ this strategy because they believe the concerned narrative is *really* a story of God. Jenson's proposal understands that God's being in his story is received both by the faith community and by God himself. In traditional theological terms, it is a question both of the difference and identity of the economic Trinity and immanent Trinity. It is a quest for a realist account of the Trinity offered by the Christian community.

In the next three chapters I will argue that, in Jenson's attempt to go beyond Barth, his theology of language, and his account of the Trinity as temporal infinity, Jenson places great emphasis on the temporality of the triune reality. This means that his understanding of narrative risks becoming *ultra-realist*, collapsing the distinction between the human knower and the God who is known. His understanding of language and ontology will eventually compel us to ask whether Jenson's doctrine of the Trinity diminishes the transcendence of God.

---

113. Jenson, *ST1*, 75.

Chapter 2

How Does Jenson Advance Barth's Doctrine of the Trinity?

JENSON ONCE SAID, "I am always afraid to propose 'going beyond' Barth, since I am always afraid that the only reason I think there is a beyond is that I have missed some point. However . . ."[1] With this "however" Jenson goes on to offer his own theological proposal: "Within an eschatological rather than protological interpretation of God's eternity and so of Christ's ontic primacy, we could say the following."[2] Jenson is not quite sure whether his theology goes beyond Barth: "I do not myself well know what to make of the speculations [of mine] in [section] (V). I am a bit alarmed at submitting them. I do not even know whether they are a critique of Barth, or a mere repetition of him."[3] But if we investigate Jenson's work as a whole, we will find his theology is no mere repetition or superficial critique of Barth. Jenson recognizes Barth's theological accomplishments and he largely accepts them. He develops Barth's insights and finally he "goes beyond" Barth. How Jenson advances Barth and the significance of this advancement is the topic of this chapter.

Jenson comes to Barth's trinitarian theology with a question. We first asked it in the introduction. The question is "how Jesus Christ, a past event, can be the decisive reality in our present life." As we have seen, the question points to the demise of classical theology. Jenson realizes we cannot tackle this problem by reaffirming a timeless and transcendental divine reality, and so he is motivated to look for an answer in Barth's doctrine of the Trinity. Also, it is the same concern that marks the point which Jenson advances Barth's theology.

1. Jenson, "Religious Pluralism," 36.
2. Jenson, "Religious Pluralism," 36–37.
3. Jenson, "Religious Pluralism," 38.

In this chapter, I argue that Jenson's Trinitarianism attempts to find a new way to articulate the triune God of Christianity in order to replace the transcendentalism effectively refuted by the Enlightenment. His concerns are similar to Barth's. Both aim to transcend the Enlightenment and the nineteenth-century Protestantism. For Barth, the doctrine of the Trinity is his resource. For Jenson, his own trinitarian project intends to continue and advance Barth's. I will show Jenson's agreement with Barth's narrative theology of the Trinity. *Jenson chooses to advance Barth's narrative theology with an unreserved commitment to the ontological function of narrative.* Jenson believes that the doctrine of analogy and pneumatology are the weak points of Barth's theology. His concern is that Barth's weak doctrine of the Spirit and his doctrine of analogy will ultimately make Barth's efforts unsuccessful. For Jenson, that the Trinity is identifiable through narrative means that God inhabits time and so may not be regarded as simply above time. That God is Father, Son, and Spirit means that God embraces three dimensions of time—past, present, and future. Therefore, I will argue that the ontological function of narrative, pneumatology and the relation of time, and God's being are the areas in which Jenson takes Barth's doctrine of the Trinity forward. I will also ask whether Jenson's critique of Barth reveals Jenson's over-reliance on the temporal dimension of reality, and whether this makes his proposals ultimately unsatisfactory.

1. Enlightenment, Liberal Theology, Barth, and Jenson

As I have discussed in the introduction, the challenge to modern theology comes from the Enlightenment's challenge to the classical theological tradition. Jenson believes that the Enlightenment is the "decisive break" between premodern and modern theology.[4] In this section, I argue that Jenson believes that he and Barth are attempting to find a reply to the Enlightenment. Both believe that the liberal theology of the nineteenth century tried to do the same thing but was unsuccessful. They are therefore aiming to go beyond liberal theology too.

1.1 Enlightenment and the Demise of Classical Theology

Jenson argues that traditional Christian theology was formed of a combination of the gospel-proclamation of the God who raised Jesus from the dead and the religious, dualist metaphysical quest for timeless deity of Western antiquity. It understood the gospel-proclamation as

---

4. Jenson, *ST1*, 7; Jenson, "Karl Barth," 22–23; Braaten and Jenson, "Introduction," 1.

"supernatural" knowledge of God and believed metaphysical speculation to be "natural" knowledge. The former was thought to be obtained only by surrendering oneself to the authority of agency of revelation, whereas the latter, by contrast, is accessible to "reason."[5] The Enlightenment challenged this synthesis of faith and reason.

Jenson believes that the Enlightenment was the declaration of independence of the individual from every limitation or authority. Enlightenment is "enlightening" because the intellectual leaders of the eighteenth century believed that the independent human mind could carry its light into all dark realms of superstition and authority. It celebrated the power of reason of autonomous free human. Kant employed the word "critique" to sum up this power of reason. Thus, the Enlightenment was also the intellectual policy of the "critique" of all "appearances" of truth.[6]

The individual, a free and thinking subject, employed critical reason to question the authority of revelation and the teaching of the church that interpreted it. Classical Christian theology insisted that the gospel taught that God was "supernatural" and he is known, not by reason, but by revelation only. The gospel is thus an "authoritative" communication from God and the church. Because revelation and the church's teaching are "authoritative," the *philosophes* of the Enlightenment rebelled against it.[7] In Jenson's view, the Enlightenment critique is religious rather than truly "natural." Jenson argues that "The Enlightenment found its lever of critique in this division [of natural and supernatural knowledge], judging 'revealed' religion by the standard of 'natural' religion. The outcome was an elite theology and worship purged of specifically Christian character."[8]

More unfortunately, the natural knowledge of the antiquity—metaphysics—was also rejected because the *philosophes* judged it incompatible with the intellectual duty of the critique of appearances. The success of natural science in the seventeenth century motivated them to thoroughly adopt the policy of critique to the problems of humanity's own life. The result is an attitude radically skeptical of all knowledge. The policy of critique as scientific ethos forbids us from introducing any absolute or unchangeable truths into our explanations of reality. The policy of radical critique does not allow us to assume any continuity or unity between the present and the past. There is no unproblematic timeless eternity. The Enlightenment rejected the

---

5. Jenson, *TI*, 132; Jenson, *AT*, 6; Jenson, "Kingdom of America's God," 54.

6. Jenson, "Karl Barth," 23; Jenson, *AT*, 5; Jenson, "What Academic Difference Would be the Gospel Make?," 78; Jenson, "On the Problem(s) of Scriptural Authority," 246.

7. Jenson, "Karl Barth," 23–24; Jenson, *AT*, 7.

8. Jenson, "Karl Barth," 24. See also Jenson, *ST2*, 134–35.

God of metaphysics, and questioned whether Jesus, a vanished historical figure, can have any divine meaning for us in the present.[9]

As a result, the Enlightenment effectively refuted the doctrine of the Trinity as "transcendental" and "metaphysical."[10]

1.2 Critiquing the Spirit of Enlightenment

In the previous section, we saw Jenson arguing that the drive of human autonomy and the policy of critique effectively challenged the classical theology's synthesis of gospel-proclamation and metaphysics. In this section, I will show how Jenson relates Barth and himself to the Enlightenment and to liberal theology.

Though Karl Barth referred to himself at the end of his life as "a child of the nineteenth century,"[11] Jenson locates Barth beyond the nineteenth century. Jenson sets Barth's theology in the context of modernity and considers the Enlightenment to be "modernity's founding event."[12] He believes that Barth's theology "is an attempt . . . to transcend the Enlightenment."[13]

For Jenson, Barth fully perceives the Enlightenment's spirit of striving for human absolute autonomy. We see Barth's position on the Enlightenment in his *Protestant Theology in the Nineteenth Century*. The defining phenomenon of the Enlightenment was the "*Mensch*"—the "absolutist" person. "This is the human person 'who discovers his own power, his own ability, the potential that slumbers in his . . . humanity simply as such, and who understands this as something final . . . , i.e., as something . . . in itself justified and authorized and mighty, and who therefore sets this potential in uninhibited motion in every direction.'"[14] However, the Enlightenment's view of human autonomy and destiny is false and misleading. Jenson and Barth both believe that this is precisely what Christian theology understands as "sin." Longing for absolute autonomy is human's "sin" because it rejects everything that may challenge its judgment.[15] Barth defines human pride as one of the three forms of sin. It is pride that makes humans refuse to

---

9. Jenson, "A Dead Issue Revisited," 54; Jenson, "Once More," 120; Jenson, *RAI*, 18–20; Jenson, *ST2*, 135.

10. Jenson, "Karl Barth," 24.

11. Zuckmayer, *A Late Friendship*, 3.

12. Jenson, "Karl Barth," 22.

13. Jenson, "Karl Barth," 22.

14. Jenson, *AT*, 4–5. See also Jenson, "Karl Barth," 23. Barth, *Protestant Theology*, 36.

15. Jenson, "Karl Barth," 23.

live in dependence upon God's grace and providence.[16] The Enlightenment's version of human absolute freedom is precisely this pride, and thus, human sin. Barth believes that, as opposition to God's work, sin is evil, and in evil, there is only "nihility" or "nothingness."[17]

Following Barth's doctrine of sin, Jenson argues that the freedom and hope granted by the Enlightenment is only an illusion, and this is also a form of sin. *It results as a threat of nihility or despair of life.* Jenson observes that the Enlightenment's radical critique and absolute autonomy does not make possible rationality or the real openness of human subjects. Conversely, the radical critique, which reaches its climax in late modernity, prevents commitment and keeps humans suspicious of everything in their life. "It is actually perfectly reactionary, since it allows everything in my life to remain exactly as it was; while it appears to be heroism it is in fact avoidance."[18] The illusion of openness allows humans to remain closed to any real future. It prevents them from being changed or challenged by any truly new possibility. Jenson believes that rationality is epistemic openness to God's future. Obedience to the divine command involves us in a change of mind, and this is a matter of virtue rather than a natural capability. Radical critique, by contrast, refuses to be challenged by God's future and thus it is irrationality. Irrationality is not incapability but that false openness and optimism that conceals the sin of despair.[19]

1.3 Enlightenment and Liberal Theology

Jenson and Barth view nineteenth-century German liberal theology, of which Schleiermacher is representative, as an attempt to counter the Enlightenment's challenge. Barth calls Schleiermacher as an "apologist."[20] This does not mean that Schleiermacher took a confrontational or antagonistic stance towards the Enlightenment. He intended that theology should fulfill the demands of the Enlightenment and thence to pass beyond it.[21] According to Barth:

> [Schleiermacher] is as a modern man and therefore as a thinker and therefore as a moral philosopher and therefore as a philosopher of religion and therefore as a philosophical theologian and

---

16. Barth, *CD* 4/1 §60.
17. In German: "*Das Nichtige.*" Barth, *CD* 3/3:351–53.
18. Jenson, *ST2*, 147. See also, Jenson, "On Becoming Man," 31–33.
19. Jenson, *ST2*, 146.
20. Barth, *Protestant Theology*, 439–50.
21. Barth, *Protestant Theology*, 433.

therefore as an apologist and therefore finally as a dogmatist determined on no account to interpret Christianity in such a way that his interpreted statements can come into conflict with the methods and principles of the philosophy and the historical and scientific research of his time.[22]

For this reason, liberal theology unfortunately articulated the Christian faith as a function of human existence. Contemporary intellectual culture determined how theology could interpret human life and decided on the appropriate form of religion. When an account of human existence had been given, Christ could be fitted in and a Christian theology offered.[23] Barth insisted that this approach could never be successful, because we may not understand God simply as a continuation of our own thought. God is "Wholly Other."[24] Therefore, he comments that:

> The Gospel of Christ is a shattering disturbance . . . For this reason, nothing is so meaningless as the attempt to construct a religion out of the Gospel, and to set it as one human possibility in the midst of others. Since Schleiermacher, this attempt has been undertaken more consciously than ever before in Protestant theology—and it is the betrayal of Christ.[25]

Jenson, following Barth, considers Schleiermacher's to be one of two great attempts (the other was Hegel's) to meet the challenges of the Enlightenment.[26] Along with Barth, he also recognizes that liberal theology cannot transcend the Enlightenment. He points out that the "nineteenth century response to the Enlightenment harbored a particular flaw," which was its acceptance of "the Enlightenment's elevation of the Greek element of our thinking to be unilateral judge of the whole."[27]

Barth and Jenson believe that liberal theology fails to meet the Enlightenment's challenge. Since they believe that the modern theological problem is directly related to the Enlightenment, they offer their own proposals to go beyond both the Enlightenment and liberal theology.

---

22. Barth, *Protestant Theology*, 431.
23. Barth, *Protestant Theology*, 461–73; Jenson, *GAG*, 5.
24. Barth, "The Righteousness of God," 24.
25. Barth, *The Epistle to the Romans*, 225. See also Jenson, "Karl Barth," 25.
26. Braaten and Jenson, "Introduction," 4; Jenson, *ST1*, 8.
27. Jenson, *ST1*, 9.

1.4 Transcending the Enlightenment and Liberal Theology Dialectically

Barth's theology is not just the opposite of the Enlightenment or liberal theology. In Jenson's view, the relation between Barth, the Enlightenment, and liberal theology is far more complex than this. Regarding the drive of human independence from authority and the policy of critique of the Enlightenment's spirit, Jenson argues that "to neither aspect of that spirit does Barth's theology have an undialectically antagonistic relation."[28]

Jenson argues that Barth rejects the Enlightenment's version of human autonomy. Barth teaches that true human freedom is found in an ontological relationship—with Jesus Christ. For Jesus, being human and being lord and judge coincide, so Jesus he is truly autonomous and free. Similarly, Christian faith is not grounded on the human experience of religion or search for meaning. It is determined by Jesus as the "Lord." *Trinitarian theology is therefore not about divine reality only, but about the proper ontology of human being.*[29]

For the spirit of critique and the refutation of timeless metaphysics, Jenson argues that Barth's "polemic was initially a straightforward *continuation* of liberalism's polemic against 'metaphysics,' that is, against claims for theological assertions's meaningfulness outside of a religious relation to Christ." Thus, Barth's theology is as critical and christocentric as liberal theology. It is also anti-metaphysical, which puts it in agreement with the spirit of Enlightenment.[30] Barth sets himself against liberal theology because its complacent belief in religion as a function of human existence makes the Christian faith simply the highest form of religion. He also rejects the liberal view that history is only what can be reconstructed by research.[31]

Jenson's theology has a similar "dialectically antagonistic relation" with the Enlightenment and liberal theology. Jenson argues that though the Enlightenment's own proposal is unsuccessful, in its spirit it shares concerns with the Christian faith:

> The Enlightenment unleashed the critical function of the mind over against all appearances of truth. Who would now wish to restrain it? Or even to challenge its autonomy? None, anyway, [it is] faithful to the gospel's insatiable critique of all religion and of all human pretensions to truth. The Enlightenment dreamed

---

28. Jenson, "Karl Barth," 23.
29. Jenson, "Karl Barth," 23.
30. Jenson, "Karl Barth," 25–26.
31. Jenson, "Karl Barth," 25–26; Jenson, *GAG*, 5.

of universal order, and set out to adumbrate it. And it dreamed of constructing humane polities in the course of the same quest. Surely [Jonathan] Edwards was right to recognize that the dreams are fitting, because the universe's Creator is *triune*.[32]

In Jenson's view, transcending the Enlightenment and liberal theology does not mean abolishing human autonomy or critical thinking. Jenson believes that Greek dualist metaphysics and reasoning poisoned the real spirit of Enlightenment. Liberal theology attempted to overcome this dualism but instead became deeply entangled in it. *Transcending the Enlightenment means upholding the spirit of reason by challenging Greek dualism as the norm by which reason, beauty, and reality are judged.* We should not suppose "the qualification of truth taught by Plato or Aristotle as more 'natural' or 'rational' than truth taught by Isaiah or Paul."[33]

Jenson believes that Barth's, and his own attempt, to transcend the Enlightenment are not reactionary. They simply relocate the Enlightenment's hope for reason, autonomy, meaning, and reality to a new ground, no longer that of Greek dualism, but of the doctrine of the Trinity.

2. Jenson's Reading of Barth

Jenson explicates Barth's attempt to meet the challenge of the Enlightenment and of liberal theology through an analysis of Barth's doctrine of the Trinity. Jenson finds that in his early work, *The Word of God and the Word of Man*, Barth made two "great systematic moves that were to shape the *Church Dogmatics*." Jenson summarizes:

> The first is the overturning of the reality-question. It is not, Barth came to see, that our selves and world as we first encounter them are real, and that we must then inquire how God fits in; what happens with God towards us is our real life, and the reality-question is properly aimed rather at what we initially take to be our selves and world. The second is the use of the inherited Trinity-doctrine to define this unexpected reality of God.[34]

For Jenson, the doctrine of the Trinity is the center of Barth's theological inquiry. The reality of the triune God determines human subjects reality and meaning. This approach to theology indeed reverses the order given by liberal theology and subverts the Enlightenment's approach to knowledge.

---

32. Jenson, *AT*, 195–96.
33. Jenson, *ST1*, 9.
34. Jenson, "Re-Review," 53.

The triune reality of "what happens with God towards us" is no speculation. Barth understands this reality christologically: "Reality is the history of Jesus the Christ of Israel—and of those who play roles in his drama, which is all men . . . [T]here is just one order of reality: the history that takes place in Jesus Christ."[35] Therefore, Christology and the doctrine of the Trinity interweave one another and depict the same reality.

Jenson shows that it is no accident that Barth develops his theological schema along such lines. Barth's early dialectical theology in *The Epistle to the Romans* already laid down the way Barth would construct his Christology and doctrine of the Trinity in the *Church Dogmatics*. Our analysis of Jenson's reading of Barth starts from the dialectical theology of *Romans*.[36]

2.1 Dialectical Theology of Time and Eternity

Jenson argues that the "systematic principle" of *Romans* can be summed up as dialectic of time and eternity. Barth said, "If I have a system, it consists in what Kierkegaard called 'the infinite qualitative difference' between time and eternity."[37] *The opposition of time and eternity is the controlling theme for Jenson's interpretation of Barth and the origin of his critique of Barth.*

For Jenson, Barth's dialectic of time and eternity is a challenge to religion. The target of Barth's polemic is the liberal theology which regards Christianity as one, albeit the highest, form of human religion.[38] God is in eternity while humans are in time. There is an infinite difference between eternity and time. As beings in time humans can only experience eternity as crisis or as the cancellation of time, and as their own death. We "stopped at 'the line of death' where eternity touches time."[39]

Religion tries to cultivate a sense of eternity from human side. It is the attempt "to experience eternity temporally, to think, discuss, depict, and represent it."[40] Barth's *Romans* denies this attempt can be successful. What religion can find is "Not-God." It is only "the God of this world (who can

---

35. Jenson, "Response," 32.

36. We should note that Jenson limits his discussion to the second edition of *Romans*.

37. Jenson, *GAG*, 8; Jenson, "Karl Barth," 26; Jenson, *ST1*, 170. From Barth, *Der Römerbrief*, xiii.

38. Jenson, *GAG*, 5.

39. Jenson, "Karl Barth," 27. See also Jenson, *GAG*, 8–9; Jenson, *ST1*, 170.

40. Jenson, *GAG*, 9. From Barth, *Der Römerbrief*, 112.

be named Life, Reality, Kingdom of God, The Beyond, etc.)."[41] Religion is human pride, lust, and betrayal of God.[42]

Despite Barth's brutal critique of religion in *Romans*, Jenson considers it still "wholly religious." In Jenson's view, *Romans* deeply stands within the great western tradition. Jenson argues that Barth describes the relation of time—the passible—to eternity—the impassible—in the moment of crisis as "the likeness of the impassible." This is very close to Platonism's concept of image. Barth's *Romans* allows no particular historical event, not even "Jesus," can be truly the union of time and eternity. This is also not dissimilar to Platonism. For Socrates and Plato, "Eros" is an unstillable spiritual energy struggling between mortality and immorality. Barth refers to the dynamic of our lives, which derives from the insoluble problem of our finitude, as "Eros."[43] These examples show, Jenson believes, that Barth in *Romans* has not succeeded in breaking free of Greek philosophy.

Jenson finds Barth's dialectics in *Romans*, as seen in its doctrine of election, eventually becomes "the final triumph of Platonic religion." Jenson believes that it immobilizes religion and the genuine Christian faith of gospel.[44]

Jenson realizes that in the *Romans* commentary Barth proposes that God can genuinely overcome the duality of time and eternity. The God who can overcome the duality, is the one "who 'justifies' the 'ungodly.'"[45] Human beings are permitted to rebel against God, because in the rebellion we exhaust all possibilities and discover that all our religion is "Not God." Facing God's "No," we are in crisis. Only when we are in this crisis, we turn to Jesus and realize the opposition between our temporal realities and God's eternity. Dialectically, the possibility of knowing God—a unity of time and eternity—opens in this crisis: "In the radical cancellation of historical . . . realities, there appears . . . their true, eternal meaning."[46] In the moment of crisis, God's "No" is indeed a "Yes." There is the oneness of time and eternity behind and above its separation. It can be found in Jesus Christ. He is Savior in that he occupies "the line of death" where eternity touches time. In him, the total denial of meaning to our temporal life binds us to eternity—to the time's truth. This unity is real only as *crisis*.[47]

---

41. Jenson, *GAG*, 10. From Barth, *Der Römerbrief*, 163–64.
42. Jenson, *GAG*, 10.
43. Jenson, *GAG*, 14–15.
44. Jenson, *GAG*, 29–30.
45. Jenson, *GAG*, 16.
46. Jenson, *GAG*, 26. From Barth, *Der Römerbrief*, 52.
47. Jenson, *GAG*, 26–27. From Barth, *Der Römerbrief*, 65, 88, 129, 280.

There can be a unity of time and eternity in Christ because God's eternity transcends the difference of time and eternity. *God's eternity is the sole reality. The temporal world does not stand over against God as a second independent reality. The relation of time of eternity is a movement or an occurrence with a goal.* The goal is to show God's ultimate transcendence in eternity: "The relation of time and eternity 'occurs *for* the second against the first, as a turning . . . *from* the first *to* the second, as a victory of the second over the first.'"[48] However, this movement or occurrence "is not *in* time, but *of* time to eternity—and so *in* eternity. It *occurs solely in God*."[49]

The result of this is that we cannot know or experience God's act as history within temporal realm. The historical events that God's act "makes itself observable within visible history," which include "the life of Jesus," are not themselves the act of God. They are mere "empty spaces" in history. The meaninglessness of our history remains meaningless. God's saving act of uniting time and eternity is the "*actus purus*"—pure event—of an "invisible event" in God. The eternal meaning of our reality—God's saving act or the unity of time and eternity—can only be found from God's intention in it. We cannot stipulate a meaning to it, because God's saving act is solely a decision of God: "The oneness of God's will divides itself into duality, in order to prove itself as oneness in overcoming this duality . . . it is a decision which is made 'only in God himself, in God alone.'"[50] Therefore, the invisible origin of all things, including the fall and redemption, is God's eternal decision or predestination. Predestination is a "decree which is made in God *before* all time and so also *before* each moment of time."[51] Moreover, because God's eternal decree is a movement in God from time to eternity and from rejection to election; it is a *history* in God.

But Jenson believes that this proposal is "the final historicizing of Platonism." In Barth's proposal, the saving event of the history between God and us "becomes a history in God *alone*, an *eternal* history, a history which *cannot be narrated* . . . a history 'of which no history can be narrated, because it occurs . . . eternally.'" Jenson concludes that *Romans* can be seen as "the final triumph of platonic religion."[52] Because it cannot be narrated, Jenson complains that Barth's doctrine of election immobilizes the Christian faith, and his polemics against religion become a dialectics of abstractness.

---

48. Jenson, *GAG*, 27. From Barth, *Der Römerbrief*, 143. Italics Jenson's.
49. Jenson, *GAG*, 28. Italics mine.
50. Jenson, *GAG*, 28.
51. Jenson, *GAG*, 28. Italics Jenson's.
52. Jenson, *GAG*, 29. From Barth, *Der Römerbrief*, 50. Italics Jenson's.

Jenson is alarmed by Barth's dialectic of eternity and time in *Romans*. Jenson believes that though the dialectic is a polemic against religion, it is the polemic of Socrates: "Barth's dialectics are born of a basic contradiction between time and eternity. So also were Socrates' . . . Barth's dichotomy of time and eternity came to him at the end of the same tradition in which Socrates stood."[53] This makes the doctrine of election expressed in *Romans* an historicized version of Platonic timeless divine eternity. Jenson fears that this "immobilizes" the faith of gospel and cannot satisfactorily answer the question of reality and meaning. Dramatic alterations to Barth's proposals on this theme of time and eternity are needed.

2.2 Barth's Christology and Reality

Though Jenson is not satisfied with Barth's dialectic of time and eternity in *Romans*, he claims that neither Barth nor himself should give up on dialectic. It is only the abstractness of the dialectic that we need to overcome. Barth's Christology in *Church Dogmatics* gives him the answer he is looking for.[54]

Jenson believes that the problem of modern theology is the radical critique and historicist consciousness of the Enlightenment. The issues of time and eternity have to be dealt with. Jenson's concern with time rightly impacts on his reading of Barth's Christology.

From his opening gambit that "Christianity is an historical religion," Jenson develops three questions:

> (1) To what end does God rule human history, and what is the course of the history of salvation? (2) In what sense does God have a history, and what is the relation between this history and ours? That is, *how* does God guide human history? (3) What is the reality to which talk in the Church bears witness?[55]

These questions guide Jenson's reading of Barth's Christology. They related it to the issues of time and eternity, of meaning, and of reality, raised because they represent the modern theological problems represented by the Enlightenment and liberal theology. Through their exploration Jenson gathers the elements of his own means of improving on Barth.

---

53. Jenson, *GAG*, 11.
54. Jenson, *ST1*, 170.
55. Jenson, *A&O*, 17–18.

Jenson believes the initial part of the first question can be rephrased as "why did God create the world?"[56] Barth's answer is in his doctrine of covenant. "Creation," in his definition "is the . . . external basis of the covenant . . . It prepares . . . the sphere in which the institution and history of the covenant take place."[57] God is love. Making this covenant is God's act of loving and demonstrates the reality of that love. Creatures are God's others. God's Creation shows he is real lover, for he makes a loving covenant with the others who are beyond his own triune fellowship.[58] In his eternal decree God decides to love the creature and make covenant with him; therefore, he decides to create him. Thus, the creature exists solely because of this eternal decision of God.[59]

The covenant of creation is precisely the covenant of reconciliation. God's covenant of creation is an eternal decision to love his creatures and have fellowship with them. The covenant we now know and live is God's fellowship with sinners and thus it is a covenant of reconciliation. Thus, God's eternal decision to love the creatures—the covenant of creation—takes the form of the covenant of reconciliation with sinners in the crucifixion and resurrection of Christ.[60]

So, the incarnation of the Son is the content of God's eternal decision to love his creatures. God's eternal decree is a "double" predestination. In eternity God chose to live for us and we for him. We, as sinners, are not chosen by God for our merit, but for God's grace. God chose to lose that we might gain, to be himself burdened with sin and evil in order that we might be blessed.

God eternally chose to be one with sinful man in the personal existence, that is, he chose to be incarnate Jesus Christ. This eternal election determines the course of salvation.[61] Since God's choice to be one with us is in itself a self-determination of God, and since it was decided eternally, Jesus Christ—the God-*man*—exists in eternity before all time. The preexistence of Jesus Christ is God's chosen eternal reality.[62] At this point, we get the answer to the second part of Jenson's first question. Salvation is God's eternal election to be Jesus Christ, to be the electing God. The course of

---

56. Jenson, *A&O*, 22; Jenson, "Karl Barth," 30.
57. Barth, *CD* 3/1:97.
58. Jenson, *A&O*, 22; Jenson, "Karl Barth," 30.
59. Jenson, *A&O*, 24.
60. Jenson, *A&O*, 25; Jenson, "Karl Barth," 30.
61. Jenson, "Karl Barth," 30.
62. Jenson, *A&O*, 66–68; Jenson, "Karl Barth," 30–31.

salvation is the event that starts with the preexistence of Jesus Christ and is directed to the final fulfillment of God's covenant.

Then, we come to Jenson's second question of God's history and the relation between this history and human's history. Jenson observes that, for Barth, history is:

> Something other than itself and transcending its own nature encounters it, approaches it and determines its being in the nature proper to it, so that it is compelled and enabled to transcend itself in response and in relation to this new factor.[63]

Jenson shows that this definition of "history" has three features: (1) History is self-transcending. History happens when one leaves one's own security of the present and moves out toward what we are not yet, and thus, is self-transcending. (2) Only when there is the reality of others, can there be history. History is only possible in communion between persons because we cannot move from our own reality unless there is another reality other than ourselves. (3) History with its transcendence is in time. Only in time can persons meet each other. Timeless being has no history.[64]

Accordingly, God's being as the triune is itself a history. All of God's works outside himself are in history. They are the overflow of eternal interpersonal communion within God. The event of God's eternal decision to be with us in Jesus Christ must be history too. As this decision is made eternally, the preexistence of Jesus Christ is necessarily preeminently event. It is an eternal history of God. Because this eternal history is God's own history and his eternal covenant with human at the same time, it is the basis of all other history between God and Man. It is the "inner basis" of the covenant. God's eternal history of choosing to be Jesus Christ is the "principle and essence of all happening."[65]

An analysis of God's eternal personal history sets the platform for Jenson's answer to the third question. From Barth's doctrine of eternal election, it can be seen that "Reality is the history of Jesus the Christ of Israel."[66] The "history of the man Jesus with God, *is our real history.*"[67]

Jenson's point is striking. He appreciates Barth's Christology as a brilliant attempt to overcome western metaphysical tradition. He calls it a "christological metaphysics," a "christological reversal" of western

---

63. Jenson, *A&O*, 75. From Barth, *CD* 3/2:158.
64. Jenson, *A&O*, 75.
65. Jenson, *A&O*, 77–78. From Barth, *CD* 2/2:183.
66. Jenson, "Response," 32.
67. Jenson, *A&O*, 133. Italics Jenson's.

metaphysics, or an assertion of the "ontological priority of Christ."[68] From Jenson's description, the triumph of Barth's christological metaphysics is to insist the "Ground of Being" is personal and temporal.[69]

Because Christ is the eternal event in God's life and the Ground of Being of human's life, the meaning of human existence cannot be sought as an independent phenomenon: "There is no human life in itself, and surely no meaning of such a life. Rather, the event of Jesus Christ's life, because it is the central event in the life of the eternal God, is the eternal presupposition of all else that happens."[70]

Jenson argues that Barth's Christology shows us the reality and meaning of human beings without recourse to the timeless eternity of classical theology. It is not a religious discourse of reality which turns to be a function of human experience as liberal theology. Unsurprisingly, Jenson's comment is that "Barth has solved the problem of the disappearance of the timeless."[71] He believes that Barth has overcome the challenge of the Enlightenment and liberal theology in this respect: "In Europe, it was Karl Barth who finally broke through to a post-Enlightenment recovery of authentic Christian vision: of Christ's story as the encompassing story of all reality."[72] We will see later Jenson does follow and continue Barth's insight in this area.

2.3 The Knowledge of God and Barth's Doctrine of the Trinity

In Jenson's interpretation, Barth's christological metaphysics is interwoven with his doctrine of the Trinity: "Karl Barth has reachieved an authentic doctrine of triunity by what amounts to a christological inversion of Hegel's. Only put *Jesus* in place of Hegel's 'world,' and you have the doctrine of Barth's *Church Dogmatics*, volume 1/1."[73] But the most important achievement of Barth's doctrine of the Trinity is that he adheres to his christological reversal and thus breaks through the traditional metaphysical Trinitarianism. In Jenson's view:

> Barth puts the doctrine of the Trinity at the very beginning of theology in order to have it clear from the start that we are not talking about the class of entities called, by some criteria or

68. Jenson, "Karl Barth," 30–31; Jenson, "Response," 32.
69. Jenson, "Karl Barth," 31.
70. Jenson, *GAG*, 69.
71. Jenson, *A&O*, 140.
72. Jenson, *AT*, 42.
73. Jenson, *TI*, 136.

other, "God," but about the particular being revealed in Jesus Christ—as God. He puts the Trinity in the prolegomena, in the discussion of revelation, to make it clear that we are not discussing a general idea of "revelation," of what *a priori* it would mean were a god to reveal himself, but the particular event of God's revelation in Jesus.[74]

For Barth, the "question which is the doctrine of the Trinity is to answer" is "*Who* is God?"[75] Jenson suggests that the task is then to provide a set of descriptions that identify God. Barth offers as his fundamental identifying description: God is the one "*who has revealed* himself in Jesus Christ."[76] The doctrine of the Trinity is an interpretation and analysis of revelation: this is the argument of Barth's theological prolegomena and discussion of revelation. Moreover, the revelation of God is in fact the particular historical event, Jesus Christ, in the Bible. From revelation we arrive at the biblical doctrine of the Trinity: God is the Father, Son, and the Spirit.[77] Jenson sums up Barth's entire position with one sentence in *Church Dogmatics*: "The name of Father, Son, and Spirit says that God is the one God in a triple repetition, and in such a way that this repetition itself is grounded in his deity, that is, in such a way that . . . only in this repetition is he the one God."[78]

Jenson identifies two particularly significant elements in Barth's doctrine of the Trinity. First, the triune reality is identified by the narrative of the Bible as revelation. The form of revelation, which is the biblical narrative, is not separated from the content of revelation, which is God as the Trinity. As Jenson puts it, "*What* is revealed is no more or less than that revelation *does occur* and therefore *can* occur."[79] The Trinity is identified by the biblical narrative, and what the narrative depicts is the triune reality.

Secondly, Jenson argues that Barth's doctrine of the Trinity closes all possibilities of identifying God by religious projection. Barth's answer to all three questions is simply God himself. This leaves us with no opportunity for religious quests for God of the sort launched by liberal theology. Barth's doctrine of the Trinity denies the validity of the Enlightenment's critique of the doctrine of God and so removes the problem identified by liberal theology.

---

74. Jenson, *GAG*, 97.
75. Jenson, "Karl Barth," 32. From Barth, *KD* 1/1:316–17.
76. Jenson, *GAG*, 99.
77. Jenson, *GAG*, 99–102; Jenson, "Karl Barth," 32; Jenson, *TI*, 136–38.
78. Jenson, *TI*, 138. From Barth, *KD* 1/1:369.
79. Jenson, "Karl Barth," 33.

In short, God is knowable. He is known through the biblical narrative by temporal events.

3. How does Jenson advance Barth's Doctrine of Trinity?

Jenson's attempt to re-establish the ontological validity of Christian account of God has many similarities with Barth's. Like him, Jenson wants to overcome the challenge of the Enlightenment with narrative trinitarian theology. In opposition to the Enlightenment, Barth and Jenson argue that the real otherness of the triune God is not established through positing God as a timeless, eternal, and transcendental entity. For Barth, the triune reality is revealed in Jesus Christ as "Lord." Like Barth, Jenson emphasizes that apart from the gospel, we cannot retrieve the epistemological validity and the religious meaning of the Christian faith. The life, death, and resurrection of Jesus Christ in the gospel show that the Christian God is trinitarian, so Jenson insists that trinitarian theology is grounded on the biblical narrative. He agrees with Barth that the biblical narrative "depicts" the triune reality.

Jenson pushes forward Barth's argument that biblical narrative (including the story of Israel in the Old Testament, and Jesus's life, death, and resurrection) is a trinitarian story of promise. Through the biblical narrative, the triune God promises, acts out, and accomplishes true freedom and hope. Because of the trinitarian story of promise, humans can hope for freedom and meaning. Through this story of promise, we discover that "God is love." The triune reality is a communion of love within the triune God and between the Trinity and the creatures.

Jenson promotes Barth's narrative Trinitarianism by a radical commitment to the ontological function of narrative. According to him, "God himself is identified by and with the particular plotted sequence of events that make *the narrative of Israel and her Christ*."[80] The "phrase 'Father, Son, and Holy Spirit' is simultaneously a very compressed telling of *the total narrative* by which Scripture identifies God."[81] In other words, the Divine narrative is not merely a pointer to divine reality: it *is* the Divine reality. The triune God is not only identified *by* it but also *with* it. God is an event, and thus the biblical narrative is Divine history: "God is an *event*; history occurs not only in him but as his being."[82] We can see that Jenson's formulation resembles Barth's "*God* reveals himself. He reveals Himself *through Himself*. He reveals *Himself*." However, it does not maintain the dialectical asymmetry between God's

---

80. Jenson, *ST1*, 60.
81. Jenson, *ST1*, 46.
82. Jenson, *ST1*, 221.

revelation and human utterances of Barth's trinitarian theology, because Jenson emphasizes that God "is identified *by* and *with* . . . the *narrative*." Barth's emphasis is on God's own veiling and unveiling event while Jenson's is that God is *really* identified *by* and *with* the biblical narrative.

Jenson has a strong reason for making this move: only when we recognize that the triune God is identified by and with biblical narrative, do we realize that God's being is in time and takes time. While Barth is keen to emphasize the *Realdialectic* of God's veiling and unveiling event, Jenson is keen to show God is not impassible but in time and that he unfolds himself through time.

Jenson uses narrative as the key of his trinitarian theology because he identifies being and time as the most acute issues for contemporary trinitarian theology. In his view, the Enlightenment can effectively challenge the validity and meaningfulness of Christianity mainly because, after Augustine, the traditional Christian religion identified God as an eternal, timeless, immutable entity in line with Greek philosophy. When the Enlightenment's challenge of the existence of this entity came to predominate, a realist view of God is made impossible by transcendental metaphysics, and religious experience is only meaningful when it is shaped accordingly.

Jenson commends Barth's theology for its forceful polemic against the Enlightenment's challenge. For Barth, the divine event in Jesus is eternally determined by God's eternal decree of election. Creation and reconciliation form one whole meaningful history. Jenson appreciates Barth's move for correcting the *extra calvinisticum* and allowing us to understand God's being as event and decision.[83]

But Jenson believes that Barth has not entirely avoided the crisis. He fears that Barth's doctrine of eternal election and doctrine of analogy will undo his efforts and return his theology to the traditional position in crisis. Barth states that God's eternal decree is located in God's eternal history. Temporal history is only the *knowledge* of the reconciliation—of God's eternal decree. The *fact* of reconciliation is correlated to God's eternal history. The narrated event of temporal history is related to the eternal history *analogously*. Therefore, we know and experience our true being in God because Jesus Christ, the God-man, "exists *analogously* to God's way of existing."[84] Our experience of our own lives and knowledge of our own being and existence is an "image," "analogy," or "reflection" of Jesus Christ in God.[85] More

---

83. Jenson, *ST1*, 221–23.
84. Jenson, *GAG*, 74. From Barth, *KD* 4/2:185.
85. Jenson, *GAG*, 74–75.

ambiguities arise when Barth says Jesus's time is the "prototype" of our time and the revelation "falls into time from above."[86]

In this way Jenson believes that Barth is in danger of prioritizing the eternal history over the temporal history.[87] Though Barth states that his doctrine of analogy is an analogy of relations rather than between substances with partly similar and partly dissimilar attributes, Jenson contends that this doctrine puts Barth in danger of removing reconciliation itself—the inner reality of Jesus's life—from our history.[88] It tends to make every event in time refer back to be timeless and eternal. He fears that the "notion of the analogy of the whole of time to something else is itself the grin of the timeless cat."[89] Jenson is not satisfied by this regression to eternity and believes that it undoes Barth's attempt to face the challenge posed by the Enlightenment.

Jenson points out that the difficulty comes from the way that Barth approaches God's transcendence and freedom.[90] He suggests that we should drop Barth's doctrine of analogy and not use it to defend the transcendence of God. God's transcendence is rather the sheer futurity in which he transcends all possibilities, and so is unlimited and free.

Jenson's objection to Barth's doctrine of analogy shows how he understands theological language. The decision that theological language is analogical language creates a problem. It imports the unsurpassable gap between temporal reality and eternity of Greek philosophy into Christian faith. Theological language is not analogical in the sense of traditional western metaphysics. God-talk is possible because it is grounded on God's self-revelation. God's self-revelation is narrated as a story of God. This narrated Divine history is the reality of all history. But how can we know that a character who appears in different places in the story is the same character? Jenson believes that the continuity of their acts will indicate that they are the same character. God is hidden, not because of the distance between time and timelessness, but we are still in the course of God's story, which is the history of our salvation. Jenson believes that as the Divine story fully unfolds, we will find that the narrated history adequately signifies the Divine history.[91]

---

86. Jenson, *GAG*, 152–53.
87. Jenson, *TI*, 180.
88. Jenson, *A&O*, 162–63; Jenson, *GAG*, 152–53.
89. Jenson, *GAG*, 154.
90. Jenson, *GAG*, 153.
91. Jenson, *ST2*, 36–38, 161–62. I will analyze Jenson's theology of language in details in next chapter.

Jenson believes that Barth's weak pneumatology means that he cannot do without the traditional doctrine of analogy for his account of God's freedom and transcendence. Without a developed pneumatology Barth has no choice but to cling to the timelessness of eternity, even though it endangers his attempt to overcome the metaphysics of timelessness. Jenson argues that Barth prioritizes the Father, the past, or the Beginning over the Spirit, the futurity, or the End: "Barth displays the doctrine that the Father is 'the fount of the Trinity' . . . This gathering to the past, to the Beginning . . . pervades all Barth's thinking."[92] Jenson complains that he sees that "the shadow of religious direction to the past, of the 'analogous' notion of eternity, is dark and well defined" in Barth's weak Pneumatology.[93] He wants to give Barth's Trinitarianism what it needs by adding that the "Spirit is the goal of the Trinity . . . The Spirit is the hypostasis of God's futurity."[94] If we clearly assert this futurity in the doctrine of the Trinity, the challenge of timeless metaphysics can be finally overcome.

We have seen that Jenson is in whole-hearted agreement with Barth's attempt to get beyond the Enlightenment and its resultant liberal theology. He adopts Barth's narrative Trinitarianism and Christological reversal of metaphysics. Jenson's distinctive advance is the emphasis on the temporality and futurity of God. These he makes central to his doctrine of the Trinity.

However, what Jenson cannot accept is Barth's doctrine of analogy. He fears that the doctrine brings back the timeless entity as the Ground of Being. Barth introduces this doctrine into his discussion of God's self-revelation because he wants to articulate God's transcendence. Jenson's interpretation does not miss this point. According to Bruce McCormack, Barth reconstructs Christian theology in critical realistic terms. The doctrine of analogy and the dialectic of time and eternity are Barth's theological devices for his grand project of a critically realistic theology. Its main thrust is that:

> Barth now regarded God as a Reality which is complete and whole in itself apart from and prior to the knowing activity of human individuals. He conceived of the relation of God to the world in terms of a fundamental *diastasis* (i.e., a relation in which the two members stand over against each other with no possibility of a synthesis into a higher form of being). This critical distinction between God and the world found expression

---

92. Jenson, *GAG*, 173. The passage that Jenson feels uneasy about is: "He is the Beginning, without whom there is no Middle and no End; the Middle, that can only come from the Beginning and without whom there would be no End; the End that comes altogether from the Beginning." Jenson, *GAG*, 173.

93. Jenson, *GAG*, 173.

94. Jenson, *GAG*, 173–74.

in a well-known formula as early as November 1915: "World remains world. But God is God."[95]

Barth believes the relation of God's revelation in Jesus Christ and the self-revealing God is in an analogy of relation. The analogy helps us properly relate and differentiate God and humans. It is concerned for "the freedom of God in his immanence."[96]

Jenson insists that, given the unity of God's revelation in Jesus Christ and the self-revealing God, Barth's doctrine of analogy is not required to safeguard God's transcendence from created reality. Barth's doctrine risks taking him back towards a metaphysics of timelessness, though perhaps he does not develop his doctrine of analogy far enough to take him into this danger. McCormack points out that the central concern of Barth's doctrine of analogy is not a timeless similarity of archetype and ectype of being; the concern is how the communicative event of revelation can be successful while the distinction between God and human is upheld:

> The "analogy of faith" refers most fundamentally to a relation of correspondence between an act of God and an act of a human subject; the act of divine Self-revelation and the human act in which that revelation is acknowledged. More specifically, the analogy which is established in a revelation event is an analogy between God's knowledge of Himself and human knowledge of Him in and through human concepts and words . . . It is not an analogy between the being of Creator and the being of the creature . . . The central area of theological reflection to which this understanding was applied by Barth is that of the relation of the content of revelation to human language.[97]

Alan Torrance agrees. He believes that Barth's doctrine of analogy is quite different from the doctrine of analogy of the metaphysics of timelessness because Barth shows that it is the communicative relation or communion between God and human realized in Jesus Christ the Son:

> [T]he analogy of faith was perceived by Barth as allowing an analogy of relations which challenged the more static, model of (pseudo-logical) relations reflected in the traditional analogy of proportionality. Barth's *analogia relationis* sought to bring into a dynamic correlation relations [sic] of the divine to the divine (the Father and Son) and relations of the human to the human.

---

95. McCormack, *Karl Barth's*, 129.
96. Barth, *CD* 2/1:320.
97. McCormack, *Karl Barth's*, 16–17.

> *In this way it pointed to a relational foundation which lay not in the supposition of proportionalities confirmed speculatively from within the created order but rather in terms of "personal" interrelations affirmed concretely of the One who participates in the eternal communion of the Godhead and who also creatively realises this in the created order as the dynamic and "koinonial" vinculum between the sphere of intra-divine communion and that of inter-human mutuality.*[98]

The analyses of McCormack and Torrance seem to agree with Barth's own formulation:

> We say . . . that the analogy in question is not an *analogia entis* but according to Rom. 12.6 the *analogia tes pisteos, the likeness of the known in the knowing, of the object in thought, of the Word of God in the word that is thought and spoken by Man*, as this differentiates true Christian prophecy in faith from all false prophecy.[99]

Analogical language for Barth is not based on a static conception of Being. It comes from the mystery of God's personal act and the dynamic interaction of God and humans. Analogy is a way to speak of *the transcendence of God* in the on-going communicative act of revelation.

Jenson does not seem to acknowledge the possibility of understanding Barth's doctrine of analogy in terms of this communicative dimension, and so without the time and eternity schema. The incarnation of the Word of God provides a dynamic but still distinct—analogical—relation and interaction between God and humans. Analogy needs not be a remnant of Greek metaphysics. Analogy may mean the communicative correlation (that is, the co-relation) of different beings within the totality of reality. They bear resemblances not because they are images of the metaphysical timeless Ground of Being, but because they participate and communicate with each other, within other's life, while remaining distinct from one another.

Barth's doctrine of analogy implies that God's revelation is not only a temporal event but a *communicative* event in temporality. I believe that an adequate account of the relation and differentiation between God and humans must understand the multi-dimensionality of reality. Space, agents, speech, act, and time come together and interact with each other to form a real story. Jenson suggests however that the transcendence of God can be formulated in terms of his sheer futurity only. One may wonder how

---

98. Torrance, *Persons in Communion*, 188–89. Italics mine.
99. Barth, *CD* 1/1:243–44. Italics mine.

the sole emphasis of temporality can adequately articulate the relation and differentiation of God and other agents in reality.

Whether Jenson's own doctrine of God places so much emphasis on temporality that it subsumes all other dimensions of reality into it is the question I will explore in the next two chapters.

Chapter 3

Jenson's Theology of Language and Narrative Trinitarianism

FOR JENSON, GOD IS identified by and with the Gospel narrative. We cannot have narrative without language. How Jenson understands the nature of language will therefore directly affect his understanding of the relation between narrative and the triune reality. In this chapter I will argue that the modern assertion of God's death leads Jenson to believe that theological language is in danger of becoming meaningless. This concern is the basis of his theology of language.

Jenson locates the problem of meaninglessness in three areas: the assumption of divine timelessness, the problem of the verifiability of information about God, and the problem of historicity. I will argue that Jenson offers a proposal that establishes the meaningfulness of language through a close relationship between *language, reality,* and *time*. His proposal asserts that narration *is* the totality of historical reality, and it *is* God's word. This word *is* God's history. To some extent this is one version of ultra-realism.[1] I argue that Jenson's position makes theological language become a metaphysical reality rather than a linguistic communicative activity. Finally, theological language is in danger of becoming God's monologue.

---

1. Here, I should provide my definition of realism, and ultra-realism. I would follow T. F. Torrance: "A realist position is one in which signs are naturally correlated to, and are ontologically controlled by, the realities they signify, *but* when signs and realities signified perfectly coincide, or when statements are absolutely adequate to their objects, so that they substitute for them or are mistaken for them, then an ultra-realist position is set up." Quoted from: Torrance, *Reality and Evangelical Theology*, 66.

1. The Unintelligibility of Language about God and the Traditional Timeless Metaphysics

Jenson's theology of language aims to tackle the contemporary challenge of the meaninglessness of theological language. Jenson recognizes that "Christianity's language about God has become unintelligible to its hearers is finally apparent also to us who speak it—in that we find it increasingly unintelligible to ourselves."[2] "Formulated explicitly: statements in the form 'God is . . .' are meaningless; they are pseudo-statements, improper language."[3] But for Jenson the problem is not inherent in Christianity itself but is a result of traditional metaphysics, and is made acute by the rise of "scientific critique."

Jenson believes that the early church had no problem in conceptualizing the relation and meaning of God and Christian speech of God. This view of the experience of the early church is the basis of Jenson's theology of language. We will therefore start by looking at Jenson's view of the relationship of God and Christian speech about God in the early church.

1.1 The Flexibility of Language in Primary Trinitarian Discourse, and the Identity of Narrative and Reality in Religious Life

Jenson calls the early church's trinitarian discourse "primary Trinitarianism"[4] and refers to the trinitarian "logic," "life," and "experience" of the early church.[5] He starts his interpretation of this primary Trinitarianism with a discussion of how the writers of the New Testament dealt with the identity of God and relationships of Christ, the Son, and the Spirit. For the writers of the New Testament, Jenson asserts that they do not need to argue for the identity and singularity of Spirit.[6] He believes that the logic and rhetoric of the identifications, "God" and God's "Spirit," and of "Christ" and Christ's "Spirit," were easily understood by the Christian communities because the conceptual or linguistic usages of these terms in the New Testament are consistent to that of the Hebrew Scriptures.[7]

---

2. Jenson, *KTHF*, 3.

3. Jenson, *KTHF*, 10.

4. Jenson, *ST1*, 91; Jenson, *TI*, 40; Jenson, "Triune God," 105; Jenson, "Jesus in the Trinity," 309. For Jenson, the period of primal church is from the apostolic church to around 150 AD. See Jenson, *ST1*, 95; Jenson, *TI*, 45; Jenson, "Triune God," 108.

5. Jenson, *ST1*, 91; Jenson, *TI*, 21, 28; Jenson, "Triune God," 99.

6. Jenson, *ST1*, 91.

7. Jenson, *TI*, 40; Jenson, "Triune God," 106.

These writers also identified Jesus Christ with God. Jenson points out that "a semantic pattern in which the uses of 'God' and 'Jesus Christ' are mutual determining . . . is firmly established before the earliest Pauline writing."[8] Jenson gives various examples. First, in Paul's writing, the "[t]heological predicates take God or Christ or both simultaneously as subject: for example, 'grace' is interchangeably 'of God' or 'of Christ' or 'from God our Father and the Lord Jesus Christ.'"[9] Besides, there are parallel constructions which have "God" and "Christ" side by side.[10] The Gospel of John also unambiguously narrates the course of Jesus's life in Israel with his disciples and his life with the Father as the Son in a simultaneous and identical manner.[11] Yet, Jenson notes that, "'God' and 'Christ' are not simply identified; thus prayer and thanksgiving are always directed *to* God, *through* Christ or 'in his name.'"[12]

Jenson also points out that a notable eclecticism and interchangeability can be found in the usages of the titles and dramatic images of Christ. Through this eclecticism, we are told that the trinitarian theology of these images and titles is located not so much in their conceptual or iconic contents but in the logic they display.[13] The logic of these titles and dramatic images is constant even though at first glance their iconic contents seem quite diverse. Jenson states the logic in this way: "Christ's relation to God is such that God himself is identified *by* the relation and *as* the one so related . . . Also, the titles . . . are more narrative than conceptual . . . they stipulate his roles with the Father and in Israel."[14]

He then uses one of Jesus's titles, "Lord," to illustrate how this logic works. He shows that "Lord" at first merely was the term which Jesus's disciples used to address their rabbi. However, after Jesus's resurrection, the disciples's Lord was enthroned at the Father's right hand and was the giver of the Spirit as well. This address then is resonant with the biblical use of "Lord" for God himself; and "Lord" became the title to identify the human Jesus and Jesus as God at once.[15] Notably, they do not ask, or have no need to ask, whether the risen Jesus's "being" is divine, human, or mediating

---

8. Jenson, *TI*, 41.

9. Jenson, *ST1*, 91; also ref. to Jenson, *TI*, 41; Jenson, "Triune God," 106.

10. Jenson, *ST1*, 91; Jenson, *TI*, 41; Jenson, "Triune God," 106. Jenson's examples are 2 Cor 5:20; Rom 14:17–18.

11. Jenson, *ST1*, 93.

12. Jenson, *TI*, 41. Italics Jenson's.

13. Jenson, *ST1*, 91.

14. Jenson, *ST1*, 91.

15. Jenson, *TI*, 42; Jenson, "Triune God," 107; Jenson, *ST1*, 92.

when they truly address him as Lord.[16] In Jenson's view, they can do so because they are not strongly confronted with Hellenism and the Hellenic concept of God.[17]

Therefore, for Jenson, the logic of the primary Trinitarianism is laid down by a dramatic and narrative understanding of the relationship of Father, Son, and Spirit, and of the salvation they bring. *Language of God is not merely a sign which inadequately and statically refers to a fixed signified thing. It is God's story with Israel and church.* Its plot is salvation and its characters are the persons of God and the humans who are caught up in this story. By means of this story, Christians can speak of God meaningfully. He confidently summarizes the following as "a standard Pauline trinitarian conceptuality":

> "God" is named as the agent of salvation, which is accomplished in an act described by such phrases as "in Christ Jesus," the purpose of which act, both eschatologically and penultimately, is a "sending" of the Spirit with "gifts" (e.g., 1 Cor. 1:4–8).[18]

Thus, according to Jenson, the trinitarian logic provides the early church a rule to articulate the Trinity; and it can be formulated as "when the specific relation to God opened by the gospel is thematic, God the Father and Christ and the Spirit all demand dramatically coordinating mention."[19] Similarly, he asserts that "Christians bespeak God in a triune coordinate system; they speak *to* the Father, *with* the Son, *in* the Spirit, and only so bespeak *God*."[20]

This trinitarian logic was not only a grammatical or regulative rule for articulating certain facts of God, it was also a *life* that can be learned and experienced by the primal church through the church's liturgy.[21] He cites various New Testament passages as evidence.[22] He points out that one can find the early Christians taught, experienced and reflected on the triune logic and its rhetorical space naturally and unproblematically through its liturgy.[23] Language is therefore, not merely a sign, but a *life* lived.

---

16. Jenson, *ST1*, 92. Also ref. to Jenson, *TI*, 42; Jenson, "Triune God," 107.
17. Jenson, *TI*, 40; Jenson, "Triune God," 105–6.
18. Jenson, *TI*, 44; Jenson, "Triune God," 108.
19. Jenson, *ST1*, 92.
20. Jenson, *TI*, 47; Jenson, "Triune God," 109. Italics Jenson's.
21. Jenson, *ST1*, 92.
22. E.g., Rom, 1:1–4; 5:1–5, 18–20; 8:1; 11; 2 Cor 1:21–22; Eph 5:18–20; 2 Tim 4:1; Jude 20–21; Rev 1:4–5; 4:2; 5:6.
23. Jenson, *TI*, 31–33.

Because the ontological dimension and the experiential dimension of the primary church's trinitarian logic are so closely related, Jenson believes the primary Trinitarianism illustrates that:

> The triune name and the trinitarian logic and iconology determine the language of Christian faith. Within discourse not so governed, the conceptually more explicit teachings to which we will next turn become in fact the arbitrary puzzles they are often thought to be. Christians can live only in a dramatic and linguistic space determined by the coordinates of the triune name: to the Father, with the Son, in the Spirit.[24]

Jenson's interpretation of the New Testament passages may be bold but it is commended by one renowned biblical scholar, Francis Watson: "Jenson's correlations of the triune divine identity with divine self-communication and with scriptural narrative are among his most significant theological achievements."[25] Watson reminds us that we should be "patient, diligent, and attentive" when we approach to Jenson's theology. He assures us that we will find "the sheer oddity of Christian faith is one of its chief glories and the clearest proof of its divine origin" from Jenson's works.[26] Indeed, Jenson's theology of language develops a close relation between God's reality and ours.

In summary, in his interpretation of the primary Trinitarianism Jenson persuades his readers to recognize that the narrative and dramatic relationship among Father, Son, and Spirit was the logic by which the primal Christian communities articulated the Trinity. This theological discourse was coherent and consistent with that of Hebrew Bible, for both articulate God as the one who acts in history. This primary Trinitarianism was also the liturgical practice of the early church. The Trinity was experienced and learned through church's liturgy. This primary Trinitarianism shows that it is possible and meaningful to speak of God. Theological language is meaningful when we understand it as God's story and the reality of our life in God.

1.2 The Incapability of Language in Greek Religion

Jenson believes that as the Gospel spread throughout the Greek world by the second century, converted Greeks found the gospel identifies God in a manner quite different to Hellenism. Because of this "cognitive dissonance," they

---

24. Jenson, *ST1*, 93–94.
25. Watson, "America's theologian," 216.
26. Watson, "America's theologian," 215.

were obliged to struggle to articulate the biblical God in the Greek world. We must see how Jenson accounts for the encounter with Greek religion.

Jenson figures out five characteristics of the Greek religion. First, Jenson believes that Greek religion was precisely the quest for an immutable and changeless realm which was resistant to the flow of time. To counter the threat of temporality, Greek religion was determined to not accept the power of time. Therefore, "immortality, immunity to destruction" was one defining character of Greek gods. The Greek gods's eternity was established by their abstraction *from* time.[27]

Second, Greek religion taught that the acts of the Olympian gods can be understood and predicted from their motives. The human history is likewise plotted in a humanly comprehensible pattern. The events of the history are in principle predictable. For Jenson, "Greek religion and reflection were an act of human self-defense against mysterious power and inexplicate contingency."[28]

Third, the Ionian philosophers were religious thinkers and the successors of Homer. These philosophers reduced all godly characteristics to a concept of "the Divine." The Divine is one and immortal. It includes and controls the gods and all events within one comprehensible scheme. It is a unitary abstraction of divine explanatory power. For Greeks, ἀθάνατοι (immortals) is the gods's other name.[29] From Homer to Plato, changeless patterns or forms are the foundations or principles of what happens in the temporal world, even when the anthropomorphic characteristics of deities are removed by philosophical religion.[30]

The object of true cognition for Greek philosophical religion is "a being which is timeless and immutable, not coming into being or passing away."[31] Jenson finds that, for the educated class of Greece's classic period, "this abstraction, often called 'Zeus,' was the true religious object: Timelessness simply as such."[32]

Fourth, in Greek religion, the experiential world is contingent. It is always unstable and in the danger of losing its meaning. Conversely, the Divine, as the Foundation of the world, it is eternal and stable, timeless and changeless. The Divine is a quite different sort of being from anything we encounter in the experiential world. Because one cannot accomplish the

---

27. Jenson, *TI*, 58; Jenson, "Triune God," 116.
28. Jenson, *TI*, 58–59; Jenson, "Triune God," 116.
29. Guthrie, *The Greeks and their Gods*, 115; Gilson, *God and Philosophy*, 9.
30. Burkert, *Greek Religion*, 323.
31. Burkert, *Greek Religion*, 322–23.
32. Jenson, *TI*, 59; Jenson, "Triune God," 116.

quest of timeless reality solely on the basis of the experiential world and the Divine is a sort of being other than this world, Greek religion and reflection of the Divine were "metaphysical."[33]

Finally, because Greek religion taught that the timeless Ground is not directly presented in experience, we have to search for it. Thus, "Greek apprehension of God is accomplished by penetrating through the temporal experienced world to its atemporal Ground."[34]

From the fifth characteristic, Jenson then deduces four assertions on Greek theology.[35] They are the "whole complex of motifs that will be centrally important for our story."[36] First, Jenson asserts that Greek theology is essentially a negative theology. Only the negations of the predicates which apply to temporal experienced reality can be considered as the true predicates of deity. Thus, God is "invisible," "intangible," "impassible," and "indescribable."

Secondly, this theology articulates God with analogy. Though Greek theology is a negative theology, it cannot avoid using the predicates that apply to the temporal world in its articulation of God. In analogical discourse of God, the pattern is always "Deity is F, only not as other, temporal, reality is F." Thus, Jenson states that the analogical method is not a theologically neutral device. It is the theological method for positing a particular God, the Deity of Greek religion.[37]

Thirdly, this theology asks what the *true* deity is and is determined to find the marks of the *real* Ground—the quality of being divine. The search for deity is only possible if we are able to recognize it when we find it. Thus, it leads us to ask what the authentic marks of Divine are.[38] Jenson sums up the basic quality of Greek deity as "immunity to time plus whatever are its necessary conditions." For Aristotle, the condition is being sheer undistracted self-consciousness. For Plotinus, it is being One above the plurality.[39]

Finally, this theology believes mind is the faculty that enables humans to penetrate to true deity. Human speech and argument cannot accomplish this penetration because deity is timeless and cannot be sufficiently grasped by language. Thus, the theological penetration to deity

---

33. Jenson, *TI*, 59; Jenson, "Triune God," 117.
34. Jenson, *TI*, 59; Jenson, "Triune God," 117.
35. Jenson, *TI*, 59–60; Jenson, "Triune God," 117.
36. Jenson, *TI*, 59; Jenson, "Triune God," 117.
37. Jenson, *TI*, 60; Jenson, "Triune God," 117.
38. Jenson, *TI*, 60; Jenson, "Triune God," 117.
39. Jenson, *ST1*, 94;

can only be comprehended "by instantaneous intellectual intuition, by a sort of interior mirroring."[40]

The above analyzes can be summarized as follows: (1) The dichotomy of time and timeless eternity; being divine is being timelessly eternal; (2) No theological language or temporal reality can grasp the reality of God adequately because they are contingent. The second point is the result of the dichotomy. Thus, in Jenson's view, the overarching concern of Greek religion is deity's timelessness: "Greece identified deity by metaphysical predicates. Basic among them is timelessness: immunity to time's contingencies and particularly to death, by which temporality is enforced."[41] Jenson states that the God of Greek religion, according to Aristotle, is "the absolutely *present* being . . . He is the purely Present to himself and all things, without past or future. He is the exemplary fulfillment of the meaning of all beings: never not to be. In him, the denial of death is triumphant."[42]

In this dichotomy of the time and eternity, the relationship of the latter to former therefore was grasped by mere negation. The difference between eternity and time could simply be regarded as discontinuity between two sorts of reality. However, this discontinuity threatened to deny there is any meaning in our lives within the temporal world because all life and truth are located in timeless eternity.

In this way, all temporal phenomena, including language, risk meaninglessness. When the gospel came to Mediterranean antiquity Greek religion was trying to solve this "desperate" situation by "invoking *relative* divine and so also relatively temporal beings" to mediate the gap between time and timeless eternal deity. When the gospel came to Greek world, "Christ" was inevitably considered to be one of these "mediators" by Greeks.[43]

In Jenson's view, the God of Israel is the exact opposite of the deity of Greek religion. The God of Israel is not immune to time, but transcends time's discontinuities and absurdities, not by immunity, but by overcoming them in time. He is eternal God not because he is merely immortal, but because he lives through death. More importantly, "God is, indeed, himself, as the Son of the Father, a temporal creature and the cherishing brother of temporal siblings."[44] Therefore, it is "apparent that the

---

40. Jenson, *TI*, 60; Jenson, "Triune God," 117.

41. Jenson, *ST1*, 94. In *God after God*, Jenson has a similar remark: "positing a timeless reality set above our stories in time has remained the structure of what we have in the West called 'religion.'" See Jenson, *GAG*, 12.

42. Jenson, *GAG*, 13. Italics Jenson's.

43. Jenson, *ST1*, 95; Jenson, *TI*, 61; Jenson, "Triune God," 118.

44. Jenson, "A Call to Faithfulness," 91. Also see Jenson, *TI*, 58; Jenson, "Triune God," 116.

interpretation of deity as immunity to time fits ill with the stories that Jews and Christians tell of God."[45]

There is an inevitable "clash," "confrontation," and "struggle" between Christian church and Greek religion in the early centuries because the opposition of Hebrew/Christian and Greek understanding of God. It is to this that Jenson attributes the contemporary problem of theological language. After the early church, Christian theology of language was disastrously bound to the Greek religious heritage. Language, because it was a phenomenon of temporal reality, was considered inadequate to express the inexpressible timeless Divine. Theological language is a feeble, though inevitable, means to articulate this truth. When this timeless metaphysics disappeared, theological language became not only inadequate, but meaningless and irrelevant. To illustrate this difficult historical development in theology of language Jenson offers the examples of Origen and Thomas Aquinas.

1.3 Image: Jenson on Origen's Theology of Language

For Jenson, Origen is both a theological giant and villain.[46] Jenson believes that Origen made a great contribution to theology: Origen "set the basic system and created the language for the entire high patristic theology of the East and . . . for the West as well . . . And it will become plain that in nothing are we all so much Origenists as in the *way* we have gone about speaking of God."[47] He was "the creator of hermeneutically self-conscious biblical exegesis." He initiated a consistent and explicit method to study the meaning of the Bible. Moreover, "he was the first great christologist after John the Evangelist." Jenson observes that all Origen's theological reflections were done through meditating and analyzing the reality of Christ.[48] In trinitarian theology, Jenson recognizes that "Origen can speak in a way not to be achieved generally for a century; it is 'the blessed . . . *Trinity*' as such which is 'the good God and benign universal Father.'"[49]

However, in Jenson's opinion, Origen was at the same time the one who "carried subordinationist Trinitarianism to its unstable perfection and created a way of thinking that dominated the Eastern church for the

---

45. Jenson, "Logic of the Doctrine of the Trinity," 246.
46. In *KTHF*, Jenson even states that "Origen was undoubtedly a heretic." Jenson, *KTHF*, 24.
47. Jenson, *KTHF*, 24.
48. Jenson, *TI*, 74.
49. Jenson, *TI*, 77.

remainder of its theologically creative history."[50] Moreover, his theology of language is found on the basis of Platonism. It eventually asserts the difficulty of speaking God rather than the possibility. More unfortunately, when the traditional metaphysics demises in the modern society, his approach is discredited.[51]

Jenson calls Origen "the last true apologist." Thus, like his predecessors, Origen's theology cannot escape from the philosophical and religious framework of the late antiquity.[52] For Origen, the mediation of the knowledge of God was his central theological concern. God the Father is utterly beyond the temporal material world, and utterly undifferentiated. God is ontologically different: He is timeless and other reality is temporal. God can only be known by the intuition of mind (νοῦς) which is liberated from time. However, human is bound within temporality. Accordingly, there are two modes of knowing or beholding: "sensory and intellectual."[53] For this ontological gap, God is essentially unknowable to men. Only the one, who is "perfected in virtue" and not limited by time, knows God.[54] God's eternal timelessness is his eternal simultaneous presence. It means that God is one. The Word that can speak of God is *one*. However, humans, being temporal beings, are in the plurality of the succession of time. Our words are inevitably many. Our language inevitably fails when we use it to speak of God.

Humans need a medium to bridge the gap between temporality and eternity in order to speak of God. Jenson points out that "image" (εἰκών) is the conceptual tool that Origen uses to achieve his theological mediation. Origen's move was obviously influenced by the Platonism because Plato was the pioneer to use the term "image" as an ontological notion for the temporal world.[55]

50. Jenson, *TI*, 74; Jenson, "Triune God," 123.
51. Jenson, *KTHF*, 92, 96–97.
52. Jenson, *ST1*, 98.
53. Jenson, *KTHF*, 27.
54. Jenson, *KTHF*, 26–27, 33–34, 37; Jenson, *TI*, 75; Jenson, "Triune God," 124.
55. Jenson, *ST1*, 98. Recently, Mark Edwards has argued that it is unfair to label Origen as a Platonist. He contends that "the Platonic tone" in Origen's works does not mean Origen was a Platonist. Rather, Origen was a critic of Platonism. We are told that Origen "roundly declares the Ideas or Forms of Plato to be chimerical . . . if he suggests that forms and genera of all species and particulars have subsisted eternally in the divine intelligence, he means no more than Paul meant when he wrote that the whole creation is fulfilling the plan of God, and that he elects his saints to glory before the foundation of the world." Edwards even can assert that "it is those who are most conversant with fashions of the age who are least enslaved to them, and if Platonism was such an epidemic in Alexandria as scholars have supposed, the surest vaccine was to read Plato . . . we may say that, far from exhibiting the symptoms of contagion, Origen's

"Image" had been posited as an intermediate between being and non-being or a bridge between time and eternity in Plato's philosophy. It is like a statue or painting, which is a replica of its archetype. Accordingly, the world can be understood as the image of its eternal Ground. Though the world is not its own ground, it still is an image of that ground; just like an artist's imitation of a model. Middle Platonism developed this mediation concept into a plural hierarchy of levels of being. In this hierarchy, each intermediate level is an image of the reality above and an archetype of the reality below.[56] Jenson says that, in Platonism, "image" "came to be the name for the whole principle of mediation between transcendent and given reality and for the intermediary metaphysical realities through which that mediation was to take place."[57] Likewise, it is "the key word of Origen's theory of language and of his ontological and soteriology."[58] In Jenson's viewpoint, Origen is a great Christian member of the platonic tradition.[59]

For Origen, the Son is "*the* image of God." The Father and the Son are "two entities as to existence, but only one in likeness and harmony and identity of will—so that he who has seen the Son who is 'the reflection of his glory' and the 'stamp of his nature' as seen in Him, since He is the Image of God, God Himself."[60] The notion "image" provides the possibility of having both sameness and difference with other beings in one being.

---

work contains the antibodies to Platonism." See Edwards, *Origen against Plato*, 160–61.

However, one should note that Edwards's assertion limits the term "Platonic" in a very narrow sense. Though Origen's theology has divergences with Platonism, it agrees with Plato in a fundamental point: Both assert that there are two kinds of existence, Being and Becoming. The former is the motionless and timeless realm of truth. The latter is the temporal reality, which is involved in time, change, and error. The former is the invisible and spiritual world. The latter is the visible and material world. Hence, Being is a "higher" kind of existence and Becoming is a "lower" kind (Origen, *Against Celsus*, 7.46. One may refer to Richard Norris for an illustration on this point: Norris, *God and World in Early Christian Theology*, 116–18). Thus, while on various aspects Origen's viewpoints are different from Platonism or even refute the terms that Plato used, the dualist view towards reality shows that there is an obvious influence from Platonism in Origen's theology. From this viewpoint, Jenson's assertion is valid. Indeed, Henry Chadwick has made an excellent observation for Origen: "He wanted to be a Christian, not a Platonist. Yet Platonism was inside him, *malgré lui*, absorbed into the very axioms and presuppositions of his thinking. Moreover, this penetration of his thought by Platonism is no merely external veneer of apologetic. Platonic ways of thinking about God and the soul are necessary to him if he is to give an intelligible account of his Christian beliefs." See Chadwick, *Early Christian Thought*, 122.

56. Jenson, *KTHF*, 34–37; Jenson, *TI*, 75; Jenson, *ST1*, 98–99.
57. Jenson, *KTHF*, 37.
58. Jenson, *KTHF*, 29.
59. Jenson, *TI*, 75.
60. Jenson, *KTHF*, 29.

The reality of an image depends on its archetype. It indicates a creative-expressive procession from the transcendent to this world. An image reveals its archetype and thus it is a soteriological cognitive return to God. Jenson asserts that the concept of image can explain creation, salvation, and knowledge of God within the schema of Platonic dichotomy of time and eternity: "An image hierarchy is thus a circulation of being and of knowledge from the transcendent to this world and back, which can bridge yet not deny the complete difference of ontological mode of the two poles."[61]

Accordingly, the Son—*the* image of God "has his own Ground in the Father and is in turn the Ground of all other being."[62] The creatures that were created after the image of God have their Ground of being in the Son. The creatures are the ectypes of their archetype—the Son. As the ectype would not exist without the archetype; the creatures would not exist without *the* image of God. Therefore, creation is a "creative-expressive procession from transcendent to the world."

Also, the Son, *the* image of God, is God's permanent revelation—the Word.[63] Because God does not have knowledge of himself through a medium, he knows himself by positing self-relatedness through self-expression. Thus, the Word is God's self-expression and self-knowledge at once. As God's self-knowledge, the Son returns into God in that he knows God.[64] Accordingly, we can know the unseen God through the Word. Finally, we can be fulfilled as images of God and thus our being can be brought into God when we know God in the Word. Therefore, the Image provides us a soteriological cognitive return to God. The creative-expressive procession from God and soteriological-cognitive return to God has been summed up by Jenson thus: "As God reflects himself in the Image and the 'images of the Image,' the world is created. As creatures know God, each in the next image up, the world is saved."[65]

However, Origen still needs more "mediators" to bridge the timeless spiritual and temporal physical world. In Jenson's opinion, Origen asserts that, besides the Son, there are "images of the Image" of the Son. Among these images, the human soul of the man Jesus of Nazareth is the most important. *Logos* and Jesus's souls are in a perfect mystical union. Soul is one's personal act of existence in one's inner life. It is an "intelligible" and not a "sensible" entity. However, at the same time Jesus's physical life, which includes his

---

61. Jenson, *KTHF*, 30–31.
62. Jenson, *TI*, 75; Jenson, *KTHF*, 32.
63. Jenson, *TI*, 76; Jenson, *KTHF*, 30.
64. Jenson, *KTHF*, 31.
65. Jenson, *TI*, 76. See also, Jenson, *KTHF*, 30–31.

teachings, and death, is the image of his soul. Jesus's physical history is the image of that other history of his inner self-transcending existence. In this way, Jesus's life in both the hidden reality of its soul and the visible reality of its deeds is the mirror of the reality of the Son's life.[66]

With Origen's concept of image, Jenson investigates Origen's theology of language. Jenson asserts that Origen is "a radically biblicist theologian."[67] He identifies exegesis of the Bible with our speaking of God. For Origen, the subject of the whole Bible is Christ. The Bible is the narration of the life of Jesus Christ and his pre-incarnate history in Israel. Because we can know of Christ only through this narrated history, it is the sole source of the knowledge of God. The spoken and written text is the image of God, in which God is present to us, and thus we may speak of him. However, the Bible is only an image. The historical experience is imperfect. It is an ectype of its spiritual archetype. The *spirit* of the written text is itself unspeakable and is hidden under the mere words. This hidden spiritual reality only can be known through pure intellectual intuition. Thus, there are two gospels: the visible gospels and the spiritual gospel. The former is only the shadow of the latter. Our speaking of God is to translate our understanding of the Bible from the former sense to the latter. Thus, we interpret the Bible *allegorically*.[68] For the same reason as Plato, Origen's doctrine of allegory taught that the true sense of the Bible is hidden and has to be penetrated by the mind.[69]

Though Origen's image-prototype theology of language is by-and-large Platonic, Jenson asserts that in two aspects it is fundamentally Christian. First, Jenson appreciates Origen's theology of language is utterly Christocentric. For Origen, we speak of God precisely by speaking of Christ. The Word and our words are separated by the ontological divide. There are totally different "languages" on each side. Our words cannot cross the divide to speak of the "unutterable" Word unless there is a reality which is present on both sides of the ontological divide. Jesus is the one that "somehow" bridges this ontological divide. He is the medium by which God deals with humans. Jesus Christ is the only means by which we can speak of God.[70]

Secondly, this is Origen's identification of the final transcendent reality as the *eschaton* in the Bible. For Origen, theological language is eschatological in three senses: (1) It means that the unutterable final meaning of the theological images/language is the eschaton. The theological language is its

---

66. Jenson, *KTHF*, 33–34.
67. Jenson, *KTHF*, 37.
68. Jenson, *KTHF*, 38–43.
69. Jenson, *KTHF*, 27–29, 37–47; Jenson, *TI*, 75.
70. Jenson, *KTHF*, 55.

symbols; (2) It means that when we can successfully speak about God, we arrive at the fulfillment or the consummation of our existence; (3) Every human theological word is the clothing of an eschatological word. It bears an eschatological dynamism within itself. When we live in such words, we are empowered and on the way of the final fulfillment of God.[71]

The doctrine of allegory means that we can speak of God only by an infinite succession of self-annulling discourses as they are merely images. However, because the eschatological dynamism provides us with the *plot* that governs the order of succession, we may consider allegories to be real discourse about God. For Origen, the order of temporal evangelical history, from the Old Testament to the incarnation of Christ and the final fulfillment, is the complex reality of Christ's person. In the whole evangelical history, the life of Jesus Christ is the key for understanding all the rest. Jesus is the key because he is the fulfillment of the Old Testament and the foreshadow of the "eternal gospel." This order—Old TestamentàJesusàtrue mystery of Christ—is the *plot* that constitutes the rules of theological discourse. A theological discourse is correct when "it cancels itself in the direction of the next step." In other words, a correct theological discourse is always Christocentric as Jesus Christ is the key.[72]

Moreover, Jenson finds that the eschatological nature of theological language makes the language game of allegorical exegesis more than purely descriptive. The eschaton will establish the connections of life and knowledge: "When we play it, we are not merely describing, at several removes of images, the final goal of our life; *we are, by playing this language game, moving through those images toward that goal.*"[73] Therefore, Origen's theology of language does not think our present inability to find an adequate linguistic reference to the last things is a totally desperate situation. Rather as concrete applications of our present life in Christ our words are the "foretastes," "surrogates," and "present clothing" of the final unutterable Word. Christians's earthly experience of speaking God is thus not a meaningless and endless language game. It is "a history of the refinement and enlargement of their language."[74]

The eschatological and christological concentration of Origen's theology of language is the point that interests Jenson:

> Origen, for all his Platonizing, insisted that *Jesus Christ* was the image of God, thereby directing man's pursuit of the meaning of

71. Jenson, KTHF, 34–47.
72. Jenson, KTHF, 52–53.
73. Jenson, KTHF, 45. Italics Jenson's.
74. Jenson, KTHF, 46.

life toward history. Again, there is no doubt that that exclusively Western apprehension of reality we call historical is culturally connected to this need in Christian speaking. We shall take, therefore . . . Origen's insistence that only the history of Jesus Christ makes such [theological] utterance meaningful, as our permission to go on with our search and as hints of the directions in which to look.[75]

A proper and meaningful theological discourse should be found on the history of Jesus Christ as the key of God's eschatological fulfillment. Such discourse is meaningful not only because it speaks about God. It is meaningful also because our lives are moving along God's plot towards his final fulfillment when we participate in such discourse. In other words, theological language is meaningful and proper when it integrates Jesus's life, history, and our lives together. In latter sections, we will find Jenson using this as a rule of his theology of language.

Nevertheless, Jenson asserts that the inherent Platonic influence in Origen's theology of language makes it problematic and unsatisfactory. The image ontology comes from Platonic mythical metaphysics and when the mythical tradition is discredited as mere speculation, this theological discourse that relates to a timeless metaphysics is rejected as irrelevant and meaningless. Jenson finds the same issue in the work of Thomas Aquinas.

1.4 Analogy: Jenson on Thomas Aquinas's Theology of Language

Thomas Aquinas is Jenson's second example of the traditional theology of language. For Aquinas, theology "is a theoretical, descriptive science." Correct theological speech is "a matter of uttering true statements."[76] Aquinas's assertion of the informative or realist character of theological language is compelling for Jenson. He thinks it fits the modern challenge of the meaninglessness and irrelevance of theological language.[77]

Jenson asserts that the doctrine of analogy is the means that Aquinas employed for his task of a realist theological language: "Statements about God are analogously descriptive."[78] For Aquinas, a proper theological analogy is not a conjecture. It comes from a fundamental ontological fact: God

---

75. Jenson, *KTHF*, 97.
76. Jenson, *KTHF*, 62–63.
77. Jenson, *KTHF*, 97.
78. Jenson, *KTHF*, 63.

is an absolute transcendent being while he is related with creatures as their cause and reason.

Aquinas followed the traditional metaphysics to assert that "being" is neither an empty word nor unintelligible darkness. Rather, being is "convertible" into *good, one, true,* and *beautiful.* Because all physical beings are only good, true, and beautiful to some extent and cannot be the final explanation of their own perfections; they are dependent on an absolute being which is the final cause and explanation of good, one, truth, and beauty. God is the one whose essence and existence are the same. He is one and simple. He is the Being.[79] Therefore, according to Jenson, Aquinas asserted that "'God' means: 'the first cause and reason of all that reality which we find as we look about.' 'God' means 'the eschatological Reason without which existence is absurd.'"[80]

Jenson then uses Aquinas's assertion of God as the creatures's Cause and creatures his effects to interpret Aquinas's doctrine of analogy. God is the cause of all things. All things other than God are the effects of God. Because we speak about God with our own language, theological language is drawn from our ordinary speech about creatures as God's effects.[81] Moreover, because both natural and revealed (or supernatural) knowledge of God are effects from God, their logical structure are the same. It means that there is no logical difference between natural and revealed knowledge of God. All our theological speech, whether it generates from natural or revealed knowledge, are logically the same.[82]

However, our theological language is not adequate for speaking about God. It cannot be univocal when we talk about God. Though we can speak of God because he is our cause, he is not a member of his effects. He does not belong to the class of his creatures but is ontologically different from them. This difference implies that the cause-effect likeness of God and creatures is imperfect.[83] The cause and its effects only can be named together *univocally* when they belong to same class, such as "man begets man," and "man" in the clause is understood univocally. Because God as creatures's cause is ontologically different from them, God is not a univocal cause of them.[84]

Moreover, our language works only within a certain mode of being. Humans's words are signs or names to signify something. Language works

79. Jenson, *KTHF*, 68, 79, 93.
80. Jenson, *KTHF*, 68.
81. Jenson, *KTHF*, 68–69.
82. Jenson, *KTHF*, 72.
83. Jenson, *KTHF*, 75.
84. Jenson, *KTHF*, 69, 75–76.

by the linguistic distinction between a subject and its predicate. It assumes the distinction between a thing and what it is. However, God is what he is. His essence is identical with his existence. So, when our words are used of God, their ordinary rules cannot be applied. They cannot articulate God univocally.[85]

However, this ontological difference and linguistic limitations so not make our theological language totally equivocal and meaningless. Aquinas did make theological statements, such as "God is one" and "God is perfect" which are intended to be statements about God and not merely about our language. Aquinas taught that, under the limitations of our linguistic rules, when we realize these statements "*as* stipulations of the inappropriateness of our language's mode of signifying, they are also stipulations of God's mode of being."[86] In Jenson's opinion, such contradictory claims can be valid because, for Aquinas, statements about God are neither univocal nor equivocal, but analogical.[87]

Theological language is not totally equivocal because all created things are effects of God. Jenson asserts that, for Aquinas, a cause causes what is like itself. Thus, created things are images of God that bear likeness to God. The causal logic is the reason for creatures's likeness of God because Aquinas's causal logic functions in all modes of temporality of creatures's lives. It is God's exemplar, creating power, and goal for creatures.

In this ontological-causal relation, all creatures are imitations of God's perfection in some ways.[88] The ontological-causal relation between God and creatures make our speaking of God possible. It posits a likeness-in-unlikeness between God and creatures. This likeness enables us to speak of God in creaturely-language. When our language is used theologically, it can be meaningfully because God is the exemplar of creatures. We can speak of God therefore according to the linguistic mode of our created being. Jenson explains that theological language "seeks to signify its 'that

---

85. Jenson, *KTHF*, 76–79.

86. Jenson, *KTHF*, 79.

87. Jenson, *KTHF*, 75.

88. Jenson, *KTHF*, 80. It should be noted that Jenson understands Aquinas's different theological terms (i.e., proportion, likeness, representation, assimilation, participation, and imitation) as various forms to say the same "causal and explanatory relation" for "the likeness" between God and creatures. Among them, Jenson thinks "participation" and "imitation" are the two most significant terms. In this sense, the temporal movement of creatures' perfection is the most important aspect of the doctrine of analogy in Jenson's opinion. It is interesting that Jenson's understanding does not stress on proportionality but God's teleological causality. The domination of teleology over relation indeed influences Jenson's theological thinking deeply. I will analyze this point in the section 3 of this chapter and the following chapters.

which is signified,' a perfection found (in varying 'modes') in both God and creatures, in defiance of its own 'mode of signifying,' which is appropriate only to creatures's mode of being."[89] When we speak of God in this way, we speak of him *analogously.*

Moreover, because God is creatures's final cause in this ontological-causal relation, human existence is teleologically structured. Analogical speech of God is meaningful and valid because it points to our transcendental goal of existence in the *eschaton*. Jenson even states that "God cannot be spoken of at all apart from logical-ontological reflections—apart, that is, from our strivings to find meaning."[90] *In this sense, analogical theological language is meaningful not only because it articulates God's reality through its likeness-in-unlikeness; but also it opens its speaker and hearer toward the final fulfillment of their lives.*[91]

When the doctrine of analogy is linked to eschatology or teleology, Jenson believes that Aquinas's theological language is descriptive and informative. In Aquinas's scheme, the transcendence which theological language utters is not a self-projection. It is the transcendence of God's life and knowledge, which he grants human to participate in. When the *eschaton*, the final fulfillment, comes, our theological discourses can be verified and falsified. It posits a descriptive and informative, and thus a realist, theological language.[92]

Thus, Aquinas's doctrine of analogy, according to Jenson's interpretation, is found on the ontological-causal relationship between God and human. This ontological causality inherited in creatures at the same time posits a final eschatological fulfillment for creatures. It provides the meaning and the final fact of the theological language, through which assure our analogical theological language is meaningful and informative.

Jenson rejects the ontological-causal supposition of Aquinas's doctrine of analogy because it only works within the Platonic metaphysics of image. When traditional metaphysics became obsolete, we can no longer think God analogically in Aquinas's way.[93] Moreover, even within its own scheme, it cannot do what it is intended to do. According to Jenson, "'Analogy' is hardly the name of a set of usage rules. It is rather simply a name for the difficulty. It hardly establishes a stable position between univocity and

---

89. Jenson, *KTHF*, 84.
90. Jenson, *KTHF*, 88.
91. Jenson, *KTHF*, 59, 87.
92. Jenson, *KTHF*, 63, 88.
93. Jenson, *KTHF*, 96.

equivocity. Rather, it simply says, 'Theological language must not be either.' Thus it points rather to the problem than to a solution."[94]

Our discussion has shown that Jenson's interpretation of the doctrine of analogy, which is like his interpretation of Origen, asserts the meaningfulness of theological language through an integration of *eschatology* and *language*. He thinks that Origen's theology of language is distinctive because of its christological concentration while Aquinas regards theological language as simply fact-stating or descriptive as any ordinary language is. Though Jenson rejects the Platonic influence in Origen's and Aquinas's thought, he suggests that eschatology, history of Jesus, and a realist theological language are "hints of the directions" for contemporary theology of language:

> We shall take, therefore, Thomas's insistence on the informative character of theological utterances, and Origen's insistence that only the history of Jesus Christ makes such utterance meaningful . . . as hints of the directions in which to look. Their joint understanding of the eschatological function of theological utterances gives a starting point for our search.[95]

1.5 Summary

From his examination of the theology of primary Trinitarianism, Origen, and Aquinas, Jenson shows that theological language can be meaningful in a number ways. The meaningfulness of the theological language is found on an integration of *life*, *reality*, and *language*. Life is not abstract, for it is our present participation in our eschatological fulfillment. It has to do with our commitment or attitude to life. It is articulated linguistically in form of narrative. Reality is the history of Jesus Christ, through this history of Christ we participate in his eschatological fulfillment, and thus it is our reality as well as God's. In this integration, Jenson seems to imply that the univocity or equivocity of language is not the central issue for the meaningfulness of theological language. From his discussion of Aquinas, he seems to suggest that theological language is a realist language even if it is verified only *eschatologically*.

Jenson believes that after primary Trinitarianism theology wrongly posits God as a timeless metaphysical being. It assumes that temporal creatures cannot speak of a timeless God. The image-analogical theology of language is the product of this metaphysics. It inevitably regarded

---

94. Jenson, *KTHF*, 92.
95. Jenson, *KTHF*, 97.

theological language as inauthentic discourse about God. It can only work within traditional metaphysics. In modernity, the triumph of scientific method and our awareness of the tensed-character of human's historicity has destroyed faith in traditional metaphysics, and with it the credibility of the image analogy for theological language.

The next section will study Jenson's analysis of analytical philosophy and historicist hermeneutics. I will show how Jenson uses his analysis to construct his own theology of language that integrates language and life.

2. The Unintelligibility of Language about God, the Problem of Verifiability, and the Problem of Historicism

Along with the demise of traditional metaphysics is the rise of modern scientific thinking. Jenson lists analytical philosophy and historicist hermeneutics as two principal modern challenges of the meaningfulness of theological language. I argue that Jenson answers these challenges by asserting a close relationship between *language*, *God's reality*, and *life*. He suggests that our theological talk is a word-event that integrates the whole reality and all modes of time in the love of God. It is this that makes theological language meaningful and informative.

2.1 The Challenge of Analytical Philosophy: How is Theological Language Meaningful and Informative?

2.1.1 *The challenge*

According to Jenson, the logical positivists of analytical philosophy attack theology as a meaningless pseudo-science. He summarizes the challenge of analytical philosophy as the problem of the distinctive ontological relation of reality and the name "God." Analytical philosophy asks Christian believers why they do not regard their statements about God as hypotheses. A hypothetical statement can be refuted by objections of evidence and be shown to be false. If "God" is a name or a subject-word, statements about it are informative. They are description of that name or subject-word. In this way, one cannot judge their truthfulness or correctness until they are verified or falsified by evidence. In this way theological statements could be descriptive.

However, theology does not only use "God" as a name or an ordinary subject-word. They also use "God" as a self-sufficient and self-evident description of this "name" or subject-word. God, in this sense, means "the perfectly good, wise, etc., being." A theological statement such as "God is good" means "the perfectly good being is good." Theological statements of this sort are considered vacuous and tautological by analytical philosophers. Because theology wants the word "God" to be informative and irrefutable, or to be a name and a self-defined description at once; analytical philosophy thinks there is an inherent logical confusion in it. The difficulty is that the word "God" by itself is its own and sole referent.[96] Jenson believes that this challenge results from the ontological difference between God and all other reality: "Since God is the Creator, all relational statements about God relate Him not to some particular reality, but to the whole of it."[97]

2.1.2 *The meaningfulness of theological language and dramatic coherence*

Jenson rejects the traditional image-analogical language for speech about God. He has to provide an alternative when faced by the challenge of analytical philosophy. Jenson argues that theological language is meaningful because we grasp the ultimate meaning of life through our articulation of story of Jesus Christ as God's drama. It is informative because it is an eschatologically verifiable and a descriptive historical narrative.

Jenson admits that theological statements are not hypotheses, but this does not mean that theological language is vacuous. Jenson uses I. M. Crombie's thought to show that the origins of theological language are twofold. First, it is our search of our final meaning because our experience of the incompleteness of life. Secondly, it is the interpretation of our experience of divine reality.[98] As part of our search for the completeness of life, Christian theological language is a meaningfully evocative and expressive experience language like poetry. Yet, unlike poetry, the evocative power of religious language is not our own construction but is established by historical *narratives* of Jesus Christ.[99] According to Jenson:

> Christian utterances about God operate to posit an attitude to life exactly *as* narrative language. As a consequence the question of their truth or falsity cannot be declared irrelevant—whatever may be their evocative efficiency. For here the speaking that posits the ends of life does so not by free choice or invention but

---

96. Jenson, *KTHF*, 16–17, 103.
97. Jenson, *KTHF*, 17.
98. Jenson, *KTHF*, 135–37.
99. Jenson, *KTHF*, 104–7.

JENSON'S THEOLOGY OF LANGUAGE AND NARRATIVE TRINITARIANISM   103

by a narration that is either justified as cognition of the course of events or not at all.[100]

In this way, Jenson asserts that theological discourses "at once express an attitude and tell the truth about reality."[101] They are expressively meaningful and informative.

Jenson suggests that our longing for completeness of life and the narrative of Jesus Christ are not loose or unconnected expressive and informative statements. They are two "dramas." He calls the former as "the drama of Time" or "the drama of our lives," while the latter the drama of Jesus Christ.[102] In theological discourse, Christians try to stipulate a relation between two dramas and to speak of their meaning.[103] The meaning of such discourse does not come from the verification of hypotheses but our judgment on our expressive experience and interpretation of divine narrative reality. So, Jenson suggests that theological language is *verdictively* meaningful.[104] He then introduces that the meaning or the verdict of Christian belief, which we grasp from the theological statements, is its *dramatic coherence*:

> [W]hat the verdict is about is something like the meaning of a *play* . . . Grasping the meaning of a *drama* is . . . that we grasp the *unity* of the play . . . We see how its parts fit together, or rather, we experience them as parts. How do the parts of a play fit together? Again, presumably, in many ways. But one fundamental pattern is surely the pattern of *expectations* raised and satisfied . . . Talk of dramatic unity or dramatic appropriateness is the paradigm for talk that is indivisibly both informative and expressive of attitudes.[105]

Jenson's notion of dramatic coherence brings the problem of language back to his concern of temporality. The notion of "drama of Time" and his suggestion of valid theological meaning as "dramatic coherence" indicate that he views religion as an answer to the meaninglessness or nihility of our death. Indeed, he suggests the meaning of theology as dramatic coherence means that our expectation of the final fulfillment of life can be *appropriately* found in the story of resurrection of Jesus Christ:

100. Jenson, *KTHF*, 108.
101. Jenson, *KTHF*, 111.
102. Jenson, *KTHF*, 110, 123.
103. Jenson, *KTHF*, 114.
104. Jenson, *KTHF*, 110.
105. Jenson, *KTHF*, 111–12.

> [W]e experience our lives as incomplete *stories*, as dramas missing their climax and denouement . . . I therefore can never experience the whole play . . . The absolutely last thing has happened, in the events of Jesus's existence. His story tells of the conclusion of our lives . . . To tell Jesus's story as the story about God is to tell it as narrative of the climax and denouement of my story and your story.[106]

From the notion of dramatic coherence, Jenson suggests that to say that God is "perfectly good" is not tautological. Rather, it "is to project His goodness forward to the end of our story. It is to cry out for a certain kind of goal, and so of plot and meaning, for life."[107] Similarly, God is not a circular referential name: "Theological utterance is narration of the story about Jesus as the story about God."[108] Theological utterances about God are all about a known man, Jesus Christ. Finally, he asserts that theological language can satisfy the criterion of verifiability because its dramatic coherence anticipates our resurrection from death in Jesus Christ. This anticipation is an eschatologically verifiable assertion. Theological statements are therefore informative and descriptive statements and thus meaningful.[109]

We have seen that Jenson redefines a linguistic and analytical problem to make it the problem of our *temporality*. Language is our expression of our search of our meaning in "the drama of Time." Also, our resolution is found in "the drama of God." This move suggests that he looks for the integration of meaning, life, language, and reality.

Jenson knows his proposal is not yet complete. He needs to face some questions: "What *is* 'the story of Jesus'? . . . Is it the 'biblical Christ' or the 'historical Jesus' whose story is the content of theological utterance? . . . Is the 'story of Jesus' separable from 'told as the story of the meaning of my life'?"[110] In short, we cannot establish the meaning of theological discourse until we can determine the meaning of Jesus's story. For Jenson, this is a problem of historicist hermeneutics. With his attempt to solve his problem, Jenson is moving towards an ultra-realist position.

---

106. Jenson, *KTHF*, 135, 140.
107. Jenson, *KTHF*, 131.
108. Jenson, *KTHF*, 139.
109. Jenson, *KTHF*, 153–55.
110. Jenson, *KTHF*, 141.

2.2 The Challenge of Historicity: How Theological Language is Historical, Real, and Meaningful?

2.2.1 *The challenge*

For Christians, we know the story of Jesus from the Bible. The statements about Jesus are about an ancient history. There is a temporal distance between the biblical texts and its contemporary readers. Jenson believes that scientific thought since the Enlightenment adopts a methodology of critique to acquire the historical knowledge, which is now called as "historical-critical" method. The historical critique follows Enlightenment's spirit of "critique of appearance" to question whether the historical record of the Bible is *real history*. Moreover, in historical critical study, we put the emphasis on the meaning of the biblical statements *in their own time*. We intend to know them according to their own historical background or tradition.[111] However, when we limit the past events and their meaning in their own particular historical places; "all are relativized, shorn of their possibility of universal validity—that is, of their claim to validity for me."[112] The result of is that men find themselves are "a plurality of individuals and cannot found history as a unity."[113] Jenson summarizes his question on hand as "How does *historical* narration about God work? . . . How do the documents of historical tradition bring God to understanding?"[114]

2.2.2 *The meaningfulness of theological language and history: two unsuccessful examples*

Under the circumstances of historical-critical method, some theologians have suggested ways of bringing the present meaning of the Bible out from

---

111. Jenson, "On the Problem(s)," 245–46; Jenson, *KTHF*, 18–21.

112. Jenson, *KTHF*, 20.

113. Jenson, *KTHF*, 224. See also, Jenson, "Hermeneutics and the Life of the Church," 102–5; Jenson, "On the Problem(s)," 246. In a poem, "Epiphany," Jenson states that "the hermeneutics of suspicion" is a feature of Western theology. In this point, he is clearly inclined to commend the Eastern theology:

Our finite knowledge cuts two ways:

Can hold us frozen in suspicion

Or give one clue sufficient for the venture.

The easterners were wise because they took their chance

And won.

See Jenson, "Epiphany," 559.

114. Jenson, *KTHF*, 162.

its history. Jenson does not think they are satisfactory. His two examples are classical Liberalism and Bultmann.

For Jenson, classical liberals, following their findings in historical-critical research, did not count the resurrection as an established "historical" fact so it could not be the present object of faith. Their proposed object of faith was the moral and religious teaching of the historical Jesus. It was this teaching that was to be salvific. Again, they try to establish their viewpoint by historical-critical research, but they succeeded in showing only that the historical interpretation of the historical Jesus will always be undetermined. They thus invented another sort of history in order to find the salvific Jesus who would solve their conundrum. We are told that:

> The "*Historie*" of Jesus, that is, what ordinary folk mean by history, may be unreliably reachable, but never mind, it is anyway the "*geschichtliche*" Jesus in whom we may believe . . . And the *geschichtliche* Jesus is to be found in the New Testament, however unreliable the New Testament may be as *Historie*.[115]

Jenson believes that this proposal cannot solve the difficulty of historicity either: the actors of subsequent history, because they are too historical entities, must be equally uncertain. Therefore, *Geschichtliche* can never be known except in one's present here and now.[116] It only can affirm the brokenness rather than provide a clear picture of the historical facts.

Jenson's second example is Bultmann. For Jenson, Bultmann does not invent another history as the present theological interpretation of our historical-critical findings. He insists that the author of a text and its reader are in the same historical world. The possibility of understanding is based on "that the interpreter has *a life-relation to the matter which comes to word . . . in the text.*"[117] An interpreter of a text approaches the text with a concern for understanding of human life. The whole interpreting process is carried out in this way:

> We ask about a text: ". . . does an apprehension of human existence show itself in this text, which . . . proposes a possibility of understanding also for today's . . . man? Which . . . means a genuine decision also for him?" To face such a decision in a text is existentiell understanding; to ask about it in this way is existential interpretation. Existential interpretation has the task of

---

115. Jenson, "Once More into the Breach," 123.
116. Jenson, "Once More into the Breach," 123.
117. Jenson, *KTHF*, 163. Italics Jenson's.

bringing existentiell understanding to clarity... The difference is between *hearing* and *asking*: "Did I understand?"[118]

Bultmann believes that we must interpret a historical text *existentially*. It is the interpretation about interpreter's "questioning, deciding, future-seeking character of life."[119] The same rule can be applied to the theological interpretation of history. One may even say that theological question is the basis of all existential interpretation. Because we interpret historical text theologically we are questioning and deciding our *final* future. On this point Jenson agrees with Bultmann, so he integrates Bultmann's thought with his own concept of *dramatic coherence*. Bultmann's theological interpretation, according to Jenson, is a way to interpret of our life story coherently:

> To question a text historically means to question it with reference to my own future... To question a text theologically is to question it about my *final* future, about what is to come of my life. And this is also the question about myself, about that final decision in which I am myself—for there must be a conclusion to my story if the occurrences of my life are to be a *story* at all, are to cohere as a life. Therefore the question about God is the presupposition of all historical questioning; and all historical questioning is implicitly the God-question.[120]

Bultmann not only rejects the concept of two-histories, but even radically asserts that there is no subject-object ontological division in historical reality. We experience a historical event and interpret it accordingly only when it poses a challenge for my future.[121]

But Jenson does not accept Bultmann's existential interpretation because it finally becomes an *ahistorical* interpretation. Bultmann suggests that humans cannot open themselves freely to the future because they are entangled by their past. Humans can find their proper final question or *eschatological existence* in Jesus Christ's proclamation. Jesus's proclamation—*kerygma*—is God's word that speaks to humans, but this proclamation is always an eschatological event. It is never the past but always the present. Therefore, the historical narrative is irrelevant to the proclamation.[122] Jenson rejects Bultmann's proposal because it cannot fulfill the criterion of verifiability:

---

118. Jenson, *KTHF*, 123, 163–64.
119. Jenson, *KTHF*, 164.
120. Jenson, *KTHF*, 165–66.
121. Jenson, *KTHF*, 167.
122. Jenson, *KTHF*, 168–73.

> In the proclamation we meet the Christ who lives in the event of the proclamation; to do this we do not need to learn about the historical Jesus . . . In general, the whole problem of verifiability recurs . . . as the problem of the relation between the "Jesus of historical research" and the "Christ of the proclamation."[123]

2.2.3 The meaningfulness of theological language and history: God's word-event and historical reality

We now know that Jenson refuses to solve the problem of the relation of historical distance and present meaning between Jesus's story and us by proposing two kinds of history or by a subjective existential interpretation. He suggests that all history is an event. In that, there is continuity between the narrated history of God and our theological discourse. Then, we can concretely determine the meaning of Jesus's story.[124]

Jenson's first step is to provide a conceptual tool to integrate language, time, and reality. His tool is Gerhard Ebeling's concept of word-event. As we have seen that, for Ebeling, language or word is basically "the spoken word," an event of one person addressing another. It is also an act that brings effects. Jenson does not put the emphasis on the interaction between linguistic beings of the concept of word-event but points out that when we define word as word-event, we view "language as something that is done, as an act that changes things."[125]

Jenson points out that because humans live in temporality, they formulate their identity through asking themselves whether they "will confess his past and decide for his future." In this way, one's existence and existential meaning is indeed a word-event because it is the act that interprets the past and decides a future. We can regard the function of the word in this event, as "the illumining of existence."[126]

One should note that not only is our life a word-event, but so is all reality. Because our question to ourselves "belongs not only to our existence but to the world in which our existence is given us," we meet the world in our lives in that we meet it as a "bespoken reality." The whole reality as the world's presence to us is already a word-event. In this way, historical reality is also a word-event that questions the human about his or her past and asks them to decide their future. In this sense, human existence and the whole of

---

123. Jenson, *KTHF*, 174.
124. Jenson, *KTHF*, 235.
125. Jenson, *KTHF*, 177.
126. Jenson, *KTHF*, 176–77.

reality—its past, presence, and future—are "inwardly related."[127] Jenson then argues that the historical reality is *real* and is a *word-event* in that it *speaks of* a future. It is "an *act* that *changes things*": "In the correlation of existing and meeting, having and counting as . . . we see also the word-character of historical reality: That is real which has a future—and it has a future in that it is spoken, in a word that aims at something."[128]

But Jenson does not follow Bultmann or Ebeling in understanding the relation of historical reality and human life as a subjective *existential* relation. He believes that historical reality comes to us as something other than us. Historical reality comes to us as our tradition. Our tradition is the language we are taught and by which we may speak about reality. In other words, historical reality comes to us as interpreted traditions, as stories. The historical distance between the historical text and its reader, Jenson asserts that, is not a brokenness but a relation between human and reality: "The language I speak is my relation to reality. And it is a particular, materially determined relation to reality, determined by the history in which this language has come to be the particular language . . . The specific possibilities of understanding my life and the world I live it in . . . are given by the language I am taught."[129] "The distance in time between the text and us is not a hindrance to understanding, to be 'bridged over'; it is the very condition of understanding."[130] In this relation, the past, the present, and the future are mediated by the tradition-in-language. So we experience temporality through the mediation of language.[131]

Jenson suggests that if humans experience existence through the "question" of the reality, God must be the most original word-event which initiates questions and opens conversation. In this sense, all reality as the historical tradition-in-language and our existence are in a unity which leads back to God who is the first speaker.[132]

Then, Jenson emphasizes that God's word is not a mysterious word. It is "normal," and "natural." Because it is not different from other word-events, God's word comes to us through our tradition, as do all other realities. In other words, God's word-event comes to us as the story of Jesus Christ: "And since God is there for us as a word-event, God-utterance is inherently dependent on

---

127. Jenson, *KTHF*, 177–78.
128. Jenson, *KTHF*, 177.
129. Jenson, *KTHF*, 180.
130. Jenson, *KTHF*, 182.
131. Jenson, *KTHF*, 181.
132. Jenson, *KTHF*, 181.

tradition . . . Christians confess that this true word-event, God's word occurs as the Gospel, as the proclamation that points to Jesus."[133]

Up to this point, human historicity is understood as an ontological structure. It indicates the unity of language, temporality, reality, life, and God. In this way, historical distance does not cause brokenness between present meaning and past event. Rather, it is understood as a question puts humans from the past, in the present, for the future. More importantly, one should note that in this schema language is not something other than reality, because for humans, reality always comes as *words*.

In this schema, "all history is real as said, as narrated."[134] The difference between historical-critical research and the proclamation of Jesus's story is not a difference of objective reality and subjective interpretation. All true telling of history can be researched. Jenson asserts that proclaimed Jesus— "Jesus is risen"—must be a historical narrative about a historical Jesus. Therefore, proclamation cannot be merely subjective.[135] However, historical research can only establish the probabilities of the apostles's experience of Jesus's resurrection. The "statement of the Resurrection *itself*, 'Jesus is risen,' cannot be affirmed or denied in a report of historical research."[136]

There is still a difference between historical research and proclamation, which Jenson calls the difference of Law and Gospel. He asserts that if all historical reality is interpreted reality, and if its origin is God's address to us, it implies that the historical Jesus can be interpreted according to Law or Gospel. The difference of the Law and the Gospel is that the former has *no promise* of future while the latter is a *promise*.[137] The Law is the interpreted history *as such*, while Gospel is the interpreted history with *eschaton*: "All history is real as said, as narrated. The existentiell meaning of the word in which Jesus is *proclaimed* as the eschaton is indicated by calling this word the Gospel. The existential meaning of the narration of history *as such* is that it is God's *Law*."[138]

Jenson believes historical research refuses to make the connection between past events and the final goal of history. It opens the historical past as an *object*, and creates distance between past, present, and future.[139] Because historical research views the historical Jesus as a past event that *distanced*

---

133. Jenson, *KTHF*, 184.
134. Jenson, *KTHF*, 208.
135. Jenson, *KTHF*, 211.
136. Jenson, *KTHF*, 229.
137. Jenson, *KTHF*, 232.
138. Jenson, *KTHF*, 208. Italics Jenson's.
139. Jenson, *KTHF*, 230, 232.

from us, and insists it should be studied *disinterestedly*; Jesus, whether he is risen or not, is irrelevant to us:[140] "Historical study does not let the tradition lay claims or promises on us here now . . . If Scripture—or any body of tradition—is to be authoritative, we must read it historically-critically. If we do, methodically rather than by undeliberated necessity, it falls existentially silent."[141] Historical research does speak of history. However, it speaks history as Law: "The Law throws us back on ourselves and on the past and so opens . . . the past as a past without hope."[142] In this way, the proclamation cannot be verified or falsified by the historical research and its meaning cannot be determined by such research.

According to Jenson, "The Law does not lead to the Gospel; it is *overcome* by the Gospel."[143] The Gospel fulfills and overcomes the Law by opening the *eschaton* through Jesus's past story.[144] It is a narrated *prophecy*. "The proclamation narrates the story of Jesus as the story of the End."[145] It can be summarized as "He is risen and will come again."[146] It is God's promise that "grants us the future as God's future."[147] With the Gospel, our language about God is meaningful because we can sort out the projection of the whole history.[148] However, the Gospel is not a mere subjective conjecture. It comes to us, like the Law, as word-event, and interpreted *reality*. In this way, he tackles the historicist hermeneutical question of the meaning of God by an integration of time, language, and reality. The problem of historical research is finally posited as a problem of *preferred* interpretation:

> The event of saying and hearing the proclamation belongs to the reality as historical event of that which is proclaimed. Thus, the beginning of that proclamation, the Resurrection, itself belongs to the story to be narrated . . . And this is not a claim that our existentiell projects are real because we project them: it is the claim we take up by speaking the Gospel; and the Gospel is at every step an attempt at accurate statement of the facts about us as we have become, as we are by the Law . . . Finally, if all historical reality is interpreted, bespoken reality, and if the word in

---

140. Jenson, *KTHF*, 212.
141. Jenson, "On the Problem(s)," 246.
142. Jenson, *KTHF*, 232.
143. Jenson, *KTHF*, 211.
144. Jenson, *KTHF*, 212.
145. Jenson, *KTHF*, 231.
146. Jenson, *KTHF*, 236.
147. Jenson, *KTHF*, 232.
148. Jenson, *KTHF*, 226, 231.

question is Law *and* Gospel, so that interpretation is interpretation-as-Law or interpretation-as-Gospel, then historical reality is irreducibly ambiguous and at odds with itself.[149]

2.3 Summary

In short, Jenson answers the challenges of verifiability and historicity through an integration of *language, God, reality*, and *time*. Either *dramatic coherence* or *reality as word-event* asserts that the theological language can *really* speak of God. Moreover, Jenson's notion of word-event and rejection of Bultmann's existentialism suggest that the existence of God's reality does not depend on our subjective will or thinking. In this way, Jenson's theology of language can be considered as realist, if we follow Andrew Moore to define realism as follows:

> *Ontologically*, the realist holds that there is a reality external to human minds and that it exists as it does independently of the concepts and interpretative grids in terms of which we think about it . . . *[E]pistemologically*, the realist holds that reality can be (approximately) known as it is and not just as it appears to us to be (as empiricism holds). *Semantically*, the realist holds that it is possible to refer successfully to, and so make (approximately) true statements about, reality.[150]

3. The Relation of Narrative, History, and Metaphysics: Jenson's Theology of Language and Ultra-realism

If Jenson's theology of language allows that there may be the conflicting interpretations of the reality of Law and of Gospel, his position cannot be ultra-realist. But Jenson does not think his theology of language should stop at that point. He wants to go on to assert an identity of word, history, and God. With this identity, I argue that Jenson indeed suggests an ultra-realist position of theological language.

Recalling his notion of word-event, we must remember that for Jenson theological language speaks of God because God *speaks*. He believes that the "story the Bible tells is asserted to be the story of God with His creatures; that is, it is both assumed and explicitly asserted that there is a true story

---

149. Jenson, *KTHF*, 232–33.
150. Moore, *Realism and Christian Faith*, 1.

about the universe because there is a universal novelist/historian."[151] If there is a story, the readers can get to know characters and plot. If the author of this story is alive, still acting in time, they are still directing their story towards their goal. So, though our knowledge of God is finite, the biblical narrative, in which God is identified by and with, gives us sufficient information for our quest to know God.

For Jenson, the relation between language and God is not just like that of a creative work and its writer. He suggests a tighter ontological tie between language and God. Language and God finally come so close to each other that the history which God writes in the created realm is God's own history. "The only history that in fact occurs is Jesus's history."[152] "The God whose Word is Jesus is the Creator, who creates by speaking. That is, the Word that is Jesus determines how things actually will be, are, and afterward will have been. There simply *is no* 'history' independent of the Word and somehow behind it."[153]

Such a relationship of language and God is possible because language is understood as ontological word-event. In the ontological logic of word-event, word is *reality*. Finally, Jenson can assert that the word is an all-encompassing reality:

> The gospel is a word about an alleged past event, and it functions as unconditional promise. Therefore, if the gospel is true, it is a word in which past and future rhyme dependably and finally. Were the gospel fully spoken, it would be a word about every item of reality that already is: every person, every atomic particle, every galaxy, every animal. And it would be an evocation of futurity, a creation of new language, infinite in its openness.[154]

Jenson's interpretation of the concept of word-event clearly emphasizes the *eventfulness* of word. Yet his proposal does not make clear how the *addressing* and *communicative* character of word-event can be secured. How does interpretation of God's word-event prevent language and reality from being subsumed into God himself?

That God is identified *by* and *with* the biblical narrative does not only mean the narrative can adequately refer to or describe God. It also means that the narrative really does identify *with* God in that it is God's history and universal history. We have to remember that for Jenson the Gospel is not only the word that we heard and received from God, but also is the

151. Jenson, "How the World Lost its Story," 21.
152. Jenson, S&P, 154.
153. Jenson, "Once More into the Breach," 126.
154. Jenson, S&P, 76–77.

word that we speak about God. Indeed, Rauser, one of Jenson's admirers, argues that his theology may overcome the problem of perception because "the referent by which we address God *is fixed* . . . through the revelation of historical narrative . . . the Word as revealed to us."[155] According to T. F. Torrance, ultra-realism "is what takes place when a statement about the truth is identified with the truth itself, or when the truth of statement is identified in our thought with the truth of being."[156] In this sense, Jenson's theology of language is ultra-realist.

We should note that there are other terms for ultra-realism: Vanhoozer simply calls it "naïve realism," while McCormack describes it as naïve, metaphysical grounded, and uncritical.[157] Most scholars suggest that the most distinctive characteristic of ultra-realism is its literalism. It posits a literal or perfect coincidence between signs and realities signified. Jenson is clearly not a literalist. But the statement that God is identified *by and with* the biblical narrative is ambiguous and vague if it does not mean that *literally*. His assertion that it is an error if one thinks "the theological meaning of a text is something other than what it says"[158] means we have to ask whether he is arguing for a perfect coincidence of text and meaning.

Jenson's use of speech-act theory also suggests his theology of language is ultra-realist. In *Systematic Theology*, Jenson wants to use speech-act theory to explain being and language carries some sort of analogicity. He asserts that "we may adopt categories from J. L. Austin and suggest 'x is' is univocal in its 'locutionary sense,' in what it says about x, but equivocal in its 'illocutionary force,' in what is done when it is said."[159] But this is not what Austin says. He asserts that, contrary to Jenson, disagreement over the meaning of a "locutionary act" is more difficult to handle than the one in "illocutionary act":

> Yet after all, there is ample room, equally, for disagreement . . . in the nomenclature of locutions (What did he really mean? To what person, time, or what not was he actually referring?): and indeed, we may often agree that his act was definitely one say, of ordering (illocution), while yet uncertain what it was he was meaning to

---

155. Rauser, "*Logos* and *Logoi Ensarkos*," 144. Italics mine.
156. Torrance, *Reality and Evangelical Theology*, 66.
157. McCormack, *Karl Barth's*, 130; Vanhoozer, *The Drama of Doctrine*, 290; Hunsinger, "Beyond Literalism and Expressivism," 225.
158. Jenson, "Hermeneutics and the Life of the Church," 96.
159. Jenson, *ST2*, 38.

order (locution) . . . It is much harder in fact to obviate disagreements as to the description of "locutionary acts."[160]

One may wonder Jenson's assertion of the univocality of "locutionary acts" implies certain kind of literalism. It assumes the meaning of a word is stable or "univocal."

We should be aware that Jenson's ultra-realism is not simply an epistemological device but concerns the all-encompassing role of God's word. Every word and reality occurs within the word of God. It posits a metaphysical reality through a concept of language—God's word-event. Jenson makes this move because he believes that the meaning and reality can only be known through language within the drama of time or the universal history. In this way, the linguistic communicative function of theological language is overridden by the metaphysical project. Consequently, Jenson's theology of language is an attempt to construct a metaphysics of God's revelatory reality which "embraces" or even absorbs created reality. It is not epistemology but theological metaphysics which shapes Jenson's ultra-realism.

Here Jenson's view has similarities with Hegel's.[161] Vanhoozer's description of Hegel fits Jenson too, though Vanhoozer's opponent is propositionalism: "Hegel's philosophy is epiclike in that it unfolds history from one absolute perspective with a stylistic gravitas that gives to the events recounted a sense of inevitability . . . Metaphysics, the attempt to describe the nature of ultimate reality, is perhaps the clearest example of epic thinking . . . Transposed to theology, epic takes the form of a monological system that unfolds its story from an absolute perspective."[162]

If we understand God's word-event in Jenson's theology of language as God's monologue, Vanhoozer's, and indeed Jenson's own, criticism of Hegel relates to Jenson too: "The problem with Hegel's claim to have achieved absolute knowledge of the real meaning of the Christ event is the assumption that he has achieved . . . a universal and absolute point of view. But human knowers do not stand outside or above the action, for they are always in the thick of it."[163] "Hegel's only real fault was that he confused himself with the last judge; but that is quite a fault."[164]

However, this does not mean Jenson's theological of language is entirely unacceptable. Jenson's positing theological language as an outcome

---

160. Austin, *How to Do Things with Words*, 116n1.

161. Therefore, when Jenson needs to account how God's dramatic persons in God's word-event does not become tritheism, his theology finally reroutes to idealism.

162. Vanhoozer, *The Drama of Doctrine*, 85.

163. Vanhoozer, *The Drama of Doctrine*, 85.

164. Jenson, *KTHF*, 233.

of God's theo-drama is a better alternative than the traditional doctrine of analogy, historical criticism, and theological existentialism. What Jenson's theology of language needs is greater development of its anthropological dimension so that it avoids becoming the monologue of God. It should be aware that its speech of God takes place through mediated discourses because all our theological discourse is mediated and participatory.[165] In short, one can say that Jenson's theology of language does not give an adequate account of the difference between God and his human creatures. In the next chapter, I will analyze whether this shortcoming in his theology of language affects his narrative Trinitarianism.

---

165. As T. F. Torrance puts it, "But whereas in Jesus Christ the divine Word and human word are united within one Person, that is, hypostatically, in the Bible the divine Word and the human word are only united through dependence upon and participation in Christ, that is sacramentally . . . The Word of God does not come to us in the Bible in such a way that we meet it face to face unveiled of its divine Glory and Majesty, but only in such a way that 'we see through a glass darkly,' and 'know in part.'" See Torrance, *Divine Meaning*, 7–8. Also, if we come to know God only through his word-event or drama, we can emphasize that our theological language is our *performances* in response to the Theo-drama. In this way, we can properly speak of God's drama as *human* discourse and keep our distinction from God. Indeed, Vanhoozer offers a decent statement on the relation of God's drama and our performances: "The appropriate theological response to the theo-dramatic gospel should be equally dramatic: a saying/doing that demonstrates one's understanding of what God has done in Jesus Christ. Faith seeks nothing less than a *performance* understanding . . . Our performances are 'from below,' worked out in the fear and trembling that invariably accompanies one who has to speak and act in the thick of things. Our performances are neither wholly arbitrary nor fully scripted. . . . Christian performances must be creative as well as faithful." See Vanhoozer, *The Drama of Doctrine*, 102.

Chapter 4

Divine Temporal Infinity, Triune Persons, and the Problem of One and Three in Jenson's Trinitarianism

IN PREVIOUS CHAPTERS, I have pointed out that Jenson's central theological concern is to promote a "revisionary metaphysics," which asserts that the triune divine reality is identified by and with the gospel narrative; and that this reality impacts on the meaning of Christian life. Jenson's theology of language shows that his theological proposal is an attempt to posit human life, and the economic Trinity and immanent Trinity as a single undivided reality. The triune God, who is a word-event, is an all-encompassing reality. The communicative dimension of word-event is minimized for the sake of the undividedness of theological language and God's reality. In this chapter I will investigate the ontology of Jenson's account of the trinity. There are three essential objectives: (1) To illustrate that Jenson's primary concern is to show that the Nicene and Cappadocian Trinitarianism is "a new ontology of God,"[1] which recognizes that according to the gospel God is in time and takes time. God's *reality* is identified *by* and *with* the tense-structured evangelical narrative. (2) To argue that Jenson's analysis and innovations on the Cappadocians's Trinitarianism is on the whole tenable. His aim is to understand the doctrine of the Trinity with God's temporal infinity. (3) To argue that because Jenson interprets the persons of God mainly with temporality, his Trinitarianism has difficulty holding all the following three assertions at once: (a) the immanent/economic distinction of the Trinity—the transcendence and freedom of God; (b) the identity of immanent and economic Trinity—economic Trinity *is* immanent Trinity

---

1. Jenson, *GAG*, 47.

and vice versa;² (c) the relatedness and distinction between Creator and creatures—the communion of God and human. I argue that though there is nothing wrong with interpreting the reality of God temporally; Jenson's articulation of reality within this single dimension of time is not satisfactory. If the Trinity is a word-event, it should comprise of both linguistic-communication and temporal-eventfulness.

1. Nicaea and Constantinople: "Of One Being with the Father"

Jenson regards the Council of Nicaea as a triumph of the gospel's account of God over the subordinationist account offered by Greek religion. This is the starting point of Jenson's account of the Trinity.

In the phrases "God from God . . . true God from true God," he finds that the council confessed the Son—the one from God—is simply God again. So, it did not accept that the Son was of lesser status on a spectrum of divinity.

Secondly, the phrase "from the being of the Father" asserts the "Son's origin is an event not of God's contingently willed creative action but an occurrence in the Father's being as God."³ The council insisted that there is an eternal differentiation in God himself. Jenson contends that it is the most objectionable point in the Arians's eyes for the Arians asserted deity is equivalent to uneventfulness.

Thirdly, "begotten, not created" makes an explicit distinction between the modes of origin of the Son and creatures. Jenson claims that this phrase teaches that the Son is God himself and is not a creature, even though he is begotten from God the Father.⁴

Finally, the creed confesses that the Son is "*homoousion* (ὁμοούσιον) [of one being] with the Father." Jenson does not believe that the Council's original intentions for the term *homoousios* of the Council can be clearly known. Nevertheless, it is the fact that Arius could not sign a creed with that clause and explicitly repudiated it. The conflicts that followed the Council also show that *homoousios was* a safeguard against subordinationism.⁵ Jenson believes that all anti-Nicene factions contended that

---

2. Jenson, *TI*, 139.
3. Jenson, *ST1*, 102.
4. Jenson, *ST1*, 102.
5. Jenson, *ST1*, 102. See also, Jenson, *TI*, 85–86; Jenson, "Triune God," 127–28.

subordinationism had to be maintained in order to preserve the impassibility and immutability of God himself.[6]

Jenson states that, at the Council of Constantinople in 381, Athanasius's interpretation of *homoousios* was accepted. According to Jenson, Athanasius taught that the Son is "*homoousios* with the Father" because "'the Son is the same *one* (*as* the Father), *by* resemblance' *to* the Father." Jenson emphasizes that "the relationship marked by the prepositions needed to state the Son's status as image is taken as itself constitutive for the one being of God."[7] The Son who is the image of the Father, therefore has the same *deity* as the Father. The term "image" does not imply the Son's deity is of lesser degree than the Father's.

Jenson summarizes this:

> *Homoousios* of the Father and the Son means *both* that the differentiation of the Son from the Father is internal to *what* it means to be God and that the differentiation is internal to the concrete singularity of the *one who is* all that it means to be God.[8]

Finally, when the same thinking is extended to the Spirit, we are told that we can find *the Trinity* is God.[9]

The theological assertion that runs throughout Jenson's narrative trinitarian theology can be found here: the Greek timeless concept of God should be rejected. The gospel God takes time and is identified by and with the gospel narrative. Jenson believes that Nicaea was just the beginning of the establishment of this theological position. This task in Jenson's view was decisively achieved by the Cappadocians.

2. The Cappadocians's Trinitarianism: μία οὐσία τρεῖς ὑποστάσεις

Jenson believes that the *homoousios* did not allow the deity of Father, Son, and Spirit to be set in ranks within a hierarchy. The Cappadocians taught that if the Son is *homoousion* with the Father, "how one could, without simply worshiping three gods, truly differentiate the three *otherwise* than by ranking them."[10] In order to accomplish this, they systematized the usage of the terms *ousia* and *hypostasis*.

---

6. Jenson, *ST1*, 104.
7. Jenson, *ST1*, 103. Italics Jenson's.
8. Jenson, *TI*, 88.
9. Jenson, *ST1*, 103.
10. Jenson, *ST1*, 104–5.

Jenson observes that *ousia* and *hypostasis* had been used almost interchangeably for "something that is" in the philosophical tradition as well as in theology of the church fathers. The Cappadocians decided that "*ousia* is for the one deity of God, *hypostasis* for each of Father, Son, or Spirit."[11] Jenson claims that the Cappadocians's decision was not arbitrary. This distinction had already been discernible in philosophical use. In Greek philosophy *ousia* had tended to be used for "a real thing" in articulating "*what* it is." *Hypostasis*, on the other hand, tended to be used to distinguish the thing itself from anything else. For example, *ousia* can be used for "Peter, Paul, and Barnabas *as instances of* what they have in common—humanity"; and *hypostasis* "for each of Peter, Paul, or Barnabas *as distinguished from* the others."[12] Similarly, the Cappadocians used *hypostasis* "for an identifiable individual" and *ousia* "for what such an individual is with others of the same sort." Jenson believes that "the Cappadocians said, deity is common to the three hypostases, who are identified over against each other by 'being unbegotten,' 'being begotten,' and 'proceeding.'"[13]

Why are the three hypostases of God not three gods as Peter, Paul, and Barnabas are three humans? Jenson claims that the Cappadocians offer two answers: The first is to understand *hypostases* as relations in the mode of substance. The second is that it interprets God's *ousia* as divine infinity. Jenson commends their theology for its creativity and the significance of its contribution to the doctrine of Trinity, and he uses their insights to develop his own trinitarian theology and revisionary metaphysics.

2.1 Hypostases as Relations in the Mode of Substance and Triune Identities

In Jenson's account, the Cappadocians determined that the individuals who share humanity are distinguished from each other by "characteristics adventitious to that humanity," for examples, by short stature, Athenian ancestry, or the like. Under the circumstances, the characteristics that make Paul, Peter, and Barnabas distinct human beings do not belong to their humanity. The Cappadocians contended that God, however, cannot be conceived to receive merely accidental or privative characteristics. The distinguishing characteristics of God, Father, Son, and Spirit, "belong to singular Godhead itself."[14]

---

11. Jenson, *ST1*, 105. See also, Jenson, *TI*, 104–5; Jenson, "Triune God," 136–37.
12. Jenson, *ST1*, 105. See also, Jenson, *TI*, 104–5; Jenson, "Triune God," 136–37.
13. Jenson, *ST1*, 105.
14. Jenson, *ST1*, 105–6. See also, Jenson, *TI*, 105–6; Jenson, "Triune God," 136–37.

This is so because "the three can in fact be individually identified, by their relations to one another, precisely with respect to their joint possession of one and the same deity."[15] It is the particular relations in God, not the contingent characteristics, enable us to identify God is the Father; God is the Son; and God is the Spirit. The particular relations are how they are three. The Cappadocians described the relations of the three hypostases as: "being unbegotten," "being begotten," and "proceeding."[16] In Jenson's paraphrase of them: "God is the Father as he is the source of the Son's and the Spirit's deity; God is the Son as he is the recipient of deity from the Father; God is the Spirit of the Son's reception of deity from the Father."[17] The three are the different relations of the one God. More importantly, these relations are "the different ways in which each is the *one* God."[18] The *hypostasis* is *tropos hyparxeos* (τρόπος ὑπάρξεως), "way of having being."[19] The three *hypostases* are "modes of being, not elements in being."[20]

While we worship all three hypostases of God: Father, Son, and Spirit, we confess that there is only one God. Jenson employs the insights of Western scholasticism to summarize this finding, "the hypostases simply *are* 'relations subsisting in God.'"[21] A trinitarian *hypostasis* is "a relation . . . in the mode of substance."[22]

Jenson goes on to unpack that the relations in God—"begetting," "being begotten," and "proceeding"—as "biblical terms for temporal structures of evangelical history."[23] The temporal events happen between "Father," "Son," and "Spirit" in the Gospel, and the relations that these events show are *constitutive* of God himself. Jenson argues that this assertion works because in the gospel narrative:

> Jesus or his Father or the Spirit refers absolutely from himself to one of the others as the one God that he is in a specific way a

---

15. Jenson, *ST1*, 106. See also, Jenson, *TI*, 105–6; Jenson, "Triune God," 136–37.
16. Jenson, *ST1*, 105. See also, Jenson, *TI*, 104–5; Jenson, "Triune God," 136–37.
17. Jenson, *ST1*, 106.
18. Jenson, *TI*, 106. See also, Jenson, *ST1*, 106; Jenson, "Triune God," 137.
19. Jenson, *ST1*, 117.
20. Prestige, *God in Patristic Thought*, 245.
21. Jenson, *TI*, 106. Italics Jenson's.
22. Jenson, *ST1*, 108. Jenson quotes from Aquinas, *Summa Theologiae*, 1.29.4. Jenson indicates that Aquinas's own word is "*Persona*" for it is the standard Latin equivalent of *hypostasis*.
23. Jenson, *TI*, 106; Jenson, "Triune God," 136–37; Jenson, *ST1*, 108.

perfect correlate to that other, and so himself God within and of the history plotted by these referrals.[24]

As to how Father, Son, and Spirit, the characters (*personae dramatis dei*) of the gospel narrative, constitute *one* God and are God himself, Jenson simply asserts that "What happens between Jesus and his Father and our future *happens in God*—that is the point."[25] "This narrative, asserts the doctrine of Trinity, is the final truth of God's own reality."[26]

In the biblical narrative the Father, Son, and Spirit are the three *personae* and three *agents* of one God. Through their agency, we see what the one God does with his creatures. Crucially, these three agents do not become three gods because there is a prefect *mutuality* of the agencies of Father, Son, and Spirit. Quoting Gregory of Nyssa Jenson believes that the Cappadocians laid down the true rule: "All action that impacts the creature from God . . . begins with the Father and is actual through the Son and is perfected in the Holy Spirit. *Therefore*, the attribution of the action is not divided among the plurality of actors."[27] Thus, the three agencies of God are undivided—*opera ad extra sunt indivisa*. As it is undivided, we can confess that there is only one God. Jenson summarizes his interpretation of Cappadocians's concept of hypostasis and their rebuttal to the charge of tritheism as followings:

> According to Gregory of Nyssa, when we speak of God we may think first of the three identities [i.e., Jenson's term for *hypostases*], each of whom is God. Then there is the life among them, the complex of their "energies," which, according to Nyssa, is the proper referent of phrases such as "the one God."[28]

Jenson's insistent theological assertion is that *trinitarian language perfectly corresponds to the reality of God*. Christian God is not a timeless God. God is identified by and with the Gospel narrative which takes time. *The relations that had been unfolded in the Gospel narrative indeed are the relations subsisting in God.*

---

24. Jenson, *ST1*, 109.

25. Jenson, *TI*, 106; Jenson, "Triune God," 136–37.

26. Jenson, *ST1*, 108.

27. Jenson, *ST1*, 110. Italics Jenson's. It should be noted that Jenson's notions—perfect mutuality and undivided agency of God—indeed are different terminologies for what Prestige suggests the Cappadocians taught: in God, there is only "one 'energy' (principle of action)." See Prestige, *God in Patristic Thought*, 256. Also see, Kelly, *Early Christian Doctrines*, 266–67.

28. Jenson, *ST1*, 152–53.

2.1.1 Replacing *hypostasis* with identity

Jenson believes that main advance made by the Cappadocians was their differentiation of *hypostasis* from *ousia*. But the Cappadocians did not use the word *in the sense either the* ancients did or as the modern world does. Jenson wants the concept of "identity" to do the work of the Cappadocian concept of *hypostasis*. "Identity" better conveys the ontological function of *hypostasis* in the trinitarian theology. Jenson believes that *hypostasis* carries special ontological function in the Cappadocian trinitarian theology. This function now can be exactly captured by the concept of identity while *hypostasis* cannot. He illustrates this point through three steps.

First, an identity or a *hypostasis* is what enables us to pick something "out from the maelstrom of actuality." An identity is means of indicating or pointing something out. It helps us to figure out "this, and this, and then this" from the numerous and jumbled realities. Since we often cannot point to a thing, Jenson states that an identity can be established through two linguistic resources: proper names and identifying description. Since there are three proper names and three set of identifying descriptions of God in the biblical narrative, we can find there are three identities—Father, Son, and Spirit in God.[29]

Secondly, an identity or a *hypostasis* is what enables us to pick something out as it "otherwise known" or to repeatedly recognize something. The identity "is the possibility of the repeated 'it.'"[30] Jenson reminds us that there are two kinds of repetition. In Hellenic metaphysical tradition, "the possibility of repeated identification lies in the prolongation of some *one* identification."[31] If something is *real* and exists as itself during a period of time, it can be repeatedly identified through *one* identity—a complex of timeless characters which it possesses. Conversely, Jenson thinks that the doctrine of Trinity teaches us that God is repeatedly identified through three identities of *one* dramatic reality with a structure of tenses and not through a set of timeless characters in *one* identity.[32] Jenson contends that for a living person, "faithfulness, rather than sameness and predictability" is the mode of one's self-identity through time.[33] The continuity of God's identity "is not that of a defined entity, some of whose defining characteristics persist from

---

29. Jenson, *TI*, 108–9; Jenson, "Triune God," 138; Jenson, "Three Identities," 6–7; Jenson, *S&P*, 112–13.

30. Jenson, *TI*, 109; Jenson, "Three Identities," 7.

31. Jenson, *TI*, 109. Italics mine.

32. Jenson, *TI*, 109–10; Jenson, "Three Identities," 7. It should be noted that Jenson does not mention this second aspect in "Triune God."

33. Jenson, *S&P*, 43.

beginning to end." Rather, "it is established in his words and commitments, by the faithfulness of his later acts to the promises made in his earlier acts."[34] As a result, he simply asserts that, God, through his promise, "is not only in fact identified by certain temporal events but is apprehended as himself temporally *identifiable*."[35] God can be repeatedly known as "the one and not another" because he is identified by and with the events in time as a story of promise. This way of identifying God is utterly different from that of Hellenic metaphysics. One should be aware that there is resemblance between Jenson and Ricoeur on the concept of identity.

Third and finally, in the modern sense, which Jenson relates to Existentialist thought, identity has to be sought within our personal existence. To be a person or to establish a personal identity in this sense is a specific *act* of presenting oneself in and through time. A person is conceived or a personal identity is established through the *acts* which enact or evoke one's own existence: "I am what I am only in that I remember what I have been and hope what I will be." This act "names the mode of repeated identifiability proper to certain entities, those we currently call 'personal.'"[36] Existentialist thought describes this act as "existence" or "*Dasein*."[37] For Jenson, this third aspect of identity's ontological function is related to the first two aspects: naming and repetition. Naming and repetition are *acts* done *in* and *through* time. In this aspect, I argue that there is a difference between Jenson and Ricoeur. For Jenson, *one* single personal agent acts and establishes his or her own identity, while for Ricoeur, one's narrative identity is open-ended and incomplete and is shaped by "the network of interweaving perspectives" of personal agents. This difference shows that Jenson's narrative theology prioritizes event or act over communication.

Jenson argues that the term *hypostasis* did not carry this three-folded meaning in the period before the formulation of trinitarian and christological doctrine. But this is precisely the reality that trinitarian theology sought to articulate for an individual *hypostasis* or person of the Trinity in Cappadocian theology. For this reason, identity is a more suitable word than *hypostasis* for the three in God.

---

34. Jenson, *TI*, 40.
35. Jenson, *ST1*, 49.
36. Jenson, *TI*, 110; Jenson, "Triune God," 138–39; Jenson, "Three Identities," 8.
37. Concisely speaking, *Dasein* "is not an object with properties, but is rather the 'happening' of a life course 'stretched out between birth and death.'" Also, *Dasein* "is always already taking some stand on its life by acting in the world . . . *Dasein* is future-directed in the sense that the ongoing fulfillment of possibilities in the course of one's active life constitutes one's identity (or being)." Cf. Guignon, "Heidegger."

From this "modern" sense of personal identity, Jenson finally acquires his explanation for how the three identities of God can be one God (or one identity of God) at the same time:

> [T]here is even one identity of God means that God is personal, that he *is* God in that he *does* Godhead, in that he chooses himself as God. That there are three identities in God means that this God's deed of being the one God is three times repeated, and so that each repetition is a being of God, and so that only in this precise self-repetition is God the particular God that he in fact is. God does God, and over again, and yet over again—and only so does the event and decision that is this God occur.[38]

2.2 God's Being as Infinite

2.2.1 *There are not three Gods*

Now we turn to the second Cappadocian answer to the question of why three instances of the divine *ousia* do not make three gods. Then we will see how Jenson develops this answer for his own trinitarian theology and revisionary metaphysics.

According to Jenson, Gregory of Nyssa taught that "God" is a predicate. The numbers of gods which we can assert depends on how many subjects are attributed to that predicate. "There are three instances of the divine *ousia*" does not mean "There are three gods," because "divine *ousia*" and "God" do not have the same referent. "Divine *ousia*" is not the subject of the word "God." The proper subject of the predicate "God" is "the mutual *action* of the identities" divine "energies"—"the perichoretic triune *life*." Because all divine action is an undivided mutual work of Father, Son, and Spirit, there is only one such life. Finally, we find there is only one subject of the predicate "God."[39] The Father, the Son, and the Spirit should be considered as one God instead of three.

2.2.2 *Divine temporal infinity*

If we identify that the triune life is God and not something else, we imply there must be a divine "nature" or *ousia*.[40] In this case we need to establish

---

38. Jenson, *TI*, 110–11; Jenson, "Triune God," 139; Jenson, "Three Identities," 8.

39. Jenson, *ST1*, 214. Italics Jenson's. See also Jenson, *TI*, 113; Jenson, "Triune God," 140.

40. Jenson, *ST1*, 215; Jenson, *TI*, 111; Jenson, "Triune God," 139.

what the divine *ousia* is. According to Jenson, Gregory taught that the divine *ousia* is "infinite."[41] We can identify God's *ousia* "as and only as the life that knows no boundary and that therefore will always go on to surpass each—even true—identifying description."[42] For "infinite-being cannot be something other than its own infinity," no other name is appropriate to God's *ousia*. If it were "*some*thing," it would be limited and bounded. But Jenson reminds us such infinity "must somehow be the infinity *of* something" as it is the *ousia of* God. In the Cappadocians's theology, infinity—the *ousia* of God—is attributed to the undivided action of Father, Son, and Spirit.[43] We can therefore say that "What Father, Son, and Spirit have from each other to be three identities of *God*, and what characterizes their mutual action *as God*, is limitlessness."[44]

Jenson contends that Gregory is teaching "in an astonishing and utterly anti-Greek fashion."[45] Hellenic thought understood infinity in terms of the analogy of space and lacked all boundaries.[46] An infinite something would therefore be nothing at all because it would have no boundaries, no spatial shape, no form, and so on. But Gregory taught that the infinity as God's deity is *temporal* infinity. Such infinity overcomes all boundaries. God is infinite because "no temporal activity can keep up with the activity that he is . . . he *overcomes* all boundaries."[47]

41. Jenson, *ST1*, 215; Jenson, *TI*, 111; Jenson, "Triune God," 139.
42. Jenson, *TI*, 111; Jenson, "Triune God," 139.
43. Jenson, *ST1*, 215.
44. Jenson, *ST1*, 216.
45. Jenson, *ST1*, 215.
46. Jenson, *ST1*, 216; Jenson, *TI*, 163.
47. Jenson, *ST1*, 216; Jenson, *TI*, 165. Jenson quotes two passages from *Against Eunomius* as his evidences: "But the transcendent and blessed life, having no accompanying timespan, has nothing to measure or assess it. All things that are made, being circumscribed by their own limits, are confined to their appropriate size by a sort of boundary as it pleased the wisdom of their Creator, in order to fit the design of the universe." From Gregory of Nyssa, *Against Eunomius*, 1.366.

"The eternity of the divine life, if one were to apply some definition to it, is something like this. It is apprehended as always in being, but does not allow the thought that it ever was not or will not be. It is the same as with the shape of the circle: when the line has gone round at an equal radius from the center and joined up to itself, those who draw geometric figures say that the beginning of the figure is indefinite, since the line does not extend to either a recognized beginning or an apparent end, but when the line joins up with itself because of the distance from the center being the same in all directions, recognizing a beginning and end is impossible; in the same way no one should object to the argument if we compare the infinite nature with a circumscribed figure. It is not with regard to the limited circumference of the circle, but observing the similarity of the life which is in all respects beyond our grasp, that we say the idea is of such a kind, but with an eye to what resembles something which enjoys a life from

TEMPORAL INFINITY, TRIUNE PERSONS, & THE PROBLEM OF ONE AND THREE   127

Jenson argues that Gregory interpreted God as temporal infinite in deliberate contrast to the Arians's timeless God. In Jenson's opinion, Gregory charged the Arians with injudiciously adopting the Greek immutable and timeless deity. They refused to call the *Logos* God because the *Logos* acts and suffers in time. But Gregory asserted that it is exactly the *Logos*'s activity in time qualifies him to be God. Immutability to time merely makes this activity "inactive." According to Jenson, Gregory argued that the Arians wrongly defined God's being by having no beginning. It should be defined as having no end because it is futurity determines God's infinity.[48]

Jenson points out how different this makes Gregory's understanding of God from that of Aristotle and Plato. For the latter two, divinity is the stillness in time. For Gregory, the being of God is that "he keeps things

---

every point of view beyond our grasp. If we extend our mind from the present moment as from a central point and take it round, we may well be drawn around in the same sort of circle by what is impossible to apprehend, as we perceive that the divine life is continuous with itself and unbroken in every direction, and can appreciate that there is no limit anywhere. We say of the eternity of God what we have heard from prophecy, that God is 'King before ages,' and 'reigns for the age,' and past the age and beyond, and that we therefore declare him superior to every beginning and extending beyond every end. Holding such a concept of him as befitting the God of the universe, we proclaim our thought by two titles, using 'unbegotten' and 'endless' to express the infinity, perpetuity, and eternity of the life of God. If only one of these were contemplated in the mind alone, and the other not referred to, then the meaning of the one would surely be impaired by the omission of the other. It is not possible to express correctly the meaning of either through just one of them: to say 'endless' is to show only the absence of any end, but tells one nothing about the beginning; to use the term 'unbegun' demonstrates that the object denoted is superior to a beginning, but leaves ambiguous the question of the end. Since then these names equally express the eternity of the divine life, this might be the right point to enquire how these people cut up the meaning of eternity, and say that the concept which denies a beginning concerns essential being, while they reckon that what negates an end is a matter outside being. They use some device or other to make this distinction, that to have no beginning is a matter of being, while to have no end is excluded as external to being. Surely, since the two concepts apply to the same thing, either they ought to have included both in the definition of the being, or else, if they judged that one was to be rejected, they should have rejected the other with it. But perhaps they are quite determined to split the idea of eternity, classing one part with the essence (*ousia*) of the divine nature, and reckoning the other with those that are not—for they will use base concepts in considering such matters, and like birds with injured wings, are not able to raise themselves up to the sublimity of thoughts befitting God. If so, my own advice to them would be to turn their doctrine around the other way, so that they reckon 'endless' as part of the being, and leave out 'unbegun' rather than 'endless,' giving priority to future expectations rather than to the stale past." From Gregory of Nyssa, *Against Eunomius*, 1.666-72. English translation from Brugarolas, *Gregory of Nyssa*.

48. Jenson, *ST1*, 216; Jenson, *TI*, 165.

moving."⁴⁹ As Jenson puts it, "To be God is always to be open to and always to open a future, transgressing all past-imposed conditions."⁵⁰ He transcends "any limit imposed on what can he be by what has been, except the limit of his personal self-identity, and any limit imposed on his action by the availability of time."⁵¹ In other words, when we say God's *ousia* is infinite, we recognize that God is temporally unhindered. If eternity is "transcendence of temporal limits," we have to concede that the deity who is temporally limitless or unhindered is eternal. Consequently, we have come back to Jenson's favorite theme: "the true God is not eternal because he lacks time, but because he takes time."⁵² Though Jenson commends the Cappadocians for the breakthrough they made, he points out that they did not overcome Greek metaphysics entirely. Jenson states that: in the Cappadocians's theology, "the assumption that deity is equivalent to impassibility, remained unchallenged in itself."⁵³ This limitation caused the "vicissitudes" of the subsequent developments of the doctrine of Trinity.

2.3 Jenson's revisionary interpretation of Cappadocian Trinitarianism: A Critical Analysis

Having set out Jenson's position on the triune identities and divine infinity, we can begin to investigate whether his innovations on the Cappadocian Trinitarianism is defensible.

In Jenson's discussion of the Cappadocians's Trinitarianism provokes one criticism. Is Jenson right to replace *hypostasis* with identity? To a great extent Jenson follows Cappadocian teaching. Zizioulas points out that one of the most important contributions of Cappadocian Trinitarianism was to understand *hypostasis* as identical with *prosopon*. The Cappadocians taught Divine *hypostases*—the relations within the triune God—should be understood ontologically, for *to be* and *to be in relation* are identical. As a result, "the word *person/hypostasis* became capable of signifying God's being in *an*

---

49. Jenson, *ST1*, 216; Jenson, *TI*, 165. Jenson here quotes Jean Daniélou's finding: Daniélou, *L'être et le temps*, 95–115. However, it should be noted that Daniélou argues that the reality of God is "unchanging" while the intelligent and material beings are moving: "Il y a trios orders de réalité. Dieu qui est ἄτρεπτος, l'esprit qui est animé du mouvement historique, la matière qui est animée du mouvement cyclique." Daniélou, *L'être et le temps*, 94.

50. Jenson, *ST1*, 216; Jenson, *TI*, 166.

51. Jenson, *ST1*, 217.

52. Jenson, *ST1*, 217.

53. Jenson, *ST1*, 108.

ultimate sense."⁵⁴ Jenson does indeed follow the Cappadocians's teaching here. His theology of triune identities intends that the *hypostases/persons/ identities* of God should be grasped ontologically.

Jenson insists to replace *hypostasis* with identity because the term can convey the three—Father, Son, and Spirit—in God are relations subsisting in time and who take time. But does this distort the Cappadocians's teaching of *hypostasis*? Various studies suggest that though the Cappadocians asserted the triune *hypostases*—the relations of God—indeed signify God's being, they taught these relations are posited without temporal distance. Thus, we could argue that Jenson's interpretation in terms of temporality cannot adequately interpret the Cappadocians's concept of *hypostasis*. For example, Balás analyzes Gregory of Nyssa's teaching in *Against Eunomius* and finds that: "Since the Persons of the Trinity (the Son and the Spirit) are πρὸ τῶν αἰώνων and thus ἄχρονοι, no temporal distance is possible between them."⁵⁵ However, Jenson insists that the relations in God—"begetting," "being begotten," and "proceeding"—are "biblical terms for temporal structures of evangelical history."⁵⁶ The "life of God is thus constituted in a structure of relations, whose own referents are narrative. This narrative structure is constrained by a difference between whence and whither that one cannot finally refrain from calling 'past' and 'future.'"⁵⁷

Similarly, in the discussion of triune infinity, the main challenge to Jenson's interpretation is whether temporal infinity properly accounts for Gregory's teaching on divine infinity. Jenson states that his finding is influenced by Ekkehard Mühlenberg's work, *Die Unendlichkeit Gottes bei Gregor von Nyssa*.⁵⁸ Mühlenberg, as B. Otis and David Balás report, argues that "Gregory conceived God's eternity, which could be identified with his infinity, 'as the infinite extension of time.'"⁵⁹ However, there are examples to show that Gregory suggested God's eternity is "timeless."⁶⁰ Otis and Balás believe that they have

54. Zizioulas, *Being as Communion*, 87–88. Italics Zizioulas's.
55. Balás, "Eternity and Time," 135.
56. Jenson, *TI*, 106; Jenson, "Triune God," 136–37; Jenson, *ST1*, 108.
57. Jenson, "Does God have Time," 195–96; Jenson, *ST1*, 218.
58. Mühlenberg, *Die Unendlichkeit Gottes*. See Jenson, *ST1*, 215n44.
59. Balás, "Eternity and Time," 146. See also Otis, "Gregory of Nyssa," 340–41.
60. 1. "The nature, on the contrary, which is self-sufficient, eternal (ἀίδιος), and contains all beings (τῶν ὄντων ἐμπεριεκτική) *is neither in place nor in time*, but being before these and above these in an ineffable manner, αὐτὴ ἐφ' ἑαυτῆς can be contemplated only be faith, not measured either by αἰών or by time, but remains by itself (ἐφ' ἑαυτῆς ἐστῶσα) resting in itself (ἐν ἑαυτῇ καθιδρυμένη) not divided into past or future, for nothing of it is outside of it (οὐδε γὰρ ἔστι παρ'αὐτὴν ἔξω αὐτῆς), the passing of which (οὗ παροδεύοντος) could make something past and something future. These (i.e., past and future) are τὰ πάθη proper to those (beings) within creation, whose life

disproved Mühlenberg's thesis.⁶¹ The argument made by Otis and Balás seems to threaten Jenson's case for the divine temporal infinity.⁶²

But we may find Jenson's interpretation tenable if we try another approach. Let us use Gregory of Nyssa as an example. We will begin our analysis of Gregory's thought from his doctrine of human salvation and participation in God, and then go back to his doctrine of God.

David Bentley Hart points out that if we take Gregory's teaching of human participation in God's goodness seriously, we have to see the relationship between God and man, established by God's self-disclosure of his divine infinity and human participation, as "a real event." He contends that a real trinitarian "economy" is essential to a fruitful participation of human to God's goodness. It is worth quoting him at length:

> After all, were the relation between God and humanity simply that between the infinitely hidden and the finitely manifest, it would be no relation at all, but only an impossible interval, posed between the ontological and the ontic, the actual

---

is split into hope and memory according to the division of time, whereas that transcendent and blessed power, to whom everything is always equally present as if it were now (ἡ πάντα κατὰ τὸ ἐνεστὸς ἀεὶ πάρεσιν ἐπτίσης), is seen as comprehending by its all-circling power (τῆς περιεκτικῆς τῶν πάντων δθνάμεως) both past and future." Gregory of Nyssa, *Against Eunomius*, 1.370-72. Cf. Balás, "Eternity and Time in Gregory of Nyssa's *Contra Eunomium*," 135. Italics mine. 2. "[The created essence (ἡ κτιστὴ οὐσία)] is stretched out within a certain dimensional extension (διαστηματικῇ τινι παρατάσει), enclosed by time and space; the latter [i.e., the uncreated nature (ἡ ἄκτιστος φύσις)] transcends all notion of dimension (πᾶσαν διαστήματος ἔννοιαν) . . . In this life we can apprehend a beginning and an end for all beings, but the Beatitude which is above the creation admits neither beginning nor end, but is beyond all that is connated by either, *being ever the same, firmly established by Itself, not passing from one point to another by a distension of Its life* (οὐ διαστηματικῶς ἐκ τινος εἴς τι τῇ ζωῇ διοδευόσα)." Gregory of Nyssa, *Against Eunomius*, 2.70. Cf. Balás, ΜΕΤΟΥΣΙΑ ΘΕΟΥ, 138. Italics mine. 3. "For since human life, being moved in a distended manner (διαστηματικῶς κινουένη) . . . but *not as if God would leave in his life some distance* (διάστημα) *behind himself and would again proceed living toward the future* (πρὸς τὸ προκείμενον πάλιν ἐν τῷ ζῆν διοδεύοντος)." Gregory of Nyssa, *Against Eunomius*, 2.459. Cf. Balás, "Eternity and Time," 140. Italics mine.

61. Balás, "Eternity and Time," 146; Otis, "Gregory of Nyssa," 340-41.

62. However, we should note that Jenson does not understand God's eternity only as an "infinite extension of time": "God is not infinite because he extends indefinitely but because no temporal activity can keep up with the activity that he is." Jenson, *ST1*, 216. Also, Jenson explicitly states that theology can only apply an infinitely linear time concept which comes from Aristotle's philosophy to created events. "A stretch of linear time preceding creation must be oxymoronic." Jenson, *ST1*, 139. For Jenson, "Time is *both* the inner extension of a life, as for Augustine, *and* the external horizon and metric of all created events, as for Aristotle. For time is a 'distention' in the life that is God and just so is the enveloping given horizon of all events that are not God." Jenson, *ST2*, 35.

> and the possible, the absolute and contingent; its only true proportion would be an infinite otherness, and its only true expression the creature's eternal frustration. There must then already be in God, for Gregory's "dynamist" theology of the image to be meaningful, the ground of possibility that would allow the hiddenness of God at once to remain inviolable and yet to unveil itself in a created icon; there must be a Trinitarian "economy" (to use an entirely inappropriate word, given the infinite self-donation of the Father in the Son and Spirit) of invisibility and disclosure, and the created image of God must participate at once in this invisibility and in this disclosure: it must acquire its brightness "within" the Trinitarian order of relations, according to an economy (the word being here appropriately employed) that, in keeping with Gregory's language, might best be called the economy of glory. And, for Gregory, glory means more than an "attribute" of God: it is his light, his splendor, and—most importantly—his Son and Spirit ... Or, to phase it differently, God's light is always Trinitarian; his glory is inseparable from his triune being.[63]

In other words, if there is a fruitful human participation in divine life, we should confess that the triune being can be found in the event of the divine economy. We cannot posit that the "real" divine being is separated from the economic event and at the same time teach human is meaningfully participating in divine life. Hart's statement shows that triune economy should be a "real" event in temporal world if we are to take Gregory's doctrine of salvation seriously.[64]

Likewise, the life of participation in God's goodness, according to Gregory, can be understood as an experience of temporal unhinderedness. In other words, the divine infinity experienced by the blessed is a *temporal infinity* in Jenson's sense. Even Balás admits that:

> Gregory clearly teaches elsewhere, such a painful distention by memory and hope is absent not only from the life of God, but

---

63. Hart, "Mirror of the Infinite," 121–22. However, we should note that Hart is fiercely against "all simple oppositions" between Trinitarianism of "Greeks and Latins." Hart, "Mirror of the Infinite," 126.

64. I should point out that Hart's position is little different from Jenson. For Hart, God the Father is hidden. He is understood through "the infinite self-donation" of himself "in the Son and Spirit." Thus, trinitarian "economy" is "an entirely inappropriate word" in some senses. Jenson recognizes God is "hidden." Jenson, *ST1*, 233–34. However, he would not say it is "entirely inappropriate" if we ascribe Father in trinitarian economy. He states that we can identify Father because Jesus addresses the God of Israel is his "Father."

also from our future beatitude, where only love remains. We do not think, however, that Gregory's insistence on the essential "distention" of all created existence is due simply to polemical exaggerations in his struggle against Eunomius. Eternal beatitude excludes distressing memories and unfulfilled hopes, yet also our future blessed life is a life by participation, consisting in an essentially progressive partaking of the Infinite Good, a continuous "forgetting what is behind and being stretched out for what is ahead," i.e., for further increase in perfection, "in all eternity of the ages."[65]

So we may say that there is a divergence between immanent Trinity and economic Trinity in Gregory's theology. For Gregory, the infinity of God himself is transcendent and *atemporal*. There is no temporal distance and distension in God himself: God is "being ever the same . . . not passing from one point to another." The three *hypostases* of God, who are God himself, act in time. Moreover, human participation in God experiences an infinite perfection in temporal sense: "a continuous 'forgetting what is behind and being stretched out for what is ahead,' i.e., for further increase in perfection, 'in all eternity of the ages.'" From this divergence, we find that, as Meredith claims, Gregory "is wrestling with an intractable problem" of the sharp opposition between the doctrine of Trinity and then generally accepted concept of divine simplicity from the time of Parmenides.[66]

One may wonder how Gregory can hold these opposite assertions at once. Hart has shown us "a link" between the hidden immanent God and his economy is necessary for a true and meaningful human participation in God. He claims that such "link" can be found in Gregory's teaching of divine glory. But Hart's interpretation may easily slip into modalism or subordinationism, so he does not represent a satisfactory answer to our question. We can look at this issue via another doctrine—the unity of divine nature and power—to see how Gregory constructs this link.

Gregory, in his polemics against Eunomius's subordinationism, taught that there is a unity between God's activity (ἐνέργεια), power (δύναμις), and nature/being (φύσις/οὐσία). He understands power as the capacity to act and manifest the nature of that existence. Heat is a connatural power of fire, for example.[67] Because the Father and the Son manifest the same power,

---

65. Balás, *ΜΕΤΟΥΣΙΑ ΘΕΟΥ*, 138–39.

66. Meredith, *Gregory of Nyssa*, 20. See also, Meredith, "The Divine Simplicity," 339–51.

67. Barnes, *The Power of God*, 13, 305. See also, 220–307 for Barnes's careful exposition of Gregory's thought.

they must share the same nature. Notably, the power of God is the capacity to produce or create:[68]

> [I]f they agree that the one activity [of creation] is exercised by the Divine Power [δύναμις] without passion, let them not quarrel about the other: for if He creates without labor or matter, He surely also begets without labor or flux.[69]

Because the paradigmatic divine power is production, we can say that "God is first and foremost a God who acts."[70] Since God's power is connatural to God, and, as part of his nature, "wherever one finds the power of producing, one must also find God, just as wherever one finds seeing or burning, one must also find an eye or fire."[71] Thus, one can know God through his power—his acts and his *Logos*, who is indeed God himself—in time.

More interestingly, Gregory taught that God is perfect in power and goodness. Therefore, God cannot be hindered by any limits—which is close to infinity in Jenson's sense. When Gregory mentioned the Son and the Spirit, he said:

> [They] are indefectably perfect in goodness and power [δύναμις] and all such things. For all good things, as long as they do not admit their opposite, have no limit to their goodness, since they are naturally circumscribed only by what is opposite to them . . . [for example,] power stops when weakness takes hold, life is limited by death, light's boundary is darkness, and all in all individual good things cease when they meet their opposites.[72]

However, the power of God does not possess any sequence and interval. Thus, it is "transcendent." Its transcendence is atemporal.[73]

---

68. Barnes, *The Power of God*, 223: "The first Person is productive (that is, is God) by generating the Second; the second Person is productive (that is, is God) by creating."

69. Gregory of Nyssa, *Against Eunomius*, 3.2.63. Cf. Barnes, *The Power of God*, 248.

70. Barnes, *The Power of God*, 259.

71. Barnes, *The Power of God*, 234.

72. Gregory of Nyssa, *Against Eunomius*, 1.167–69. Cf. Barnes, *The Power of God*, 271.

73. "Therefore, however great God is, the Word, who is with him, is surely equally great: so if God has limits, the Word to be sure is limited too; but if the infinity of God transcends limitation, then the Word, envisaged as simultaneous, is not comprehended in limits and measures either." Gregory of Nyssa, *Against Eunomius*, 3.2.19. "The indivisible, immeasurable, uncircumscribed Power, containing in itself the ages and all the creation that is in them, and by the eternity of its own nature exceeding in every direction the infinity of the ages, either has no mark to indicate its nature, or has one quite different from that which the creation has." Gregory of Nyssa, *Against Eunomius*, 3.6.68.

Consequently, one should find that the "link" between the "becoming" in the flux of time and the transcendent "divine being" without temporal sequence falls upon the assertion of the power which is connatural to the divine nature/being, just as heat is connatural to fire. Gregory assumes that God's power is a timeless "substance" or "entity" outside temporal reality but which works within this reality at the same time. Under this teaching of divine power, even the simplicity of God can mean the different operations of God show the Father, Son, and Holy Spirit possess the same power; and thus must have the same nature.[74]

Barnes believes that Gregory's teaching "stands in stark contrast" to both the anti-Nicene and the Platonic doctrine of mediation.[75] But we can see that although there is no doctrine of mediation, such understanding of the divine transcendence is a kind of timeless eternity and impassibility of Hellenic thought in Jenson's view.[76]

Gregory taught that the power of God who acts in time indeed is God himself. A meaningful human participation in God requires a real event to establish the relationship between God and human. The infinity of the divine power and goodness is a kind of unlimitedness. The infinity experienced by the blessed in God is a continuous perfection which triumphs over the unrecoverable past and unfulfilled hope. Besides, the teaching of a unity of divine act and being is a great success of breaking through the predicaments of Hellenic influenced subordinationism. In Gregory's time, Eunomius was the most obvious example of this subordinationism. In his debate with Eunomius, Gregory taught that divine economy in time is God's own reality in order to defend the full divinity of Christ. In this viewpoint, Jenson legitimately argues the unity of God's act and being and the temporal infinity are the distinctive characteristics of Cappadocians's theology.

On the other hand, Gregory did teach God should be without sequence, interval, and temporal distension. God is ἄχρονος. Thus, as Jenson states in his earlier work, *God After God*, Gregory "automatically identifies God's infinity with changelessness and timelessness" when "he steps outside the trinitarian argument."[77] In his opinion, it shows that "the assumption that deity is equivalent to impassibility, remained unchallenged in itself."[78]

English translation from Leemans and Cassin, *Gregory of Nyssa Contra Eunomium III*. Also see Barnes, *The Power of God*, 236.

74. Barnes, "Divine Unity and the Divine Self," 50–51. Barnes cites Gregory of Nyssa, *On the Making of Mankind*, 6.1–2.

75. Barnes, *The Power of God*, 234.

76. See Jenson, *ST1*, 208–10.

77. Jenson, *GAG*, 122.

78. Jenson, *ST1*, 108.

In summary, Jenson develops his own doctrines of triune identities and divine temporal infinity through his interpretation of the Cappadocians's theology. He highlights the Cappadocians's breakthrough and at the same time points out the limitations of their theology. He employs the Cappadocians's trinitarian insights to his own trinitarian proposal selectively. His analysis and revision of their thought, which is the intellectual resource for his revisionary metaphysics, can be justified. We have seen once again from his discussion of the Cappadocians's thought that the relation between God's reality and time is the central theological issue of his Trinitarianism.

3. Jenson's Trinitarian Proposal and Revisionary Metaphysics: Analysis and Criticism

After we have discussed Jenson's interpretation and revision of the Cappadocians's Trinitarianism, it is time for us to sketch Jenson's trinitarian proposal and revisionary metaphysics as they are developed under the light of that interpretation. I will briefly sum up Jenson's Trinitarianism in terms of triune identities and divine temporality. I will point out the issues that his proposal raises. I will argue that over-reliance on the temporal dimension means that his Trinitarianism is in danger of blurring the distinction between God and creature, and paradoxically even creates a danger of modalism.

From our discussion, we know that for Jenson the Gospel has already taught that we can identify the triune God by and with the biblical narrative. We have also learned that from its very beginning, the Christian church lives in a culture that considers divine eternity as timeless and persistence. Thus, searches of "attributes" of divine "being" and "mediators" of the deity are the foremost tasks of its religion. This situation eventually causes the continuous "struggles" and "clashes" between Christian doctrine of the Trinity and Hellenic Philosophy. For Jenson, the Nicene decisions and Cappadocian theology were a triumph of Christian church over Hellenism. The most two important successes are that: (1) all three *hypostases* of God—Father, Son, and Spirit—were firmly recognized as God himself; (2) the being of God can be grasped in a manner of temporal infinity.

3.1 Triune Identities and Divine Temporality

Jenson insists that the doctrine of Trinity can only be developed correctly when we recognize that "God himself is identified by and with the particular plotted sequence of events that make the narrative of Israel and her Christ."

He warns of the danger to Christian faith when our discourse about God precedes the exposition of Trinity.[79]

In Jenson's opinion, the biblical narrative "asserts the doctrine of Trinity, is the final truth of God's own reality."[80] "All aspects of the Lord's hypostatic being appear in Israel's Scripture."[81] Thus, based on the insights of Cappadocians's theology, he asserts that the temporal events happen between "Father," "Son," and "Spirit" in the Gospel and the relations shown from these events are *constitutive* for God himself. The Cappadocians called these *dramatis dei personae* as *hypostases* of God. I have shown that Jenson believes that "identity" is a more appropriate term in modern sense than *hypostasis* because the Cappadocians gave the word a meaning quite different from its sense in the Hellenic philosophical tradition. Undoubtedly, the concept of identity is an important innovation. In this concept, Jenson emphasizes that God is *a* person and he establishes his personal identity through *acts* of presenting himself in and through time.[82]

Through the concept of identity, Jenson proposes a Trinitarianism that tries to avoid the pitfall of static divine attributes of Hellenic metaphysics. At the same time, his proposal maintains that God is an objective person or reality and not merely the subjective projection of human beings. The Christian God is therefore not the God of normal religion which comes, as Feuerbach contends, from human projection. The "revelations" of normal religion which are products of our religious projections and quest are, in Jenson's view, *idolatry*.[83]

3.2 The Complication of how many Divine Hypostases, Persons, or Identities

Jenson's introduction of the concept of identity attempts to explicate the mode of existence of three hypostases in a temporal manner, and so to bridge the gap between economic Trinity and immanent Trinity. But this does not mean our trinitarian reflection has been accomplished. We still have to deal with the difficulties caused by his innovative replacing of the Cappadocians's *hypostasis* with identity.

In the previous section, we saw Jenson attempting to show that there are three identities of God—Father, Son, and Spirit—and one personal

79. Jenson, *ST1*, 60.
80. Jenson, *ST1*, 108.
81. Jenson, *ST1*, 63.
82. Jenson, *TI*, 110–11; Jenson, "Triune God," 139; Jenson, "Three Identities," 8.
83. Jenson, *ST1*, 60.

identity of God—God himself—at the same time. It should be remembered that Jenson was trying to establish his arguments for replacing *hypostasis*, whose Western equivalent is "person," with identity there. There may be some confusion at this point. On the one hand, he explicitly states this existential sense of "personal" identity is "in a sense—note well—very different from the trinitarian 'person.'"[84] On the other hand, he immediately asserts that "there is even one identity in God means that God is personal . . . there are three identities in God means that this God's deed of being the one God is three times repeated." It looks as though Jenson is suggesting there are four identities, or one personal identity and three identities in God. Eventually, what the terms *hypostasis*, person, identity, and personal exactly meant are unclear. Unfortunately, throughout *TI* and "Triune God," he does not provide further explanation of his position.

This complication helps us realize that Jenson needs to do more than replace of *hypostasis* with identity. In his later work *ST1*, Jenson puts the question explicitly in the following form:

> Is the Trinity itself a *personal* reality? Is "itself," as just used, the right word? Should it not be "himself"? But if the Trinity is personal, as are Father, Son, and Spirit, how many divine identities are there? Four rather than three?[85]

In other words, this is a problem about the relationship between the divine oneness of Trinity and the three persons/*hypostases*/identities of this divine reality. The Judeo-Christian faith confesses there is only one God—the God of Israel. God is the personal reality that the Israelites and the Christians pray and praise. In the gospel narrative, Father, Son, and Spirit were described as concrete dramatic persons of this God. The church teaches that these three persons are mutually and fully *homoousios*. Thus, Trinity is the one God. However, one should note that Jesus addressed the God of Israel as "my Father." The Father is therefore at the same time the God of Israel and the one among three identities of the God of Israel. His problem is how to hold all these assertions together. Jenson calls it "the patrological problem."[86] He points out that one would avoid the whole problem by positing Trinity as impersonal[87] but such attempt will "compromise the thoroughgoing per-

---

84. Jenson, *TI*, 110; Jenson, "Triune God," 139.

85. Jenson, *ST1*, 116.

86. Jenson, *ST1*, 115.

87. This is what Pannenberg suggests Jenson should do. See Pannenberg, "Eternity, Time, and the Trinitarian God," 70.

sonality of God as he appears in Scripture."[88] Therefore, it is better to regard God is personal and to deal with the problem directly.

Because the assertion of a personal God should not be given up, and because the terms *hypostasis*, person, and identity can be equivalent to each other, Jenson has to explore the meaning of these terms to develop a platform for what comes next. He begins his task with an analysis of the concept of person.

3.2.1 Person

In *ST1*, Jenson suggests that the marks of personhood are individuality and social relation of address and response. The standard Western definition of person was invented by Boethius: "a person is an individual entity endowed with intellect."[89] However, an intelligent being is not necessary a personal being. Jenson provides his own modified definition: "a person is one with whom other persons—the circularity is constitutive—can *converse*, whom they can *address*."[90] In this definition, he emphasizes both individuality and the conversation that is social existence. According to Jenson, these two defining components are biblically and theologically appropriate. Father, Son, and Spirit are called *personae* because the term "apparently came into theology by way of exegetical use: biblical instances of God's speech were said to be God speaking 'in the person of' Father or Son or Spirit." The term refers us to the individual characters which "are individuated by role differentiation" within the biblical narrative.[91]

Merely role differentiation could imply modalism. An individual can play several social roles, and more than one individual can play the same role. Obviously, both options cannot be the appropriate meaning of person in trinitarian theology. A social person proper to the trinitarian theology should point to its specific reality. Therefore, Jenson's second defining component—a person is in a social relation of converse—is clearly important. When we say "something *is* a social *persona*" in trinitarian theology, it should not be a merely role playing. Conversely, it should refer us to "specify

---

88. Jenson, *ST1*, 117.

89. Jenson, *ST1*, 117.

90. Jenson, *ST1*, 117. Italics Jenson's. One should note that Jenson mentions he has "tried to ignore this plain fact, and developed a very different position" of person in "Triune God."

91. Jenson, *ST1*, 118.

an identity that is *constituted* in a particular set of social relations of address and response."[92] Jenson gives us an illustration of this logic of person:

> The Father's speaking his Word, the act in which the Son is constituted, is itself a call for response, thereby constituting the Son as himself a speaking being like the Father. The Father's breathing the Spirit, the act in which the Spirit is constituted, is in itself the Father's entry into the communal freedom that the Spirit gives, to constitute the Spirit a personal agent also over against the Father.[93]

Jenson finds that his position exactly agrees with Tertullian's concept of *persona*. Tertullian taught a *persona* "is a subsistent social relation."[94] He understood the three *personae* in God are "the relations of address and response found in Scripture between the Father and Jesus and the Spirit, establish reality in God, just as such relations do among human individuals."[95] Finally, Jenson concludes that using the concept of person to articulate the triune reality is definitely legitimate. In his viewpoint, defining person as *individuality* and *relation of converse* are precisely in accord with biblical and theological reflection of Trinity.

3.2.2 Hypostasis and identity

After redefining the concept of person, Jenson comes to discuss *hypostasis* and identity. According to his line of thought, one should expect he would highlight the inadequacy of *hypostasis* and instead favor identity. Indeed, he admits that the Cappadocian fathers's teaching of *hypostasis* as *tropos hyparxeos* is a powerful means of explaining how the triune relations can be the different ways of existence in which each is the one God. However, he insists that the term was considered primarily as "enumerable instance of a certain sort." We are told that an *hypostasis* was principally referred as "something that can be counted and to which characteristics can be attributed, some of these characteristics generic for all hypostases of the same *ousia*, and some differentiating the hypostasis from other hypostases of the same *ousia* and so making it countable among them."[96] Furthermore, the divine relations in the Cappadocian teaching of *hypostasis* are the relations of origin—the

---

92. Jenson, *ST1*, 119.
93. Jenson, *ST1*, 119.
94. Jenson, *ST1*, 119.
95. Jenson, *TI*, 73; Jenson, "Triune God," 123; Jenson, *ST1*, 119.
96. Jenson, *ST1*, 117.

Father is unbegotten and not proceeding, the Son is begotten from God the Father, the Spirit is proceeded from God the Father—and not the relations of address and response. Thus, he finds that a *hypostasis* may not adequately articulate the divine personhood—the reality of divine converses.

On the other hand, Jenson defines a divine "identity" as "a *persona dramatis dei* who can be repeatedly picked out by a name or identifying description or by pronouns, always by relation to the other two."[97] Under this definition, the three identities are identified by and with the biblical narrative which records these identities's addresses and responses. Thus, he believes that the term identity is more suitable for trinitarian discourse, because it "is obviously chosen with persons in mind."[98] Person prevails over *hypostasis*, in his view, because it must be construed on the horizon of time. Though the temporal dimension is not explicitly demanded by the definition of person, he thinks that it is indeed important for our trinitarian reflection.[99]

3.2.3 *The correlation between person and identity*

From the above discussion, we know that God is personal. There are three *personae* of God. Also, these three persons can be identified as three identities of God alternatively. Then, we come back to the question we have previously met: "If the Trinity is personal, as are Father, Son, and Spirit, how many divine identities are there? Four rather than three?" Jenson puts this question in another way and highlights its crux—the complication in the connection between person and identity, "must one identity always be one person or one person one identity?"[100]

The crux that we have pointed out requires Jenson to further clarify the conceptual relationship operated within his terminology. In Jenson's terminology, "identity" is indeed an equivalent of "person" or "*hypostasis*" in traditional theology. It usually refers to the concrete divine characters—Father, Son, and the Spirit—in God's story who reveal God himself. In other words, the term serves as *a pointing system* to *point* the reality of triune God. The trinitarian faith requires that such "system" should be "a relation in the mode of substance." As a result, an identity of triune God points to a specific person of his own—Father, Son, or Spirit. In *TI* and other earlier works, Jenson seems to argue that the Trinity is personal and this personal Trinity

---

97. Jenson, *ST1*, 106.
98. Jenson, *ST1*, 118.
99. Jenson, *ST1*, 118.
100. Jenson, *ST1*, 119.

bears his own identity as well. He employs the existentialist concept to argue that one establishes one's own "self-identity" or "personal identity" through acts "of positing oneself in and through time."[101] As God does reveal himself and let others know him through acts "of positing oneself in and through time," Jenson inevitably says that "there is even one identity of God means that God is personal, that he *is* God in that he *does* Godhead, in that he chooses himself as God."[102] Finally, the argument leads to the problem of "four identities" that Jenson himself raised.

Obviously, Jenson is aware that as long as the correlation between identity and person is one to one, it would be problematic to hold the indicative function and the "existential" or "personal" function of the term "identity" at the same time. He makes a maneuver in his usage of trinitarian terminology in *ST1*. We are told that "Father, Son, and Spirit are three identities, and the Trinity is not an identity."[103] We should note that this later work presents this slight but significant difference from his earlier works in the concept of identity. In *TI* and other earlier works, Jenson claimed that "there is even one identity of God."[104] In *ST1*, Jenson conversely states that "Father, Son, and Spirit are three identities, and the Trinity is not an identity." He explains he does not treat the Trinity as an identity because "the Triune God is always identified by reference to one or several of the three identities. Were it otherwise, there would be four divine identities; the Trinity would then have to be taken for the 'real' God, and we would be back with modalism."[105] *In short, Jenson's maneuver clarifies that an identity is a person. However, a person who presents itself through its own temporal deeds does not need to be an identity. In this sense, identity is obviously a pointing system. It points to an individual person. However, a person can be something broader than an identity.* However, we may question whether this assertion works or not.

3.2.4 *Triune identities, the monarchy of Father, and the Trinity as a person*

In order to make his assertion valid, Jenson needs to loosen the connection between identity and person in *ST1*. First, he argues that the one to one

---

101. Jenson, *TI*, 110; Jenson, "Triune God," 138–39; Jenson, "Three Identities," 8.
102. Jenson, *TI*, 110–11. See also this statement: "God is indeed describable as personal in the modern sense . . . The person . . . is the Trinity." Jenson, *TI*, 175.
103. Jenson, *ST1*, 119.
104. Jenson, *TI*, 110–11; Jenson, "Triune God," 139; Jenson, "Three Identities," 8.
105. Jenson, *ST1*, 119.

correlation is not come from the gospel narrative. Such framework is rooted in the Western philosophical conception of the selfhood.

In the standard Western interpretation, a person is an individual entity endowed with intellect. Personality is possessed by a self-enclosed thinking entity—"I." Identity and personality is inevitably one to one. Identity and personality are an outcome of a self-thinking consciousness.[106] However, in Jenson's opinion, this interpretation cannot be maintained in the late/post-modern world. Phenomenology, Post-structuralism, and Psychiatry demonstrate the traditional understanding of personhood cannot work. If selfhood is merely a self-enclosed thinking entity, it will be inevitably broken and muddled.[107]

More importantly, Jenson argues that this one-to-one correlation does not correspond to the Christian faith. He claims that various Christian doctrines teach that a person can be something more general than a concrete individual identity. The correlation between identity and person may not be one to one. In other words, "there may be *more than one way to be personal*."[108] We are told that in the doctrines of original sin and the indwelling of Christ in the believer, there is "certain looseness in the connection between identity and personality."[109] For this reason, Adam and his descendants, or Christ and believers, are treated as one person in these doctrines though they are clearly distinct identities.[110] In one way we may be one person with Adam and Christ while in another way different from then both by identity and person.

Jenson argues that Christian speech to God shows there is flexibility in the correlation between identity and personhood. In Christian speech to God, we address God in hope of his response, which therefore meet God in a personal way.

According to Jenson, in "the primal pattern" of Christian worship and prayers, we address God the Father, with the Son, and in the Spirit. In this pattern, we do not address the three divine persons one by one but *simultaneously*. When we address Father, Son, and Spirit simultaneously, we indeed address the Trinity as *community*. As the one whom we address and in hope of response, the Trinity as *community is a person in sociological sense*. This pattern of Christian speech to God "allows and mandates some flexibility" in

106. Jenson, *ST1*, 120.
107. Jenson, *ST1*, 121.
108. Jenson, *ST1*, 120.
109. Jenson, *ST1*, 119.
110. Jenson, *ST1*, According to Jenson, Jonathan Edwards is the one who plainly wrote his theology of sin on this line. Indeed, Edwards's concept of personhood has influenced Jenson's trinitarian theology.

the correlation between identity and personhood. Eventually, we can at the same time address to the Trinity as a person; and to Father, Son, and Spirit as three identities and as three persons without difficulty.

Jenson then suggests that in order that a community to be capable of converse "there must be *someone* who can be addressed *as* the community."[111] The Father is this someone in the Trinity and therefore, in this pattern of Christian speech to God, Father can be addressed as an identity of the triune God and as Trinity concurrently without problem.[112]

Jenson explains that when Christians address God in worship, we praise *the Father* "with" the Son, "in" the Spirit. When we praise the Father in doxology as *arche*; we are "enveloped" by God, and praise the Father as the unified and inter-penetrated life of the three persons—*perichoresis*:[113]

> We may praise the Father "with" the Son, as it is the *Father* who is with the Son, so that the Son is with us. We may praise the Father "in" the Spirit, as it is the *Father* who is in the Spirit, so that we are in the Spirit. Thus, we may praise the Father precisely as the unity of equal Father, Son, and Spirit, within which we stand.[114]

In other words, as *arche*, the Father is addressed as the Trinity and as a triune identity—Father—at the same time.

Jenson therefore claims that if a person is defined as "one whom other persons may address in hope of response,"[115] we will find the correlation between identity and person does not need to be one to one. Then, he claims that "the patrological problem" is solved satisfactorily because there are "two ways of addressing the Father, and in one of these ways he is addressed as the Trinity." The Trinity is not "another identity than the Father, and yet the Father as Trinity is otherwise personal than he is hypostatically."[116] Besides God's three persons, the Trinity can be a person because we address God as the Trinity in terms of God's *perichoresis*. The Trinity as a person is not therefore God's fourth person. Rather, we can perceive it as God's communal whole.

---

111. Jenson, *ST1*, 122. Italics mine.
112. Jenson, *ST1*, 121–22.
113. Jenson, *ST1*, 214.
114. Jenson, *ST1*, 122.
115. Jenson, *ST1*, 121.
116. Jenson, *ST1*, 122. Hence, we can notice that Jenson has modified his position. In *TI*, he states that: "God is indeed describable as personal in the modern sense, but it is the triune event of which this is true, not the Father merely as Father." See, Jenson, *TI*, 175.

3.3 Further Questions: Consciousness, Personhood, and Reality

We may notice that the validity of the above argument assumes it is possible to define person *at the same time* in terms of both *individuality* (i.e., identity) and *social relation of address and response* (can be either collective or individual). However, can we ask how can we legitimately perceive the oneness of God through this loosened relationship of person and identity? How in this loosened relationship, can the individuality of the person be preserved? Will it not be lost in some corporate personality? What is its implication for the created reality if this model of God's triunity in work? These are three acute questions for Jenson's Trinitarianism.

In his discussion of the Cappadocians's theology, Jenson attempts to answer the first question through the concept of divine infinity. God's three relations are "the different ways in which each is the *one* God."[117] The prefect *mutuality* of the agency of Father, Son, and Spirit ascertains that God is one: *opera ad extra sunt indivisa*. "God's deed of being the one God is three times repeated, and so that each repetition is a being of God, and so that only in this precise self-repetition is God the particular God that he in fact is."[118]

I argue that Jenson's account of God's mutual agency only comes into its full force with his theology of consciousness. Indeed, *consciousness* is the means by which Jenson integrates God's communal personhood, trinitarian persons, and temporal event together to form a unity. It is interesting that Jenson explicates his realist Trinitarianism in terms of the idealist concept of consciousness. I will argue that the concept of consciousness enables Jenson to talk about God's three relations as individual persons within God's corporate personhood. Then, I argue that Jenson's Christology and theology of conversation are devices for him to express individuality and corporate identity at once. However, in all these attempts, Jenson's Trinitarianism still may be unable to avoid a certain modalism. It may also blur the distinction between Creator and creatures. Finally, I argue that Jenson's difficulties come from his lack of a theological means to delineate the distinction and relation between consciousness, reality, and time. This is the result of his over-reliance on the temporal dimension of reality to support his doctrine of God.

---

117. Jenson, *TI*, 106. See also, Jenson, *ST1*, 106; Jenson, "Triune God," 137.
118. Jenson, *TI*, 110–11; Jenson, "Triune God," 139; Jenson, "Three Identities," 8.

3.3.1 *Consciousness, personhood, and God's triunity*

Jenson employs the concept of consciousness to defend the triunity of God. For him, actions are work done by persons. Only when there is a concrete person, can we ascribe the actions to an agency: "The one God must, to be sure, be somehow a continuing subject of his acts."[119] We have seen that he insists the Trinity is *a* person through a definition of person as one who can address and response. But he is aware that he needs to further explicate his proposal "ontologically" in order to show it is "not merely our device" but "the reality of God."[120]

Jenson believes that our consciousness is an awareness of our selfhood or personhood.[121] He thinks that the traditional approach of finding one's selfhood in one's timeless, and infinite conscious intellect or thinking power is unsuccessful. He uses the Kantian insight that self-consciousness relies on a perspectival focus of the consciousness, an identifiable ego—"I"—for the focused consciousness, and the freedom that the focused consciousness finds itself in the "I" whose consciousness it is. The failure of traditional definition of personhood is exactly in positing "a primal identity" of the "I"—the diachronically identifiable individual—and the sheer focus of consciousness of that "I."[122] With these three phenomena, he claims that self-consciousness is established *relationally*. So does God's consciousness. Jenson puts the triune relations in this schema and then argues that God's oneness or selfhood can be found in terms of Father's consciousness:

> [T]his consciousness finds his "I" in the Son, just thereby becoming himself a focused locus of experience, and in such fashion that the Son and the Father are free for each other in the Spirit . . . The Father of the Son and breather of the Spirit, only as such himself a unity of consciousness, knows his "I" exactly as the *arche* of Son and Spirit, as the oneness of the one Trinity.[123]

Understanding God's triunity in terms of Father's consciousness for Jenson does not mean a return to traditional position of an immutable and timeless

---

119. Jenson, *ST1*, 220–22.

120. Jenson, *ST1*, 120.

121. Jenson, *ST2*, 49.

122. Jenson, *ST1*, 120. Though Douglas Farrow questions Jenson's definition of personhood "does not derive far enough from the Origen-Augustine-Hegel axis," I do not carry out my critique of Jenson from this theoretical ground. I would accept Jenson's definition first and analyze how it becomes problematic even we follow his line of thought. See Farrow et al., "Robert Jenson's *Systematic Theology*," 91.

123. Jenson, *ST1*, 122–23.

divine consciousness. He insists that God's consciousness is God's communal *life with history*. In other words, it is eventful:

> The triune God's consciousness is indeed a focus, but not by reducing to a mere point of timelessness or vanishing to infinity. Rather, God as Father, Son, and Spirit is a *life*, indeed a communal life with history. And by classical doctrine, each of Father, Son, and Spirit is other than the other two just and only as a *relation to* each of the other two. That is to say, each of the triune identities of God's life is precisely a perspective.[124]

Here Jenson needs to clarify the relation between God's consciousness and God's event as history. I argue that, for Jenson, God's consciousness and God's event are identical to each other. God is eventful because God is temporally infinite through his mutual agency. This mutual agency should be understood as the actuality of God's story of promise which is love. God's story of love shows that God intends to love eternally. Therefore, God, who is temporally infinite with his mutual agency, is the *consciousness* or intention of God the Father:

> If God's eternity is love, then God's eternity is personal. So we come to the *Father*, for it is the personality of the Father that is the personality of the one God. The Father *intends* himself in the Son and intends all else by the way he intends the Son. Divine infinity is . . . the infinity of this intention, that is, of a specific loving *consciousness*.[125]

Through this identity, God's triunity can be defended within his theology of divine temporal infinity. God is the event of love. It is personal and is God's eternal intention. Thus according to Jenson, God is an *event*, a *person*, and a *decision*.[126]

3.3.2 Consciousness, time, and created reality

God's temporal infinity is God's eternal loving consciousness. This consciousness is also the communal life history of God's three identities or persons. Moreover, God's history is an event in created temporal reality.

---

124. Jenson, *OTH*, 26. See also, Jenson, *TI*, 125–26.

125. Jenson, *ST1*, 220; Jenson, *TI*, 173.

126. Jenson, *ST1*, 221–23. See also, Jenson, *TI*, 176–79. Jenson has identified a fourth proposition of God's being in *ST1*: God is "a *conversation*." I will discuss the function of this proposition in the later part of this section. However, Jenson recognizes that this "proposition has not previously become explicit" in his theology. Jenson, *ST1*, 223.

The relationship between God and time is therefore ontologically important. But if time is more primary than God himself, God is not transcendental or free.

Obviously, Jenson would not understand his Trinitarianism in this way. He asserts that God is not subordinate to created time. Conversely, time is the room that God creates in himself for his creatures: "Time is *both* the inner extension of a life, as for Augustine, *and* the external horizon and metric of all created events, as for Aristotle. For time is a 'distention' in the life that is God and just so is the enveloping given horizon of all events that are not God."[127] In other words, time is not an independent ontological category outside God. It is *inside* God's triune life. As God's life is identical to God's infinite loving consciousness, time is an extension of God's infinite consciousness.[128]

If created time is *in* God, and is the extension of God's consciousness, the creatures and their reality, which exist temporally, are *in* God accordingly. Jenson states that creatures are simply "enveloped" within God: "any work of God is rightly interpreted only if it is construed by the mutual roles of the triune persons . . . This work is done between all temporal dimensions by the three persons God is." We have arrived at Jenson's idea of *envelopment*: "to be a creature is to be in a specific way bracketed by the life of the triune persons. We are 'worked out' *among* the three."[129]

Creatures, which exist *within* God's consciousness, can be distinctive from God, only if their objectivity is secured apart from God's consciousness. Therefore, if Jenson does not want to blur this distinction, his argument should not stop at the assertion that time is the extension of God's consciousness. He suggests that there is space between God and creatures in time; because space is derived from time and is a function of time: "Time is not what happens in space; space is the horizon of the present tense, that is, of one aspect of time, of what is all there for us at once . . . Space is the distention within which things can be now there for us."[130]

We should notice that space is defined by Jenson as "the distention within which things can be now there for us." In this sense, space indicates the otherness of things and persons is present to one's *present* consciousness. As a function of time, space provides the objectivity that his theology of consciousness needs. Also, because space is a function of time, which in turn is the "distention" of God's consciousness, he can assert that this

127. Jenson, *ST2*, 35.
128. Jenson, *ST2*, 34.
129. Jenson, *ST2*, 25. Italics Jenson's.
130. Jenson, *ST2*, 46.

otherness comes from God himself and is *in* God's consciousness, "space is the form of consciousness that enables distinguishing other reality from oneself... God opens otherness between himself and us, so there is present room for us."[131]

Up to this point, we can see that Jenson tries to argue space is the "locality" that marks the distinction and otherness between God and creatures. However, one may ask in *what way can* God's *present consciousness* experience space in which otherness is found? Jenson replies that God's decision to act and to converse opens the space.

> [T]here is a plain sense in which my space is the presentness spread before me as I *go about any task* or as I *enter converse* with some person or group; space is the place then *available to my agency* and for the sake of that agency *open to my immediate apprehension*. Just in this way the creation is a place open to God; the distance he sets between him and us is our placement before him *as objects of his will and knowledge*.[132]

For Jenson, space comes from God's decision to act or God's engagement in a conversation. Creatures enter converse with God through God's act of creation and redemption. Both creation and redemption are acts of God's intention and will. Because this will is an outcome of God's inner-conversation, it is not monadic but triune.[133] Jenson thinks that understanding God's consciousness as inner communication is quite different from understanding God's consciousness as mere intellect and will.[134] However, in his Trinitarianism creation and redemption are *historical* events which are within God's life. God's inner-conversation is inevitably identical to his communal life which is God's infinite loving consciousness.

Therefore, we should investigate whether Jenson's position can adequately differentiate and distinguish creatures from God in his theology of divine consciousness. It should be noted that in this Trinitarianism, God's history, God's event, Gospel narrative, God's consciousness, and God's decision are identical and interchangeable with one another: "God's history with us is one integral act of sovereignty, comprehended as his decision to reconcile us with himself in Christ Jesus."[135] If God owns language and reality directly and exclusively, God's encompassing story of promise may be conceived as oppressive of human life. Therefore, Jenson needs to establish

---

131. Jenson, *ST2*, 47.
132. Jenson, *ST2*, 48. Italics mine.
133. Jenson, *ST1*, 230; Jenson, *ST2*, 7, 27–28.
134. Jenson, *ST2*, 7.
135. Jenson, *ST2*, 178.

a secured otherness in order to maintain a proper relation and distinction between God and creatures. But what makes this distinction secure? Jenson needs to find other ways to account for our space.

3.3.3 The relation and distinction of God and creatures: Jenson's Christology and theology of triune conversation

God's inner-communication can provide space for creatures only if it is not monadic and thus only if there is a concrete other within God. Moreover, if God's inner-communication is a space for creatures, the creatures should participate in, but also remain distinct from, this conversation. Furthermore, if the space, which comes into being within conversation, is a *present* conscious experience—the presentness spread before me for others, the conversation that generates space must be a *present event*. Jenson tries to accomplish these three tasks with his Christology.

Jenson claims that he follows Alexandrian Christology and Maximus Confessor to assert that the Son *is* this human Jesus Christ:[136] "the second identity of God is directly the human person of the Gospels, in that he is the one who stands to the Father in the relation of being eternally begotten by him ... The person of the Son is the one delineated by the gospel stories of the man Jesus. Our address to him, in which we know him as personal, is that of human beings to a human being."[137] Therefore, he rejects the idea that there is Logos *asarkos* in the eternal life of the Trinity.[138] In God's eternal life, God the Son *is* man Jesus Christ.[139]

The second identity of God is a human. As a human, the Son is a real other present before God the Father: "The Son—whatever might have been—is not only God but as God also a creature, and so an other than God. Thus, he too, in his very different way as Jesus of Nazareth, stands over against the Father and the Spirit."[140] The Father's love of the Son is thus "the possibility of all otherness from God."[141]

For the human being, the Son is "the actual mediation of that possibility."[142] The Son's everlasting participation in God's communal life

---

136. For more on Jenson's interpretation of Alexandrian Christology and Maximus, see Jenson, *ST1*, 125–38; Jenson, "With No Qualifications," 13–22.
137. Jenson, *ST1*, 137.
138. Jenson, *TI*, 140.
139. Jenson, *ST1*, 141.
140. Jenson, *ST1*, 157.
141. Jenson, *ST2*, 27.
142. Jenson, *ST2*, 27.

means that, on the one hand, human can take part in God's life, and on the other hand, God as the communal life of the three persons can concretely discern the distinction of human being from God himself through the eternal Son Jesus Christ.[143] Jenson believes that the doctrine of two natures "truly guards the difference between Creator and creature."[144]

Jenson defines space as our consciousness of the presentness of others. This consciousness can be experienced when "I *go about any task* or as I *enter converse* with some person or group." God and creatures converse with each other through Son. Within this conversation, God is present as the creatures's other. It is the creatures's space:

> The eternal *Logos* is God's *address* . . . and in fact this address is Jesus of Nazareth. What God says to himself, to be eternally the triune God, is the word-event reported in the Gospels . . . [The] counterpart speaker of the triune conversation is the human Jesus . . . This is the first and foundational mystery of communion, that the triune conversation opens to creatures to be the converse of God within a historically actual human community . . . [I]t is the Son who is God's word and is so as one of us. God speaks to us and we neither die nor become his rivals because the Son is the speaker, as human and just do as God.[145]

Space is the *present* consciousness of the others. Thus, the space for creatures is the continuing presence and mediation of the Son: "Or more abstractly, we may say that the Son mediates the Father's originating and the Spirit's liberating, thereby to *hold open* the creatures's space in being. The relation of the creature to the Creator, by which the creature is, holds in *the present tense of created time* without thereby being a timeless relation, in that one of the three, the Son, has his own individual entity within created time."[146] In other words, the "world not *now* exist did not God *now* command its existence."[147] Creatures's space comes from the Son's *present* mediation. It is not a place that has its being outside God.

Because the Son's role in the triune conversation is the key for the creatures's space, Jenson brings in the concept of word to articulate the communicative nature of the Son's role. He asserts that creatures are created by

---

143. Jenson, *ST1*, 218–21; Jenson, *TI*, 173–75.
144. Jenson, "Creator and Creature," 221.
145. Jenson, *ST2*, 270–71.
146. Jenson, *ST2*, 27. Italics mine.
147. Jenson, *ST2*, 9. Italics Jenson's.

God's command which is constituted of the triune God's inner communication. This *commanding word* is the Son:[148]

> The Father commands, "Let there be . . ." *The Son, who is himself this commanding word insofar as the Father hears therein his own intention, is given to be the meaning of the creature; within creation he is the creature as intended by and for God.* And the Spirit, as the intrusive liveliness of this exchange, intrudes also on the creature who is now an item in the exchange, so that the creature is not merely in fact and statically intended for God but lives for God.[149]

God's commanding Word is a triune person. Word, on the one hand, is the *command* to create; on the other hand, he is a concrete *creature*—the man Jesus. God's creating command is thus not something abstract. It is "a word with definite content." It is the personal history of Jesus the Son.[150] Moreover, as the Son "is given to be the meaning of the creature," "to be a creature is, in christological respect . . . to be a 'created word' from God."[151]

Jenson follows Karl Barth and Jonathan Edwards in allowing that Jesus the Son is the content of God's creating word. As a result we can see creation as an outcome of God's determination to save: "precisely the work of redemption, just as it occurs in the actual event of Christ, is the purpose of creation."[152] God's conversation can therefore be understood in terms of salvation: "The divine conversation has authoritative moral content. This is true even among the three of God: the Father gives the Son a specific mission of atonement and of a 'new commandment'; the Son responds, 'Thy will be done'; the Spirit lovingly enables the mission and the obedience. The divine conversation . . . is concretely his [God's] moral reasoning and willing."[153]

We should remember that the event of our salvation is the result of God's decision, interpreted by Jenson as God's loving consciousness. In this way, word, creation, and redemption are united together in his theology. They are not to be considered separate events but as the one holistic life of the triune God. Word is not a merely communicative device. It at the same time refers to the Son, the creation, God's decision, and his communal life.

However, I argue that this identity finally undoes the function of word as a space for creatures. Even Jenson emphasizes God's word is an utterance

148. Jenson, *ST2*, 6.
149. Jenson, *ST2*, 27–28. Italics mine.
150. Jenson, *ST2*, 45.
151. Jenson, *ST2*, 45.
152. Jenson, *ST2*, 20.
153. Jenson, *ST2*, 230.

and not silent intention, the identity makes the word lose its power to distinguish itself from God, in which the space for creatures is generated: "the Word that is a triune person is God's utterance in his triune life ... [T]he Word by which God creates is not silent within him but is his address ... *God commands the world to be, this command is obeyed, and the event of obedience is the existence of the world.*"[154] If we follow Jenson's logic, we can say that this Word includes God who commands, God's word who is the command itself, God's word as the creature who obeys God's command, the event of creation as obedience to God, the event of the obedience of God's word to God's will, and the event of God's life. Can God and his creatures be referred to simultaneously in this event of the Word?

The supreme importance of the dimension of time in Jenson's concept of word eventually makes the space for creatures subsume and dissolve into God's own life. Two other pieces of evidence for my argument can be found in Jenson's account of *preexistent Logos*, and the resurrected Jesus's body as word coming to the church:

> [The incarnate *Logos*'s] preexistence ... is in one mode a narrative pattern of Israel's previous story. *Thus this mode of Jesus's preexistence is ... a specific created reality within creation, which is the Word by which God creates ... Logos is a creature* ... *he is also God* ... [I]t is the preexistent reality of the *totus Christus* ... That is, *Israel herself*, as within creation the determinate possibility of the Incarnation, spoke to her teachers ... [W]e must say that *Israel spoke to them from heaven, spoke to them from that created presence of the End within which she was already in full possession of her destiny* ... *The body of the totus Christus is a creature*, that creature that makes sense of the rest. This body is in the created heaven a self-possessed conscious creature. And *this creature speaks through* ... [its] *dependence, inferiority* ... It is thus that God reveals himself through our experience of creatures.[155]

> The subject that the risen Christ is, is the subject who comes to word in the gospel. The object—the body—that the risen Christ is, is the body in the world to which this word calls our intention, the church around her sacraments. He needs no other body to be a risen man, body and soul. *There is and needs to be no other place than the church for him to be embodied, nor in that other place any other entity to be the "real" body of Christ. Heaven*

---

154. Jenson, *ST2*, 7. Italics mine.
155. Jenson, *ST2*, 158–59. Italics mine.

> *is where God takes space in his creation to be present to the whole of it; he does that in the church.*[156]

In the first passage, the *Logos* or word as the preexistent Jesus is said to be the *reality* of Israel herself and the *totus Christus*. He emphasizes that this *creature is* at the same time God. In this sense, one must wonder whether the word is a *reality* of the Son instead of a *space* for creatures. The word, in that passage, is an all-encompassing reality from the past to the future that the Son has realized, is realizing, and will realize. What makes creatures know they are created does not come from the word-event of conversation. It comes from the reality of God's word which makes them experience creatures's dependence, and inferiority.

In the second passage, Jenson asserts that the gospel word is the risen Christ. He states that the risen Christ has no body and soul other than the church. Therefore, the church *is* the *real* body of Christ. At the same time, the church *is* God's *space* for creatures. We know for Jenson the Son "holds open the creatures's space in being." In this sense, the church is again identical with Christ. Though Jenson puts the word and the body—church—into subject and object dichotomy to try to differentiate Christ and church; one may wonder when Christ is both the subject and object of his known reality, how there can be a concrete other within it?

The ambiguous relation between Jesus, God's word, Israel, the church, and other created beings finally lumps everything together. It collapses three temporal dimensions into a mere present. It reduces or even removes the difference between language, created reality, and divine reality. In Jenson's account, the tense-structure and the reference of a word can be interchangeable simultaneously and freely.

The problem of Jenson's Christology and theology of word becomes fully obvious in his theology of sacrament. In his proposal, church's remembrance of God through sacrament, God's remembrance of church, sacrament and reality, and the triune conversation with the church are freely transposed to mean one another. Past, present, and future become one single present dimension. Jenson rejects a god who is sheer simultaneous presence because this would be a timeless god. But ironically, he seems to suggest such a god in his proposal:

> When we give thanks and share the bread and wine, we do it for the sake of Christ's "remembrance" . . . When someone remembers, this is a present act. When it is God who remembers, his answer creates what it mentions, as do all his address . . . We may generalize: anamnetic being is present reality created by a

---

156. Jenson, *ST1*, 206. Italics mine.

> word of God that simultaneously evokes a past event and opens its future, to make it live in the present . . . The middle being that is specific to sacramental reality, in which the difference is transcended between the earthly location of the sign and the heavenly and then eschatological location of the reality, is thus constituted in the logic of the triune God's conversation with his people . . . The conversation that envelopes and carries the sacramental situation is the converse of God and the congregation . . . Whether as God's address to us or as our address to God, the word in the church is at once narrative of the past and promise of the eschatological future. It is the "at once" that is ontologically crucial: the past is narrated just *as* the identity of the promised goal . . . Thus the occurrence of this word is itself the unitary present event of both.[157]

What is "the unitary present event" other than a *timeless* event and thus not an *event* at all?

Jenson argues that body is a more useful concept than Word for establishing the otherness of creatures from God. He follows Hegel in asserting that "If in the meeting between us you are a subject of which I am an object but are not in turn an object for me as subject, you insofar enslave me . . . A disembodied personal presence to me could only mean my bondage . . . were the person in question God, the bondage would be absolute."[158] Therefore, Christ should be embodied when he converses with the creatures. This embodiment can let creatures enter into a reciprocal relationship with him. This body of Christ is church. Jenson even argues that Christ does not become "a pure absolute monarchy" of the church because the church is "identified with" Christ:

> Were it merely a matter of common and even equal membership in a community that somehow belonged *to* Christ without being identified *with* him, that is, were the church properly conceived as some Protestantism does, that would have the ironic consequence that Christ would be our polity in a way analogous to the way in which a pure absolute monarch would be a polity in sheer conversation with himself.[159]

How does the identity make conversation with other possible? How does the identity become the ground for otherness? Will creatures be absorbed into God and lose their freedom? If we are one body with him, will

---

157. Jenson, *ST2*, 258–59.
158. Jenson, *ST2*, 214; Jenson, "The Church and the Sacrament," 211.
159. Jenson, "Christ as Culture 1," 328.

we be pretending to be Christ? Will we be God and not human? If the term "identified with" is used in a weak sense as "connected with" or "incorporated with," the term "belongs to" that Jenson rejects can articulate human's participation in Christ with lesser confusion.

I argue that Jenson's proposals run into difficulties because they try to articulate two dimensions of reality—God's and creatures'—without the concepts that could give them clarity. Jenson needs additional means to qualify the referential scope and direction to what is otherwise the excessive usage of "is" in his Christology and theology of word.

Maybe it is possible to speak about finding the space for creatures if we approach the question of the otherness from God rather than from his creatures. A particular space for creatures is found when *God* experiences otherness through the presentness of Christ as a creature and his mediation with all creatures. It is God's present consciousness that establishes the *space*. According to Jenson: "God sets us as other than himself, in that our accommodation in him has the present dimension of separateness . . . Just in this way the creation is a place open to God; the distance he sets between him and us is our placement before him as objects of his will and knowledge."[160]

This assertion leads us back to the point that the distinction between God and creature is established in Jesus the Son by God's will. However, as I have stated, Jenson's theology of God's consciousness is an all-encompassing reality. Jenson needs to find other means of securing the otherness of creatures in order to maintain a proper relation and distinction between God and creatures in his Trinitarianism.

3.3.4 *The problem of the relation between time, consciousness, and God in Jenson's Trinitarianism*

In the above sub-sections, I argue that Jenson uses a theology of God's consciousness to support his interpretation of the triune identities and personhoods and to articulate God's triunity. I also show that this proposal integrates God's consciousness and life with time and history. It is difficult to articulate the distinction between God and creatures in clarity. In this sub-section, I ask whether Jenson's Trinitarianism of temporal infinity and theology of consciousness is in danger of becoming modalistic, and perhaps even of threatening the transcendence and freedom of God.

For Jenson, God's eternity is God's temporal infinity. It means that God's three persons are assigned to three "poles" of temporality: "The Father is the 'whence' of God's life; the Spirit is the 'whither' of God's life; and we

160. Jenson, *ST2*, 47–48. Italics mine.

may even say that the Son is that life's specious present. If, then, whence and whither do not fall apart in God's life, so that his duration is without loss, it is because origin and goal, whence and whither, are indomitably reconciled in the action and suffering of the Son."[161] What Jenson wants to assert here is that God's eternity is not timeless. God takes time because "he is faithful to his commitments within time." What God is faithful to is his promise to Israel and the church. In other words, God's temporal reality is God's communal life as history. The triune God takes time.

Jenson ascribes the Father as the "whence," the Son as the "present," and the Spirit as the "whither" because he wants to highlight the *dramatic* roles of the three persons who constitute God's history. But because, as I have shown, Jenson's account finally understands God's communal life as a life within God's consciousness, the "whence," "present," and "whither" of God can easily turn into modalism.

Jenson argues that God the Father is the origin. He is the one who intends the actuality of his history of promise.[162] The Father is the *pre-* of all beings.[163] If the Father is the *pre-* of everything and God's life is an unfolding of his time, its modalist tone is strong already. He even can say that "the arrow of God's eternity, like the arrow of causal time, does not reverse itself. Whence and whither in God are not like right and left or up and down on a map, but are like before and after in a narrative."[164] If whence and whither, which are Father and Spirit respectively, cannot change their narrative temporal sequences; it strongly implies that the Father is the God of the past, and the Spirit is the God of the future. This is modalism.

Jenson clearly does not want to go to this direction. He may argue that God's consciousness is *communal* as we have seen. The consciousness of God involves the Father consciously finding his "ego" eternally through the Son and experiencing his freedom in the Spirit. In other words, Jenson believes that his Pneumatology and Christology protect him from modalism. I do not believe they do so.

Jenson understands the Spirit as a liberator of the I-Thou relationship between Father and Son. Jenson interprets love as an unavoidable struggle for domination even though it is the love between God the Father and God the Son. "If there is to be freely given love there must be a third party in the meeting of 'I' and 'Thou.'"[165] For God, this third party is the Spirit. In this triadic relationship of love, God's persons are concretely different and interact with each other: "the Spirit is indeed the love between two

---

161. Jenson, *ST1*, 218–19.
162. Jenson, *ST1*, 220.
163. Jenson, *ST2*, 173.
164. Jenson, *ST1*, 218.
165. Jenson, *ST1*, 156.

personal lovers, the Father and the Son, but he can be this just *in that* he is antecedently himself. He is another who in his own intention liberates Father and Son to love each other."[166] In this sense then Jenson's Trinitarianism is not modalistic.

In terms of temporality, Jenson argues that the Spirit is the one who actualizes the *spontaneity* of temporal reality.[167] In other words, the creative futurity of the Spirit prevents the events from returning to the Father and so being absorbed and lost. But, to an extent, Jenson's suppressions of the personhood of the Spirit prevent the success of this. He argues that "the Spirit . . . is inherently *someone's* spirit, so that he cannot be an autonomous someone."[168] In other words, Spirit is subordinate to the Father. One can even say that the Spirit is another name of the Father's consciousness because it is the Father's spirit and it is not autonomous someone. Therefore, it finally asserts the Father's consciousness is the sole reality of God. All events in God's history are its manifestation.

Jenson also suggests that the Father's eternal consciousness is occupied with the Son.[169] Originally, this move attempts to maintain God's consciousness as triadic and not monadic. Christ, who is a concrete other to the Father, is eternal *present* before the Father. However, this move also fails. For Jenson, the eternal preexisting Son, which the Father is conscious of, is a *pattern* of triune life. This pattern is the short-form of biblical narrative, and so God's dramatic plot.[170] In other words, the Father's consciousness is eternally preoccupied by a *pattern*, which is the dramatic plot.

Jenson's theology of actuality makes the narrative a function of someone's promise of actualization, and at the same time he follows Aristotle to think a good story or drama contains conflict.[171] There are two possible implications here. One is that the *dramatic plot* controls the way of being of God. If this is the case, God is not transcendent or free from the dramatic *plot*—the dynamics of conflict and resolution. One can legitimately argue there is a problem of the articulation of God's absolute transcendence and freedom in Jenson's Trinitarianism.

An alternative implication is that the *dramatic plot* indeed is the *room* within God's life. In this latter case, the notion of God's room implies the God outside his room is different from the God inside. In this sense, the identity of immanent and economic Trinity cannot be maintained. Because God's consciousness is a supreme consciousness that makes his

166. Jenson, *ST1*, 156.
167. Jenson, *ST2*, 43.
168. Jenson, *ST1*, 121.
169. Jenson, *TI*, 173–76; Jenson, *ST1*, 220.
170. Jenson, *ST1*, 141.
171. Jenson, *ST2*, 23.

room, it implies the whole process is the manifestation or "unfolding" of his sole-consciousness. Ultimately, this interpretation suggests Jenson's Trinitarianism is modalistic.

3.3.5 Summary and conclusion: dimensions of reality and speaking God

In this section, I continue my evaluation of Jenson's Trinitarianism through his account of God's triunity and personhood. God's temporality is Jenson's overarching concern. Because God takes time, Jenson proposes that the final triunity of God can be found in God's consciousness. But the combination of God's temporality and the theology of consciousness makes it difficult for Jenson to articulate God's triunity and freedom. For Jenson, language is an actuality or actualization or not-yet actualized promise of God's loving consciousness. It is always actual to some degree within God's temporal reality. Space is God's *present* consciousness of otherness and is derived from time. Finally, all the dimensions of reality are subordinated to and derived from time. Time is within God's consciousness. In this schema, I argue that Jenson's Trinitarianism cannot avoid the danger of becoming modalism. This blurs the distinction between Creator and creatures.[172]

---

172. In this sense, I agree with George Hunsinger's critique of the monistic tendency of Jenson's Trinitarianism. However, I do not think Hunsinger's critique of Jenson being tritheistic on the ground that "the unity of the trinity is not substantial but merely volitional" is forceful. See Hunsinger, "Robert Jenson's *Systematic Theology*," 193–98.

Chapter 5

God's Being Is in His Becoming

Evaluating Jenson's Doctrine of the Trinity with Reference to Eberhard Jüngel

ROBERT JENSON HAS MADE a major contribution to defending and promoting the centrality of the doctrine of the Trinity in the post-Enlightenment and post-modern world with Divine narrative and history. But because Jenson places so much emphasis on the temporality of being, his doctrine of God meets some problems.

I will argue that if we balance Jenson's concern of temporality of being (i.e., as word-*event*) with the linguistic and hermeneutical dimension of being (i.e., as *word*-event), we will find ways of tackling the problems in his account of the Trinity. In the following two chapters, I will develop this argument in a comparison of Jenson and Jüngel.

This chapter examines Jüngel's interpretation of Barth's doctrine of the Trinity. It will demonstrate the differences between Jenson and Jüngel's interpretations of Barth's thesis of "God's being is in his becoming." I will argue that Jüngel's assertion of God's word-event as correspondence and analogy of relation brings out the many possibilities of the concept of "word." His insight into the metaphorical nature of theological discourse clearly explicates how God and man interact in the textual/verbal-temporal-space in order to depict the relatedness and distinction of triune and human reality.[1] I argue that with Jüngel's linguistic and hermeneutical dimension of being (i.e., as *word*-event), we find valuable ways of tackling the issues of the relatedness

---

1. According to John Webster, the major dogmatic preoccupation of Jüngel's work is to develop "an account of God and humanity as differentiated and complementary realities." From this viewpoint, Jüngel undoubtedly can be a valuable theological resource for us to further and revise Jenson's theological project. See Webster, "Justification, Analogy, and Action," 106.

and distinction between Creator and creatures—the communion of God and human in Jenson's Trinitarianism.

It is not an arbitrary decision to choose Jüngel as a dialogue partner for Jenson. Both men are Lutheran and considerable scholars of Karl Barth. Both are aware that the demise of the traditional metaphysics has resulted in the contemporary nihilism of "the death of God." They both argue that the god who is "dead" in the modern world is not the Christian God, but the metaphysical god. Contemporary theology cannot and should not return to the old metaphysics but find a new way to articulate the triune reality of the Christian God.[2] Both argue that this new way is in conceiving triune reality as a "word-event" rather than a traditional metaphysical entity. More importantly, Jenson considers Jüngel to be his ally.[3] Thus, any critiques and suggestions that arise in comparison are not simply just a blunt attack from an entirely incompatible viewpoint. Rather, they suggest that there are some theological dimensions that Jenson's proposal has not fully articulated.

1. God's Being Is in Becoming and the Knowledge of God

As with Jenson, Barth's influence is observed throughout Jüngel's work. Among Jüngel's work on Barth, *God's Being is in Becoming* requires very close attention. Though Jüngel describes this book as a "paraphrase" of Barth's doctrine of the Trinity, it is regarded as "one of the finest of his writing and of all the books on Barth."[4] The discussion of this chapter will be largely focused on it. But this "paraphrase" carries Jüngel's own theological agenda.[5] Indeed, in this section, our analysis of Jüngel's interpretation of Barth aims to pinpoint Jüngel's own theological perspective. With this perspective, we can clarify the differences between Jenson's and Jüngel's interpretation of Barth. Then I will point out the significance of these differences for assessing Jenson's theology.

For Jüngel, Barth's doctrine of the Trinity indicates in what way we can come to know God and to speak God appropriately. Jüngel argues that Barth insists that our knowledge and speech of God cannot be grounded on human "speech about God." Knowledge of God can only come from God alone. It is "on the basis of God's own direction" and has to be "acknowledged as a fact."

---

2. For Jüngel's position, see Jenson, *GMW*, 43–152.

3. Jenson, *TI*, 157n172. However, I would agree with John Webster to assert that Jenson's thought is much different from Jüngel's. See Webster, "Systematic Theology after Barth," 255–56.

4. Thompson, "Jüngel on Barth," 144.

5. Webster, "Translator's Introduction," ix–x.

For Barth, knowing and speaking God concerns *God's being*.[6] We know God through his revelation. What God's revelation reveals is God himself. Thus, we know God and speak about God as a "thinking after God" (*Nachdenken*).[7] Jüngel captures Barth's position with the notion "God's being revealed." John Webster summarizes the thrust of this notion precisely:

> [It indicates] both that God's being is known only in revelation, and also that, since what is revealed is God's being, the self-communicative movement in which God makes himself present to us and for us is not alien to his being. Indeed, for Jüngel it is axiomatic that the function of Barth's doctrine of the Trinity is to state precisely this point: God is identical with himself in his self-communication, in the movement of sending the Son into the world in the unity of the Spirit, thereby setting himself in relation to us.[8]

In other words, according to Jüngel, Barth teaches that God's revelation grants the possibility of human knowledge of God. Revelation means that "the being of God has *itself already proceeded*."[9] What precedes us that makes God's being visible is the incarnation and exaltation of Jesus Christ the Son of God—"The Way of the Son of God into the Far Country" and the "Homecoming of the Son of Man."[10] Because this "movement" is an event bestowed on humanity, revelation is an historical event.[11] Also, this movement has its origin in the being of God himself, that is, in God's "primal decision." Therefore, God's being does not only "proceed" on the way into the far country. From eternity, "God's being is moved being."[12] More importantly, asserting "God's being is moved being" takes us to the doctrine of the Trinity. The Trinity is revealed in the event of the incarnation of Son of God in Jesus Christ as a primal decision of Father, Son, and Spirit: "For God's way into far country is indeed the way of the *Son* of God; in that primal decision, in the unity of the *Spirit* between the *Father* who sends the Son upon this way, and the Son who is obedient, the Son was destined to be united with man Jesus." The doctrine of the Trinity, thus, provides "an answer to the question of the God who reveals Himself in revelation."[13]

6. Jüngel, *GBB*, 1–2.
7. Jüngel, *GBB*, 9.
8. Webster, "Translator's Introduction," xiii.
9. Jüngel, *GBB*, 10. Italics Jüngel's.
10. Jüngel, *GBB*, 14.
11. Jüngel, *GBB*, 32.
12. Jüngel, *GBB*, 14.
13. Jüngel, *GBB*, 15. Italics Jüngel's.

Also, if in revelation God reveals himself *as* the one who he *is*, revelation is God's self-interpretation.[14] "Revelation means God's self-interpretation as Father, Son, and Holy Spirit."[15]

For Jüngel, Barth argues that revelation is God's self-interpretation and not illustration. The human language is not able to speak about revelation by itself. Rather the revelation of God "commandeers" human language in order to express itself in language for us. In "commandeering," God comes to speech as God.[16] Thus, it is "not that the language could grasp the revelation, but that revelation . . . could grasp the language."[17] Since God's revelation "commandeers" human language, it is an interpretation. It means "saying *the same thing* in other words." Conversely, illustration means "saying the same thing *in other words*."[18] As interpretation is saying "*the same thing* in other words," it "safeguards the identity of revelation in that it brings revelation (and only revelation) to speech as revelation." Otherwise, "revelation is no longer safeguarded as revelation *and* language is no longer safeguarded as language."[19] Then, there will be a loss of revelation as well as a loss of language.

Therefore, if revelation is God's self-interpretation, the Trinity, who is the subject of revelation, remains to be an indissoluble subject in his revelation.[20] Accordingly, Jüngel states that "The doctrine of the Trinity had to establish the fact that, as the subject of his being, God is also the subject of his being known and becoming known."[21] God is in unimpaired unity as "the revealer, the revelation, and the revealedness . . . Thus: God is subject, predicate, and object of the event of revelation."[22] God as Father, Son, and Spirit is not a human construction. God "is ours in advance." He is completely his own and it is he who puts himself forward.[23]

For the revelation of God reveals himself who he is, and for it is an historical event while its origin is in the being of God himself; the revelation as God's self-interpretation implies that God's being *ad extra* corresponds

---

14. Jüngel, *GBB*, 33.
15. Jüngel, *GBB*, 77.
16. Jüngel, *GBB*, 23.
17. Barth, *CD* 1/1:340. Cf. Jenson, *GBB*, 20.
18. Jüngel, *GBB*, 25. Italics Jüngel's.
19. Jüngel, *GBB*, 25.
20. Jüngel, *GBB*, 35.
21. Jüngel, *GBB*, 55.
22. Jüngel, *GBB*, 28.
23. Jüngel, *GBB*, 37.

to his being *ad intra*. Precisely, it means God corresponds to himself. Jüngel puts it like this:

> [A]s *interpreter* of himself, God corresponds to his own being. But because God as his own interpreter (even in his external works) *is* himself, and since in this event as such we are also dealing with the *being* of God, then the highest and final statement which can be made about the being of God is: God corresponds to himself.[24]

According to Jüngel, "God corresponds to himself" means that the being of God "reiterates itself in the historicality of revelation."[25] God corresponds himself as a relationally structured being.[26] God's "three modes of being" as Father, Son, and Spirit express the relational structure of God's being. Because the three modes of God's being are mutual relations within God's being itself, the differentiations are within the unity of God's being. It can be done because, on the one hand, according to the doctrine of *perichoresis*, the mutual relatedness of the three modes occurs as participation in each other, safeguards the concrete unity of God's being. On the other hand, the mutual differentiation of the modes is maintained by the doctrine of "appropriation," which is a hermeneutical process to assign particular attributes and operations of the Trinity to one particular mode of being.[27] Therefore, God is relationally structured as a self-related being.[28]

These relations are not impersonal structures in God. Rather, they differentiate each other because a "repetition of God" or a "repetition of eternity in eternity" is taken place. This repetition indicates that "God's being as being is pure *event*."[29] It means that God's being is in his becoming. Moreover, revelation is God's self-interpretation. The knowledge of God's being is made known to us from God's being because God's being for us is the event in Jesus Christ.[30] Thus, in revelation God is his own "double." God's essence and work are not twofold but one. "The reality of God" is God as "God in his essence and work."[31] Therefore, we understand "the one being of God in its double structure as a being in correspondence."[32]

24. Jüngel, *GBB*, 36. Italics Jüngel's.
25. Jüngel, *GBB*, 83.
26. Jüngel, *GBB*, 37.
27. Jüngel, *GBB*, 43–51.
28. Jüngel, *GBB*, 41, 77.
29. Jüngel, *GBB*, 39.
30. Jüngel, *GBB*, 120.
31. Jüngel, *GBB*, 46.
32. Jüngel, *GBB*, 83.

"God corresponds to himself" as the being of God "reiterates itself in the historicality of revelation." In short, "God corresponds to himself" means that "God's being is in becoming." Jüngel nicely explains this point which is worth to be quoted in length:

> [T]he modes of God's being which are differentiated from each other are related to each other in such a way that each mode of God's being *becomes* what it *is* only *with* the two other modes of being. The relational structuring in God's being expresses different "relations of origin" and "processions" in God's being. As the being of God, Father, Son, and Holy Spirit, God's being is thus a *being in becoming* . . . And precisely because from all eternity God's being is a being in becoming, God is already "ours in advance" . . . But already in this being of his, God is none other than the one who he is in his revelation. He is thus in this being of his already *ours* in advance, and therefore the statement is true: God's being is *in becoming*.[33]

Finally, in this correspondence we should recognize that the historical event of revelation is itself the event of God's being. According to Jüngel, "revelation is that historical event in which God's being manifests itself as a being which does not merely tolerate, but actually demands, historical predicates."[34] We are compelled to speak of God's being as divine "history": "In this correspondence the being of God takes place as the history of the divine life in the Spirit. And in this history which is constituted through this correspondence God *makes space* within himself for *time*. This making-space-for-time within God is a continuing event. The space of time conceived as a continuing event we call eternity."[35]

Up to this point, one should note the striking similarity that Jüngel and Jenson share in their interpretation of God's being is in becoming and the knowledge of God's reality as history. For Jenson, Barth's doctrine of the Trinity shows that the triune reality is "what *happens* with God towards us."[36] "[T]here is just one order of reality: the *history* that takes place in Jesus Christ."[37] "The divine being is that very lordship that *occurs* in God's act of triune revelation."[38] For Jüngel, "God corresponds to himself" means that the being of God is coming to human "in the *historicality* of revelation."

33. Jüngel, *GBB*, 77–78.
34. Jüngel, *GBB*, 109.
35. Jüngel, *GBB*, 111.
36. Jenson, "Re-Review," 53. Italics mine.
37. Jenson, "Response," 32. Italics mine.
38. Jenson, *TI*, 138. Italics mine.

Since the trinitarian theology of both men closely follows Barth, Jenson unsurprisingly considers Jüngel an ally.

For Jenson, "God's being in his becoming" is the basis to assert that God is "identified by and with the particular *plotted sequence of events* that make the narrative of Israel and her Christ."[39] It also becomes the basis for his assertion of the close-relatedness of God's reality and created reality. According to Jenson, "created time" is God's accommodation—open rooms—in his triune life for other persons and things than the three whose mutual life he is in his creative act.[40] However, this close-relatedness finally gives us an impression that Jenson blurs the distinction between each other; and raises the problem of a proper distinction and relation between creator and creatures. For instance, according to Jenson:

> No metaphor or ontological evasion should be intended. Sacrament and church are *truly* Christ's body for us, because Christ himself takes these same things for the object as which he is available to himself. For the proposition that the church is a human body of the risen Jesus to be ontically and straightforwardly true, all that is required is that Jesus indeed be the Logos of God, so that his self-understanding determines what is real ... Heaven is where God takes space in his creation to be present to the whole of it; he does that in the church.[41]

From the above passage, it seems that Jenson argues the church does not just represent but actually *is* the presence on earth of the eschatological kingdom. The verb-to-be "*is*" makes one suspect the distinction between creator and creatures, and between future and present has been distorted in Jenson's theology.[42]

2. Knowledge of God and God's Being-as-object

However, Jüngel does not stop at the point where we suspect Jenson does. He continues to explicate Barth's doctrine of the Trinity as "God's being in becoming" with two other important themes. They are: (1) God's being reveals in revelation is "God's-being-as-object"; (2) the correspondence between God and humanity is related to God's self-related correspondence

39. Jenson, *ST1*, 60. Italics mine.
40. Jenson, *ST2*, 34–35.
41. Jenson, *ST1*, 206.
42. Hans Urs von Balthasar reminds us that speaking Church as a collective person of Christ is dangerous. It may blur the distinction between Christ and the Church. See Balthasar, *Theo-Drama*, 3:342.

analogously. Indeed, these two points are the resources to reduce the obscurity of Jenson's theology.

2.1 Human Knowledge of God and God's Being-as-object

Jüngel argues that, in Barth's doctrine of the Trinity, God's being reveals himself as a "being-as-object." God's being-as-object is a very useful theological device for our conversation with Jenson's trinitarian theology. Speech of God's being-as-object helps us to identify how a human being can be a proper knowing subject in God's being in becoming. Certainly, for Jüngel, Barth's talk of God's being-as-object does not mean that by its own powers the human subject can know God as an object. Rather, because the knowing person is unavoidably the subject of knowledge of God, it is necessary for us to speak of God's being-as-object.[43] In this sense, we see there is already a distinction between God and humans.

Speak of "God's being-as-object" indicates that human person knows God as a "sacramental reality" through *faith* in his/her being-as-subject that has been made by God. Indeed, "faith" and "sacramental reality" indicate the ways that how God's being revealed can be God's self-interpretation on the one hand and can be a proper "being-as-object" for the knowing person on the other.

2.2 God's Being-as-object and the Knowledge of Faith

According to Jüngel, God's being-as-object means that God has revealed himself. God is the object of his knowledge only because God has manifested himself in his revelation as his self-interpretation. The human person does not know God through any other way than God's revelation. The human person cannot know God by his/her own capacity. The "being-as-subject of the person who knows God is the result of God's being-as-object which is actually fulfilled as self-interpretation."[44] In other words, the human person becomes the "subject" of the knowledge only because God reveals himself. Moreover, God's revelation is his self-interpretation, and thus it is an event. In this event, God's being-as-object is his being-revealed. Therefore, humans can know God *"only in the event* of the knowledge of God." Furthermore, because in the event of revelation, God reveals himself in his *Word* and he is actually known through his Word, one can find that God is *objective* in his Word. As God is known through his Word, it means that God "has become

---

43. Jüngel, *GBB*, 55.
44. Jüngel, *GBB*, 58.

speakable" and "comes to speech in human words" "in that he is considered and conceived."[45] Jüngel sums up this event of the knowledge of God as "faith": "God comes before us in his Word. Faith comes to us from God through his Word. In faith we come before God. Accordingly, God is to be perceived in God's Word. God allows himself to be perceived through his Word, in that he grants faith. In faith God is perceived."[46]

Therefore, faith is not a general human capacity. Rather, faith comes to human and man "knows God in that he stands before God."[47] Because "God distinguishes himself from man" in the event of faith; the knowledge of God in faith means "the union of man with the God who is distinct from him."[48] In faith God and humans are thus related and distinct at the same time.

2.3 God's Being-as-object as Sacramental Reality

Moreover, according to Jüngel, Barth's teaches that "God's being-as-object is *mediately* objective in his revelation 'in which He meets us under the sign and veil of other objects.'"[49] In other words, the human person can only perceive and conceive God through "the objectivity of a medium which witnesses to God's being-as-object."[50] Therefore, God's being-as-object indicates that there are two kinds of objectivity which we should make a clear distinction of them. Barth's calls them God's "primary" and "secondary" objectivity respectively.

God's "primary objectivity" refers to the objectivity in God's inner-trinitarian being.[51] For Barth, God is in himself the Lord means that he is the triune God: The "inner strength of His self-demonstration as the Lord" is the fact that God "is in Himself from eternity to eternity the triune God, God the Father, the Son, and the Holy Spirit."[52] As the triune God, God himself "stands over against himself and knows himself."[53] Therefore, in God's inner-trinitarian being, God is objective to himself.

---

45. Jüngel, *GBB*, 58.
46. Jüngel, *GBB*, 59.
47. Jüngel, *GBB*, 59. Cf. Barth, *CD* 2/1:9.
48. Jüngel, *GBB*, 60. Cf. Barth, *CD* 2/1:15, 31.
49. Jüngel, *GBB*, 61. Cf. Barth, *CD* 2/1:16.
50. Jüngel, *GBB*, 62.
51. Jüngel, *GBB*, 63.
52. Jüngel, *GBB*, 64. Cf. Barth, *CD* 2/1:47.
53. Jüngel, *GBB*, 64.

Because God is primarily objective to himself, his being-as-object reveals to us in his revelation is his "secondary objectivity."[54] It is important to note that the human knows God in his "secondary objectivity" is a "copy" or "indirect participation" of God's knowledge of himself.[55] That the human participates in God's knowledge of himself indirectly means that "God gives Himself to be known . . . in an objectivity different from His own, in a creaturely objectivity."[56] Because "God reiterates his own objectivity in the creaturely objectivity which is foreign to him, God's being-as-object is sacramental reality."[57] Jüngel then explains that, concretely speaking, God's being-as-object as sacramental reality means that God speaks with us in a human way. Accordingly, the humanity of Jesus Christ is "the first sacrament."[58] For creatures, God's sacramental reality is thus an honor; because God becomes visible and knowable in its creatureliness, and it knows God in its creaturely objectivity.[59] Conversely for God, his sacramental reality is his "renunciation of the visibility of His distinction over against the creature."[60] From God's renunciation, the fellowship between God and the human is established and continued. Therefore, God's sacramental reality, as its reveals God in creaturely objectivity, is God's grace.[61]

However, God's self-renunciation and his honoring of creatures also mean his hiddenness. In his being-as-object as sacramental reality, God reveals himself to us as He and as Thou. Thus, God "remains hidden from us as I and therefore in the being and essence of His Godhead."[62] Nevertheless, in Barth's doctrine of the Trinity, God's hiddenness should not be considered a misfortune. God's hiddenness is also God's grace. A human being is in fellowship with God because God reveals himself in revelation as sacramental reality, that is in his renunciation or hiddenness. Therefore, God's hiddenness is his grace. In this sense, God's being-as-object as sacramental reality teaches that human subject's participation in the triune God is always mediatory and indirect. However, this is not a misfortune but the grace of God. It obliges us to acknowledge that the distinction of creatures from God can be preserved by God's being-as-object in sacramental reality. God's hiddenness guarantees

---

54. Jüngel, *GBB*, 64.
55. Jüngel, *GBB*, 64.
56. Jüngel, *GBB*, 65. Cf. Barth, *CD* 2/1:52.
57. Jüngel, *GBB*, 65.
58. Jüngel, *GBB*, 66.
59. Jüngel, *GBB*, 67.
60. Jüngel, *GBB*, 65. Cf. Barth, *CD* 2/1:54–55.
61. Jüngel, *GBB*, 68.
62. Jüngel, *GBB*, 68. Cf. Barth, *CD* 2/1:58.

that the relationship of God and human is a real mutual participation and neither party has been swallowed up by the other.

In summary, the doctrine of God's being-as-object differentiates God from ordinary objectivity of the world. Indeed, it indicates God's "non-objectivity." God is irreducibly subject as Lord in himself and in revelation.[63] However, surprisingly, God's non-objectivity at the same time properly preserves the distinction between God and the human in the event of God's being-in-becoming.

2.4 Jenson's Rejection of Barth's Doctrine of God's Non-objectivity, Its Drawback, and Jüngel's Doctrine of "Word" as a Resource for Revising Jenson's Theology

Jenson does fully realize Barth's doctrine of God's non-objectivity. Jenson describes that Barth's acceptance of this methodological principle as his "fidelity" to it.[64] However, Jenson opposes this doctrine. He argues that it is an "unexamined presupposition" and eventually posits God as "non-embodied" being. For Jenson, we should not posit God as "nonobjective" or "nonembodied" because "all true mutual discourse . . . each must be both subject for and object of the other . . . and . . . a *person's* objectivity is his or her body."[65] But as we have seen, both Barth—according to Jüngel's interpretation—and Jenson are eager to articulate a true "mutual" relation between God and human.

When Jenson rejects the doctrine of "non-objectivity," and pursues a doctrine of God's embodiment, he inevitably states that the object Eucharist bread and cup, or church *is* "the body of God." Thus, he says that, "the church *is* the body of Christ for the world and for her members, in that she is constituted a community by the verbal and 'visible' presence *to* her of that same

---

63. Bruce McCormack summarizes Barth's doctrine of God's non-objectivity as follows: "The Word of God which constitutes the object of dogmatic thinking is no 'object' in the ordinary sense. The Word of God is the Subject who veils or hides Himself in ordinary objects in order to make Himself known. But in doing so, He is not transformed into those objects which veil Him. He makes Himself objective in our world without surrendering His non-objectivity, His irreducible Subjecthood. To put it in terms of Cartesian epistemology, God is never caught in the polarity of subject and object as are all ordinary objects of nature and history. On the other hand, the veils in which the Word gives Himself to be known *are* caught in that polarity, and are therefore subject to all the limitations imposed upon them by the ordinary processes of human knowing." McCormack, *Karl Barth's*, 423–24.

64. Jenson, *ST1*, 229n24.

65. Jenson, *ST1*, 228. Italics Jenson's.

body of Christ."⁶⁶ "No metaphor or ontological evasion should be intended. Sacrament and church are *truly* Christ's body for us ... Heaven is where God takes space in his creation to be present to the whole of it; he does that in the church."⁶⁷ Again, the verb-to-be "is" makes us suspect that Jenson is not aware of the difference—the "is not"—between God and created reality, and thus obscured the distinction between them.

Jenson's opposition to the doctrine of God's non-objectivity on the ground of the necessity of objectivity or embodiment in dialogue finally leads to confusion of the Creator and his creatures. In this area, it shows that Jüngel's interpretation of Barth's doctrine of the Trinity is helpful and valuable to Jenson's theology.

First, I argue that Jenson's difficulty comes from an inadequate attention to the assertion of God's objectivity as God's *Word* or God's self-interpretation in Barth's theology. According to Jüngel, Barth's doctrine of God's non-objectivity does not mean God cannot be an object of the knowledge of God. From the analysis in the previous section, one can find that, contrary to Jenson's assertion, the doctrine of God's being-as-object—God's non-objectivity—forms the ground on which God can constantly be a proper object for human knowledge of God. Moreover, Jüngel reminds us that human knowledge of God is grasped as "interpretation." A proper knowledge of God should be come from God's self-interpretation. In God's self-interpretation, "God is object in his *Word*."⁶⁸ This statement implies that if human knowledge of God is not from God's self-interpretation, this interpretation cannot be counted as authentic even if it is "objective." It suggests that in the course of human interpretation, there are two possible kinds of objectivity. First, the human can exert his own interpretation of an object as if he or she is the "Lord" of that object. Then, the object can be easily manipulated by human subject. The interpretation of the object may be only a projection or distortion of human subject's own cognition. Second, the object to be interpreted is itself the "Lord." It interprets itself and posits itself to be an "object" of—stands before—the human knower. For theology, we should insist God's objectivity is the second kind and not the first. Thus, mere objectivity, as Jenson seems to suggest, is not enough. God should be objective "in his *Word*."

When we insist "God is object in his *Word*," we may come back to Jüngel's interpretation of Barth's being-as-object or the doctrine of God's non-objectivity. However, we find that the doctrine guards the proper objectivity

---

66. Jenson, *ST2*, 168.
67. Jenson, *ST1*, 206.
68. Jüngel, *GBB*, 58.

of God and keeps a clear distinction of Creator and creatures. Indeed, from this perspective, we find Jenson is indeed following the argument of the doctrine of God's non-objectivity; because he argues that: "For the proposition that the church is a human body of the risen Jesus to be ontically and straightforwardly true, all that *is required* is that Jesus indeed be the Logos of God, so that *his self-understanding determines what is real.*"[69]

Secondly, according to Jüngel's interpretation, the thrust of Barth's doctrine of God's non-objectivity is in the assertion of "God is object in his Word." Theologically speaking, "Word" can effectively exist as "body" as it is "voice-bearing." However, it is difficult for us to conceive because it is "a highly dialectical process." Oliver Davies clearly explicates this dialectic as follows:

> In the first place, the originary voice of God, whose speaking is the creation, sets up the expectation of a divine body. Voices are produced by bodies; bodies are "voice-bearing." For God to have a voice is therefore, by implication, for God to have a body. This sets up a highly dialectical process, since it is unthinkable that the voice of the one whose speaking is the origin of the world should itself be borne by a body, for any material thing can only be the product and not the source of that creative speaking . . . The Christian belief that creation is through the Second Person, the Word who—in formula of the Prologue to the Gospel of John—"became flesh," is also expressive of this same dialectic.[70]

Accordingly, God's non-objectivity does not mean that God's Word is a nonembodied reality. Besides, we should be reminded that, for Jüngel's interpretation of Barth, God's Word is always embodied in Jesus Christ. Even God's being in sacramental reality is not said to be disembodied but embodied in ordinary world object. Therefore, Jenson's critique of the doctrine of God's non-objectivity is not established on a solid ground.

If we fully affirm that God's Word is body, the concept of Word will prevent possible confusion of Creator and creatures in Jenson's statement: "the church *is* the body of Christ for the world and for her members, in that she is constituted a community by the verbal and 'visible' presence *to* her of that same body of Christ." If God's Word is body, the church *is* truly the body of Christ; for she is constituted by the *verbal* presence to her of

---

69. Jenson, *ST*1, 206. Italics mine.

70. Davies, *The Creativity of God*, 155. However, we should note that Davies's assertion for a necessary creative process of interpretation of the "word" or "text" as "a voice-bearing *corpus* of deferred, or replicated, presence" (p.11) may not fit Jüngel's understanding of "word."

that *same body* of Christ. In short, the church is the body of Christ as it is constituted by God's Word—the body of Christ. Moreover, the church *is* the body of Christ as she speaks of God's word. It is voice-bearing as God's body. However, at the same time, God's Word is the revealed God as Jesus Christ. In Jüngel's interpretation, Word as God's being in revelation is continually in becoming. The Word always comes to humans and makes himself Lord, and so the distinction of God and human is maintained.

But Jenson also affirms that God's Word is embodied in Jesus Christ and sacrament. As we have seen, both Jenson and Jüngel come to sacrament when they speak about the objectivity of the knowledge of God. The difference between them is that Jüngel recognizes that the sacramental reality of God is both veiling and unveiling of God's being. However, Jenson emphasizes the sacrament "is" the body of God. Thus, thirdly, I argue that the problem in Jenson's theology comes from the fact that he understands the "embodiment" of God's word and its function in a quite narrow sense. More specifically, the problem is that Jenson equates God's body with the created objects of sacrament while suppressing the difference between them. Jenson defines body as person's "object-presence" and "identifiability."[71] For him, if God is a living God, "his body is not a corpse."[72] Therefore, after Jesus's resurrection, he cannot be a past historical object like "a corpse," but lively present and identifiable. Therefore, Jenson needs to identify God's body with creaturely objects to show that it is "lively" and present. He equates the sacrament and church with the body of God without making the differences between them clear.

But the body is not meaningful only when it is objectively present and identifiable. A living body continuously identifies and interprets itself and is being identified and interpreted. In this process, Barth emphasizes that a living person should be an "organic body" (*Leib*) with "independent life" to think, will, desire, and create actively.[73] The imagination is unavoidably involved. As Davies states, the "ceaselessly generative processes of self-replication, which are the life of the human body, are intimately connected with the imagination."[74] Imagination implies potential changes and differences. This does not reflect poorly on the life of human body. On the contrary, it enables "new permutations" of life.[75] Similarly, when we come to the sacrament, its transformative imagining process enables us to

---

71. Jenson, *VW*, 21, 23.
72. Jenson, *VW*, 35.
73. Barth, *CD* 3/2:378.
74. Davies, *The Creativity of God*, 165.
75. Davies, *The Creativity of God*, 165.

recognize a powerful encounter with the body of Christ taking place. It is God's imaginative transforming power that makes the creaturely object his "body." The non-identity of sacrament and Christ's body does not hamper God's availability. Only two conditions are required: (1) Christ's imaginative institution of the sacrament; and (2) an imaginative openness of the person who receives the sacrament. So, we have found our way back to Jüngel's doctrine of sacramental reality. He teaches us that the difference between the created object of sacrament and God is truly positive. We do not need to enforce an identity of the "body" of Christ and sacrament. This difference shows God's Grace and honor towards us. Our discussion shows that we should ask for a more comprehensive account of objectivity and embodiment from Jenson's theology.

After this analysis of Jüngel's interpretation of Barth, it is time for us to examine Jenson's account again.

If we keep pressing Jenson for a clear theological distinction between Creator and creatures, we find that Jenson tries to solve the problem with the concepts of "availability" and "promise." He argues that "body" does not merely mean "flesh." Rather, it is person's "availability" to be an object for another subject. The Eucharist bread and cup and the church are God's body because God is available to us there. God's availability comes to us in them because of the promise of Christ. Also, through promise we find sacrament and church *is* God's present in his body:

> No metaphor or ontological evasion should be intended. Sacrament and church are *truly* Christ's body for us, because Christ himself takes these same things for the object as which he is available to himself.[76]

> We must learn to say: the entity rightly called the body of Christ is whatever object it is that is Christ's availability to us as subjects; by the promise of Christ, this object is the bread and cup and the gathering of the church around them.[77]

> The Eucharist promises: *there is* my body in the world, and you here eating and drinking commune in it. It promises: *there is* the actual historical church, and you are she. That the risen Christ is not present merely "spiritually" is itself a vital promise of the gospel, and the one made specifically by the bread and cup.[78]

---

76. Jenson, *ST1*, 206.
77. Jenson, *ST1*, 205.
78. Jenson, *ST2*, 220.

Then, according to Jenson, "a promise has to be made,"[79] and making promise is the thing that we "do for each other."[80] Therefore, we identify God and ourselves in an irreducible subject-object relationship and are differentiated when God makes a promise to us.

For Jenson, God's promise is God's gifts that are "intrinsically *bespoken* to us" "as the church speaks the word of Christ."[81] Thus, Jenson's concept of promise leads us to notice the role of the concept of "Word" in his theology. In some sense, "Word" as God's speech to creatures marks the difference between God and his creatures in Jenson's theology. For example, he reminds us that "there is other reality than God because he speaks."[82] However, Jenson's emphasis on the "event" can be easily understood as an undone of this difference.

Jenson insists that God is a conversation and a personal event.[83] He explicitly states that "the one God is a conversation."[84] In this event, humans "are mentioned in the triune discourse *and* are called to join it."[85] The concept of conversation is good for our task of a proper distinction of God and human because conversation differentiates two subjects. However, when Jenson continues to articulate this conversational event, his argument seems to rely heavily on the on-going momentum or further development of the event. Then, God and those, such as the faithful community of the church, who participate in conversation with him, will appear to become a "single voice" towards those outside. But the constant and vital conversation between God and church has become less obvious in his discussion. Jenson can surprisingly suggest that:

> Once the conversation of God with humanity is under way, his speech to us is not another event than our speech for him to one another. Insofar as God's speech to us is the gospel, this assertion is unproblematic . . . God's word in and by the church is not an event other than the continuing antiphony of the church's own narrative in proclamation and prayer . . . What the prophet hears within his or her community can be the very

---

79. Jenson, *S&P*, 13.
80. Jenson, *S&P*, 6.
81. Jenson, *ST1*, 13.
82. Jenson, *ST2*, 6.
83. Jenson, *ST2*, 35.
84. Jenson, *ST1*, 223.
85. Jenson, *ST2*, 16.

word she or he is to speak to the community from God; and in the church it is always so.[86]

Jenson even can radically state this assertion as "hypostatic oneness of God's word and the community's word."[87] Again, the verb, "is," makes us suspect that Jenson is not distinguishing between God and his creatures. Nevertheless, we should recognize that the statement "God's word in and by the church is not an event other than the continuing antiphony of the church's own narrative in proclamation and prayer" provides some protection. However, one should also recognize that Jenson cuts down or compresses what Barth calls as the three-fold revelation of God's Word into one: "God's word in and by the church . . . in proclamation and prayer." In the task of 'antiphony,' the church requires herself to be "authentic" solely by herself. It gives us an impression that God and church speak in a "single voice." Ironically, there are examples in the Bible that the people of God can and had failed to have authentic proclamation and prayer (Isa 1:13–15; Jer 14:12).

At this point, Jüngel's doctrine of God's being-as-object is not sufficient to make a response. The doctrine of God's being-as-object clearly spells out the otherness of God's being-in-becoming in terms of the distinctive mode of God's objectivity in revelation. However, it does not explicitly articulate how the God-human relationship works in the dynamic or the eventfulness of the event of God's being revealed. Though Jenson obviously prioritizes time over space, i.e., otherness, we cannot correct him simply by reversing his account or the priorities. God's being in becoming is "word-event." It creates both the time and the space in which it takes place. Jüngel's analysis of the doctrine of correspondence and analogy provides us an account of how God and man can properly relate and interact in the event of God's revelation. Thus, it is the topic for our investigation in the next section.

3. God's Being is in His Becoming, Correspondence, and Analogy of Relation

3.1 God's Correspondence to Himself and to Humanity and His Relationship with Humanity

As Jüngel's presentation shows, Barth's doctrine of the Trinity teaches us that the relation between God and human is not static but dynamic. Because God's being is in his becoming, in which his being is in correspondence to himself and to humans, it is an "event." As this event should be

86. Jenson, ST2, 61.
87. Jenson, ST2, 61.

motivated and initiated by God himself, which is as a free event of God, it should come from his own decision. Therefore, Jüngel states that, "as event, God's being is his own decision."[88] God's self-determination is a decision that sets himself in relation. This means he has sets himself as a self-related being as Father, Son, and Spirit. Because God's revelation shows us that his being is in his double correspondence, his self-relatedness points in both an inward and an outward direction at the same time.[89] From revelation, we know God's decision is that he decides to be God for us and with us.[90] Precisely speaking, God's decision is that he determines "himself to be in Jesus Christ as the God who elects *and* elected humanity."[91] In this decision, the Son affirms the Father's will for him. In this way, the Son elects himself to be the God who elects the man Jesus and choose oneness with him. In turn, it means that the Son elects his obedience to the Father's election.[92] Then, according to Jüngel, God's decision to be electing God and elected man indicates that God's "correspondence to himself occurs as God's 'Yes' to himself. This 'Yes' constitutes God's being as *co-respondence*."[93] Jüngel emphasizes that "God does not abandon the correspondence in which he is who he is when he turns to humanity."[94] The relationship between God and human, according to Jüngel's interpretation of Barth's doctrine of the Trinity, must take the form of correspondence.

In God's eternal decision, God determines himself "to be God *as man*." It indicates that God eternally decides to be "self-giving." Thus, in Jesus Christ, God put himself unto death in order to ordain life for humanity. God says "No" to sin and "Yes" to humanity. In this way, God "maintains to the end his *Yes* to himself as his *Yes* to humanity."[95] In God's "Yes," he is in correspondence with himself and humanity. The relation of God's being for us corresponds to his self-relatedness. The correspondence establishes a close relationship between God and humanity: God's being is in becoming.

However, it should be noted that, because it is by his own free decision that God gives away for human beings's sake, humanity is in relationship with God as his other: "God's grace is rather the reiteration in relation

---

88. Jüngel, *GBB*, 81.
89. Jüngel, *GBB*, 83–84.
90. Jüngel, *GBB*, 81–82.
91. Jüngel, *GBB*, 89.
92. Jüngel, *GBB*, 88.
93. Jüngel, *GBB*, 89. Italics mine.
94. Jüngel, *GBB*, 89.
95. Jüngel, *GBB*, 93.

to something other of the *Yes* to himself which constitutes God's being."[96] Therefore, even humanity's salvation means the "taking up of humanity into the event of God's being,"[97] humanity is still "something other than" God in this relationship.

3.2 God's Relation to Us as God's Correspondence and an Analogy of Relation of God Himself

Jüngel points out that in revelation God interprets himself and reiterates himself with the help of historical predicates. Thus, it necessarily speaks in human language and unavoidably "anthropomorphic." It is truly a word-event.[98] However, Jüngel does not think the linguistic or anthropomorphic character of the revelation is a form of second best. Because he asserts that what happens in our being should take place in language. In his opinion, language can function as a "gain" for human beings.[99]

Because of his awareness of the linguistic character of human life and of the revelation Jüngel describes God's relation to us is an analogy of relation (*analogia relationis*).[100] As a process of speech, Jüngel explains that analogy enables us to have new discovery from another person's address. We cannot know something that is totally foreign to us without mediation. Thus, the analogy of another person helps us to grasp the new thing with the language which we are familiar with. As we have received something new from other person's address, which is an initial invitation to share their experience, speaker and hearer join into a fellowship in the process of speech.[101]

Jüngel argues that we know God and come to the relation with God exactly in an event of analogy. God comes to us in correspondence or analogically. At the same time, God, through his analogical "advent," enables us to have new relationship with him and with the world. In this new relation, we come to know God. Because this relation is only possible to be established through language (i.e., word); the analogy works in this process does not only deal with related things but also relation. Jüngel explains the whole process in this way:

---

96. Jüngel, *GBB*, 122.
97. Jüngel, *GBB*, 75.
98. Jüngel, *GBB*, 109–11.
99. Jüngel, "Metaphorical Truth," 52.
100. Jüngel, *GBB*, 119.
101. Jüngel, *GMW*, 291.

> One must understand analogy as an event which allows the One (x) *to come* to the Other (a) with the help of the relationship of a further Other (b) to even one more Other (c). The issue is an *analogy of advent*, which expresses God's arrival among men as a definitive event. But when the analogy contains *God* as one of its member (x:a=b:c), then, on the basis of the relation of God (x) to the world (a), the world-relationship (b:c) which corresponds to that relation appears in a completely new light . . . The world-relationship (b:c), which of itself can give no reference to God, now begins to speak for God . . . [W]hen b:c is *talked about* in such in such a way that it *corresponds* to the relation between God and the world (x→a), and God then ceases to be the unknown (x). In the event of the analogy x→a=b:c God ceases to be x. He introduces himself in that he arrives. And this his arrival belongs to his very being which he reveals as arriving. But this is possible only when this arrival itself takes place as an arrival-in-language so that in such an analogy not only the *relata* but also their relations to each other and their and their correspondence are lingual.[102]

From the analogy of relation, Jüngel illustrates that God is in a close relation with humanity in his event of coming. In this event, God comes close to man by ceasing to be an unknown x but a human understandable linguistic subject a. As this event is word-event, it is a relationship established analogically (x→a=b:c). However, though God draws to human nearer and nearer in this analogical relation, God and human never become identical. God and human are still different from each other throughout this event. Jüngel argues that this difference is vital because "[i]dentity as the ending of distance without nearness is the establishment of *absolute* distance."[103] However, this event does not cease to be temporal; because it is a *movement* of God's coming in word. Thus, analogy of relation does not return to traditional metaphysics of a timeless God. In Jüngel's words:

> The word which corresponds to God, which God lets come to earth as that word which comes solely from God and which proves him to be the one who, coming still closer from and in spite of the great distance, can thus only be a word *event*, can only be a *movement* of speech which corresponds to the self-movement of God. Human speech corresponds to the being of God, which is coming, in that it moves every statement, each of which is as such unrenounceable, on into movement again,

102. Jüngel, *GMW*, 285–86.
103. Jüngel, *GMW*, 288.

that is, it is not ashamed of its *temporality*, preferring instead some kind of timeless concept, but rather carries out purposefully that temporality.[104]

From the above discussion, one can note that Jüngel emphasizes the linguistic character of the *event* of God's self-interpretation establishes the relation and differentiation of God and human. In God's "Yes," God's self-affirmation is his correspondence to himself and human. However, God's "Yes" as self-giving and grace also differentiates God's himself from humanity. The doctrine of analogy of relation teaches us the event of God's revelation is only possible to come to human as a word-event. The event is necessarily analogical. But though it is analogical, it is thoroughly temporal. The analogical nature does not allow us to conceive God as timeless. Without this analogical advent, God cannot be known by human, and no new relationship between God and humanity is possible.

3.3 Comparison of Jenson and Jüngel

The significance Jüngel's gives to the linguistic dimension of the event of God's being in becoming helps us to see how the difficulties of Jenson's position may be addressed. Both Jenson and Jüngel would accept that God's being in becoming is a word-event. They differ in their interpretation of this word-event. For Jüngel this event comes to humanity in an utterly linguistic manner. Conversely, Jenson interprets it as God's continuous fulfillment of his promise for us in temporality with Jesus Christ the Word of God, and then by church and sacrament as body of Christ.[105] The life of Jesus Christ, which God decides in eternity, is "the sole basis for the lives of all of us." This life is described as "the overriding and *fundamental* part of each of our lifestories."[106] To put this assertion to its logical end, Jenson then stresses that "the history of man Jesus with God" "*is our real history*."[107]

For Jenson, history is already determined by God in Jesus Christ. At the same time, the event in Jesus Christ is the fulfillment of that history and itself is a history. Thus, the history of human participants, following this

---

104. Jüngel, *GMW*, 300. Italics Jüngel's.

105. For example, "What God does in the history of Jesus Christ on earth is the *implementation* and *revelation* of the eternal act of choice ... The earthly history of Jesus is the history in which God has realized His eternal decree in time, and that means, has revealed it. It is the temporal promise of our eternal election, the *revelation* that we *are* already children of God." Jenson, *A&O*, 85.

106. Jenson, *A&O*, 132.

107. Jenson, *A&O*, 133.

logic, is really the same history of Jesus Christ.[108] Therefore, we can see that it is the "eventful" or "historical" character in Jenson's theology leads to our question of a mixing up of God and human.

Indeed, Jenson himself knows that the assertion "Jesus Christ's history is our history" is problematic. He states that as Barth teaches that human being is a form of participation in God, it requires differentiation while the verb to be "is" implies identity rather than differentiation. Jenson answers that "the *knowledge* of what has happened in Christ" discerns the distinction of God and human.[109] However, if we take this answer seriously, one may suspect that it is a circular argument. For Barth, our knowledge of God is from God's revelation. God's revelation is God's being revealed. It is an event. For Jenson, this event is the history of Jesus Christ. The history of Jesus Christ is our *real* history. Then, we are asked to use the knowledge from this history, which is at the same time our real history and Jesus Christ's history, to discern a difference between Jesus Christ and us.

We may also consider another way of having knowledge to attempt to solve the problem as suggested in Jenson's work. As we have mentioned before, Jenson argues that our knowledge of God can come from his availability. Thus, we may argue that we can discern the difference between God and the human through his availability. Jenson states that church and sacrament *are* the body of Christ, and so is God's availability for us. However, at the same time we realize that we *are* church and the people who enact the sacrament. Again, we come back to our original problem.

In Jenson's later work, he provides a third answer. He argues that the difference is enforced by God's action: "God establishes himself as Creator and everything else as creature."[110] This action is God's incarnation. In Jesus Christ God precisely decides to have both divine and human natures in one unitary agent. Thus, from Jesus Christ, the difference between God and human is discerned. He emphasizes that this position is in line of the Christology of Cyril of Alexandria.[111] Likewise, he argues that the doctrine of real presence indicates the difference: "If we take 'This is my body' straightforwardly, the divine decree and the human reality are hard up against each other, and just so the difference is established."[112] In the first glance, this answer is persuading, powerful, and orthodox. However, without denying Jenson's assertion, we should remind ourselves that our difficulty is not

---

108. Jenson, *A&O*, 116–34.
109. Jenson, *A&O*, 134.
110. Jenson, "Creator and Creature," 220.
111. Jenson, "Creator and Creature," 220.
112. Jenson, "Creator and Creature," 221.

whether Jesus Christ and the sacrament can be both human and divine. Our difficulty is that, if the history and life of Jesus Christ is our *real* history and life, and if church is the body of God and is us; does it mean that Jesus Christ is me and I am Jesus Christ; or that the body of God is me and I am the body of God? Although Jenson's verdict declares that there should be difference between God and humanity in Jesus Christ and sacrament, his answer does not solve the problem of how to differentiate the difference between Jesus Christ and us; or between the body of God and church.

We may then argue that we identify the difference between Jesus Christ and us in the same way that we identify the difference of Creator and creatures in the two natures of Jesus Christ. In other words, God decides that there should be difference and thus it is established. However, one should notice that this answer finally becomes another version of Jenson's first answer: God decides that we may share in this knowledge of differentiation and so revealed in the history of Jesus Christ.

3.4 God's Consciousness as the Basis of the Knowledge of Divine-Human Difference in Jenson's Theology

Nevertheless, one should not think our analysis has pushed Jenson into a corner. He states that his theology has articulated a proper relation and difference between God and creatures. The difference is not articulated or discerned from the human side. Conversely, the difference is realized by God, Jesus Christ, himself. Jesus himself *is* his body and *possesses* his body which is discerned as other than him:

> When the church is understood with ontological seriousness as the risen Christ's body, an appropriate dialectic of identity and difference between God and the church must result. I *am* my body; yet I *have* my body. What my body does, I do; and yet I as subject must determine what my body shall do, and "in the flesh" have to struggle to make my body obey. Thus, what the church does is done by Christ the Logos; and yet he is free over against his church and, indeed, so long as the church is in the flesh, must often reform his church.[113]

Therefore, for Jenson, the difference between God himself and creatures is realized by God's *will* or his *consciousness*. From God's will, he willed us, his creatures, to be his body. He also distinguishes the difference between the body that he has and himself. Moreover, Jenson believes that our

---

113. Jenson, *UG*, 128.

consciousness[114] and knowledge[115] are come from God's consciousness. Therefore, God's will is determinative in our perception of God's relation and separateness to creatures too:

> Space . . . is the a priori of otherness . . . Thus if space is the form of consciousness that enables distinguishing other reality from oneself, we must say that this distinction is first made by God . . . [S]pace . . . is an aspect of God's enveloping conscious life . . . God sets us as other than himself, in that our accommodation in him has the present dimension of separateness.[116]

Then, we will find that Jenson has turned the usual approach to the distinction between Creator and creatures upside down. We usually start the question of distinction from human point of view. Thus, we approach the question of the ontological difference between God and creatures as an epistemological question. However, Jenson teaches that it is ontologically defined. The human epistemological question is only meaningful after one realizes God's ontic arrangement.

Following Jenson's line of thought, one may find the difference and relation of God and creatures is supposed rather than discerned. However, one may ask that, then, how does the divine consciousness come to be realized by the creatures? If it is communicable, even as a soliloquy, it should be conveyed in terms of word or sign. As George Steiner states:

> There is language . . . because there is "the other." We do address ourselves in constant soliloquy. But the medium of that soliloquy is that of public speech—foreshortened, perhaps made private and cryptic through covert reference and association, but grounded, nevertheless, and to the uncertain verge of consciousness, in an inherited, historically and socially determined vocabulary and grammar.[117]

---

114. "If active consciousness is a divine element, then by Christian lights it cannot be *my* consciousness that is active for me . . . If there is other conscious reality than God, this can only be by participation in the triune life." Cf. Jenson, *OTH*, 26–27. See Jenson, *ST2*, 98.

115. "*God* is the cause of our 'ideas'; that they are posited by his creative thinking and not by ours constitutes the otherness of what we perceive and know. God's knowing and willing constitute the 'substance' of things out there." Jenson, *OTH*, 52. Notably, Jenson argues that human does not has free-will unless we are "enraptured" by God's will. See Jenson, "An Ontology of Freedom," 251–52.

116. Jenson, *ST2*, 46–48.

117. Steiner, *Real Presences*, 137.

GOD'S BEING IS IN HIS BECOMING 183

In this point, on the one hand, we find Jüngel's teaching of God's *coming* to human as word is valuable. Although we can prioritize God's ontic decision over our epistemic experience, the communication between God's consciousness and ours unavoidably speaks of a *"coming"* of God's *word*. Therefore, it should be a *word*-event. It is proper to say that God's will of differentiating creatures from him, as it is also God's communicable will to us, is irreducibly a *word*-event. Without this word, such differentiation cannot be discerned.

Here Jenson brings in his notion of narrative. He states that our consciousness and experience can only be articulated if we are enabled by "the coherence of the narrative," which is also "the grammar of the language," of the community in which we belong.[118] According to him, "the grammar of the language" and "the coherence of the narrative" refer to "God's history with a human community actual in that history."[119] God's history in itself is the triune narrative and communal life. This history and community coincides human history and community at the life of Jesus Christ who is God's word. Accordingly, our experience does not come from ourselves, but from God's narrative as history and life. Thus, Jenson states that:

> There *are* no raw data of experience; the world that I receive and unify in my experience is always already the world interpreted in the discourse of a community, first the community of the Trinity and then the human communities I thereupon inhabit . . . With each of the rest of us the viewpoint from which consciousness stems is that of one of those *for whom* this Jew and prophet and victim lived and died (i.e., Jesus Christ), and who is some *particular one* of them as, for example, a lay deacon, a professor of physics, Susannah's child, and so on.[120]

Consciousness therefore cannot be realized without word while this word is a narrative as history. Because God's narrative is his own history, which also originates our consciousness and experience, we come back to the point that "the history of man Jesus with God" *"is our real history."* God's narrative and his history—a word-event—is not only a "coming" to human—an event from without. Rather, human history is constituted of God's history—an event within. Therefore, the verb "is" cannot be perceived from merely epistemological perspective. It only can be comprehensible if we realize it is an ontic arrangement; because this arrangement is also the origin of human consciousness.

118. Jenson, *ST2*, 99.
119. Jenson, *ST2*, 98.
120. Jenson, *ST2*, 98–99.

Jenson's argument makes close connections between God's consciousness, God's history, language, human's consciousness, and humans' history with one another. The hinge between each part is Jesus Christ the Son. One may posit that in Jenson's theology, God's consciousness is a meta-history or grand history that embraces human consciousness and history. This embrace is realized through the history of Jesus Christ, from whom each particular human historical event can be located within God's grand history and *is* this grand history.[121] Under this ontological arrangement, the meaning of some Jenson's cryptic statements on Christ's pre-existence, which also give the impression of inadequately distinguishing between God and human. They actually refer God's historical relationship with human which is initiated, embraced and then located by God's consciousness:

> [T]he "pre-existence" of Jesus the Christ is not simply that first there was a sheer divine entity who then became Jesus the Christ; somehow Jesus Christ, the God-*man* "pre"-exists himself . . . to the pre-existence of Jesus Christ there belongs among other factors his pre-existence in and as the nation of Israel. For Israel also is the human Son, whom God called out of Egypt as he would call Jesus the Son from the tomb.[122]

> In the triune life, what ontologically precedes the birth to Mary of Jesus who is God the Son, the birth, that is to say, of the sole actual second identity of that life, is the narrative pattern of *being going to be* born to Mary. What in eternity precedes the Son's birth to Mary is not an unincarnate *state* of the Son, but a pattern of movement within the event of the Incarnation, the movement to incarnation, as itself a pattern of God's triune life.[123]

From the above discussion, Jenson may argue that he does not conflate the Creator and creatures. Their difference and relationship are determined in God's consciousness, his triune narrative, and the history of Jesus Christ. Jenson describes it as the "room" that God makes for creatures in his triune life.[124]

At this point our question of a proper relatedness of God and creatures returns. From above discussion, one may find that Jenson's explanation of consciousness is a christological version of Hegel's phenomenology of Spirit. However, if Jenson's Trinity is a God of all-encompassing consciousness, and everything is interpreted and located according to his consciousness

---

121. Jenson, *ST2*, 47–48.
122. Jenson, "Christ as Culture 1," 326.
123. Jenson, *ST1*, 141.
124. Jenson, *ST2*, 34, 46–48.

and within his consciousness; how can creatures's otherness from God be protected without being finally absorbed into this consciousness? Moreover, how can something within God not be part of God? In Jenson's own logic, he may restate that the distinction is established by God's consciousness. However, it seems that the question of how something within God is not to be part of God remains untouched.

Once again, Jüngel offers another point of view. He is also interested in the role of narrative and consciousness in theological discourse and emphasizes that human consciousness is constitutive in its "story" or "narrative": "Tell me your story, and I will tell you who you are . . . I will tell you how you think."[125] We are structured *linguistically* and this linguistic structure gives us our temporality. Our story and narrative always has its past and always is entangled in the history which lies before us. The consciousness is structured *linguistically* and *temporally*, and is no merely thinking ego.[126] As monadic ego, consciousness could not know itself in *time* or in words.

For the relation of God's consciousness and human's consciousness, Jüngel agrees that if we want to understand God, we "will always be led back to narrative."[127] This narrative is God's history of creation, in which God's covenantal history with Israel and the narration of the life and suffering of Jesus are parts of that history. Therefore, God's narrative comes to human's consciousness as "a new way of thinking." It enables human's consciousness to be free from "egocentricity" of "I think," and thus, to be possible to know God.[128] However, because the story of Jesus Christ as the crucified God is always conceived as scandalous, foolish, and impossible, the knowledge of God's history cannot come from human's own general consciousness. Human's consciousness can think of God is the result of the constant coming of God's story—word in the Holy Spirit. Therefore, in Jüngel's words, "God's being remains a being *which is coming*":

> Man can correspond in his language to the humanity of God only by *constantly telling the story anew*. He thus acknowledges that God's humanity as a story *which has happened* does not cease being history *which is happening now*, because God remains the subject of his own story. To put it another way: it is the power of the Holy Spirit in which God's humanity constantly encounters human reason as a story to be told anew, although

---

125. Jüngel, *GMW*, 303.
126. Jüngel, *GMW*, 303.
127. Jüngel, *GMW*, 303.
128. Jüngel, *GMW*, 302–3; Jüngel, "The World as Possibility and Actuality," 113–14.

it cannot be captured once and for all in that act of perception. God's being remains a being *which is coming*.[129]

Jüngel argues that this coming is important to consciousness because consciousness, according to Hegel, "cannot become happy with itself in its self-certain isolation."[130] Unfortunately, human consciousness is nonetheless "egocentric." Thus, only God's coming to human as a truly other can free us from our "egocentricity."

More strikingly, when humans follow in thought the coming of God, consciousness, which is the thinking "subject" in this process, will experience itself as an "object" known by God at the same time. Jüngel argues that this reciprocal relationship demonstrates an "ontic bond" between consciousness and its object of thinking.[131] When consciousness thinks God, human is taken along by God—in communion—while they can be distinct from each other. Jüngel further explains that the bond can be established through human thinking of God because the linguistic nature of human being and God's becoming as Word allow humans to participate in God. When human responds to God's address, one can participate in God semantically:

> Rather, theology is essentially the doctrine of the word of God. As such, it is doctrine of the addressability of the human person. If man is the being who is addressed by God, and thus can be addressed about God and therefore *ontologically constituted by language*, then the presumption that one should become involved with the word of God is a presumption which accords with the very nature of man. It is certainly not something beyond presuming. *Man can engage himself in it* . . . Thought experiences itself when it begins to think God, and *is already being taken along by God*.[132]

Undoubtedly, we can find a clear distinction between God and human in Jüngel's account of narrative and consciousness. Jenson and Jüngel approach narrative and consciousness in very different ways. Jenson emphasizes that God's narrative and consciousness form an encompassing reality of himself and creatures. Human consciousness can only be located itself within God's consciousness. Jüngel also treats God's narrative as God's history, but his notion of "egocentricity" clearly sets human's consciousness as a unique whole by itself. Moreover, he emphasizes the

---

129. Jüngel, *GMW*, 304.
130. Jüngel, *GMW*, 84.
131. Jüngel, *GMW*, 163.
132. Jüngel, *GMW*, 162–63. This linguistic ontology will be discussed in depth in the second section of Chapter 6.

communion of God and human is possible because the linguistic nature of human being and God's becoming. Therefore, Jüngel's position can be seen as an opposite to Jenson's assertion of God's encompassing consciousness. Jüngel's argument clearly shows a strong anthropological-linguistic dimension that Jenson lacks. But the logic of Jenson's argument does not allow us simply to import Jüngel's position on this point. We need a more sympathetic way to revise Jenson's proposal.

3.5 Finding a "Convergence" with Metaphor

Another revision of Jenson's theology is offered by Colin Gunton. In his course of attaining "a convergence" between Jenson's theology and reformed theology, Gunton suggests that we should understand Jenson's notion of the "withinness" of creation in God *metaphorically*. He sees that both Lutheran (i.e., for Gunton represented by Jenson) and Reformed traditions aim to preserve both immanence and transcendence of God. In achieving this aim, they both try to articulate "the relation-in-otherness of God and the world." Lutherans stress the relation, while Reformed theologians put the stress on the otherness. Though there are different risks associated with each position, neither intends to deny either relation or otherness.[133]

Thus, Gunton points out that Jenson's concept of God's "roominess," which indicates creation is "contained" within God, is indeed a metaphor. Metaphor is "the *necessary* means of widening our grasp of what it is to be a creature of the good God."[134] Accordingly, the "withinness" is articulated metaphorically. When we discuss Jenson's assertion of creation within God, "we must retain in mind the fact that we are here in the realm of a metaphor in terms of which the continuing relatedness of the creation to God is being construed."[135] To bring Jenson's metaphor of "roominess" to its full force, Gunton argues that it is not only be used to describe the close relation of God and creatures, it is also used to indicate "creation as externalization"— as God's creation of something outside himself.[136]

Gunton believes that Jenson's "metaphorical containing" must allow "an element of externality, in the sense of an otherness which is established

---

133. Gunton, *Father, Son, and Holy Spirit*, 104.
134. Gunton, *Father, Son, and Holy Spirit*, 101. Italics mine.
135. Gunton, *Father, Son, and Holy Spirit*, 104.
136. Gunton, *Father, Son, and Holy Spirit*, 101–2. When Gunton argues that Jenson's metaphor of "roominess" can mean creation as externalization, he refers us to the following pages: Jenson, *ST2*, 34, 39, 47–48.

by God so that the creature shall be authentically itself."[137] He does not believe that Barth's teaching of analogy of relation between God and created world, and Jenson's teaching of the "withinness" of creatures in God are ultimately *different*.[138] In other words, God's containing of creatures is a metaphorical description of God's relatedness and distinction with creatures. As a metaphor, it implies both relatedness and otherness between God and creature.

Gunton's suggestion shows that if we understand Jenson's position metaphorically, we can preserve the whole thrust of Jenson's argument while enhancing the distinction between God and creatures in his theology. In this aspect, Jüngel's assertion of the "anthropomorphic" or "metaphorical" feature of God's *word*-event is helpful to Jenson's theology without denying his assertion of God's encompassing consciousness. With the help of metaphorical language, one can find the concept of "roominess" is "widening our grasp" of the relation and distinction of God and creatures rather than conflating the distinction. However, it demands a sharper sensitivity of the linguistic characteristics of Christian theology that Jenson's theology lacks.

If Christian theology wants to keep the relation and distinction of God and creature in healthy balance, God's being-in-becoming as both word and event should be equally upheld. On the one hand, God's history is God's coming to the world. God's incarnation and his speech to world exactly show he expresses himself anthropomorphically or metaphorically. On the other hand, Christian theological discourse undeniably is an anthropomorphic attempt to proclaim God's history with the grace of Holy Spirit in human language. This only can be done if we firmly grasp both the linguistic and eventful characteristics of God's being-in-becoming.

4. Summary

From our comparison of Jüngel's and Jenson's interpretation of Barth's doctrine of God's being in his becoming, we find that word-event is the central concept for both interpretations. While Jüngel's interpretation emphasizes the importance of the linguistic aspect of the word-event, Jenson tends to stress the historical or temporal fulfillment. In the above discussion, I have pointed out that Jenson's interpretation incurs the question of a proper distinction of God and creatures. I have tried to show the rationality of Jenson's own proposal. But my analysis suggests that Jenson's position needs to be modified. The comparison shows that Jüngel's insight of the linguistic aspect

---

137. Gunton, *Father, Son, and Holy Spirit*, 103.
138. Gunton, *Father, Son, and Holy Spirit*, 102–3.

of God's word-event makes a valuable contribution. If we balance Jenson's concern with temporality of being (i.e., as word-*event*) by Jüngel's analogical and hermeneutical dimension of being (i.e., as *word*-event), some of the difficulties of Jenson's trinitarian doctrine of God may be avoided.

Chapter 6

Theology of Possibility and Theology of Actuality

Two Approaches to the Contemporary Theological Problem of God's Death. A Further Evaluation of Jenson's Doctrine of the Trinity with Reference to Eberhard Jüngel

IN THE LAST CHAPTER, I argued that Jüngel's interpretation of God's being in becoming offers us a way to understand the word-event of God's coming to humans in a linguistic-temporal perspective. I also argued that the hermeneutical-linguistic dimension of word-event would be a valuable means of allowing Jenson's doctrine of God to articulate the proper relation and distinction of God and creatures.

In this chapter I will continue my evaluation of Jenson's Trinitarianism with reference to Jüngel. The focus of my discussion is on how Jenson and Jüngel respond to the contemporary theological problem of the "death of God" with the doctrine of the Trinity. The first section introduces Jüngel's analysis of contemporary theological *aporia* and his critique of traditional metaphysics. Like Jenson, Jüngel argues that the traditional metaphysics does not allow the modern world to come to the knowledge of God. The result is that "God is dead" for the modern world.

The second section introduces major features of Jüngel's own trinitarian theology. I will highlight Jüngel's assertion of the possibility of thinking God. I argue that the main thrust of Jüngel's theology is a linguistic ontology. He crafts an ontological account to explain that being human is a being who is addressed by God, and therefore a linguistic being. God's revelation of himself as Trinity is a *word*-event. Human participation in God is also a *word*-event. The doctrine of the Trinity re-opens the possibility of knowing God to modern theology. Jüngel's placing possibility above certainty in his linguistic ontology represents an important breakthrough in contemporary theological response to atheism. Rather than remaining within the paradigms of naïve realism and expressivism, Jüngel's linguistic ontology insists that it is this address that makes theology as *possibility* and allows it to speak of God without losing its authentic claim to be an event of encounter with God.

In the third section, I argue that Jenson also perceives his Trinitarianism as an antidote to the contemporary ethos of speaking God is dead. Jenson diagnoses the concept of divine timeless eternity as the root of the problem. He responds by constructing a narrative Trinitarianism that emphasizes divine temporality, arguing that the triune God is present in human history and as history. The presence of God is perceived by humans as they realize God's promise is being continuously actualized eschatologically in the history of Israel, Jesus Christ, and church. Jenson's emphasis is on the actuality of God's promise while Jüngel's is on the possibility of God's coming to humans.

Then, around two pivotal notions of possibility and actuality, a comparison of two theologians's thought will be carried out. Though they both consider the contemporary theological predicament has its origin in the problem of the traditional metaphysics, and both are in conversation with Barth and Hegel, their diagnosis and solution to the problem are very different. Jenson tries to correct the modern trend towards nihilism by emphasizing the actuality of God's promise in temporality. This encounters two problems. First, Jenson's emphasis of the necessity of God's presence in temporality does not completely ward off the claim of human experience of God's absence—the death of God. Secondly, Jenson's treatment of Gospel narrative as God's history cannot satisfactorily articulate the anthropological dimension of the gospel narrative. God's encompassing story of promise may be seen as oppressive of human life. Jüngel's theology of possibility may enrich and enhance the arguments of Jenson's theology of actuality for the contemporary theological problem of God's death.

1. The Death of God as Theological *Aporia* in Jüngel's Theology

Jüngel believes that talking about God in contemporary society is becoming increasingly embarrassing and impossible: "God has no place in our thought and thus has no place in our language . . . we are living in an age of the verbal placelessness of God."[1] He calls this situation as "the contemporary aporia

---

1. Jüngel, *GMW*, 3.

of the word 'God.'"² He observes that the contemporary "sensitivity to the aporia" "is expressed in the dark statement about the death of God."³ In the following sub-sections, I argue that Jüngel ascribes three problems, which are related to the traditional metaphysical concept of God, for the modern impossibility of thinking and speaking God: (1) the Cartesian formula of "I think"; (2) assuming anthropomorphism of human language as deficiency for theological discourse; (3) assuming God as pure actuality and preferring actuality over possibility. Finally, I argue that the core of Jüngel's critique is the problem of the God-man distinction. It aims to show theological thought and speech is only possible when the proper understanding of God-man distinction and relation is secured.

1.1 Contemporary Theological *Aporia* and Cartesian Formula of *Cogito Sum*

Jüngel argues that contemporary theological *aporia* or talk of "the death of God" is closely related to modern human experience of God's "non-necessity."⁴ The root of the *aporia* is Descartes's proof of God's necessity for human self-certainty of ego. In Jüngel's opinion, "this proof of the necessity of God is the midwife of modern atheism."⁵

Cartesian formula of "I think, therefore I am" (*Ego cogito, ergo sum*), according to Jüngel's analysis, suggested that human self-certainty is secured through the power of methodological doubt. Doubting is the way to render things certain. To doubt is "to distinguish true from false."⁶ If one wants to acquire the true knowledge, doubt must come first. In this way, doubting is methodologically necessary for knowing truth. At last, by the course of doubt, only the existence of the doubter himself/herself cannot be doubted. However, the certainty of reflective doubt can only assure one's present existence. At this point, Descartes asserts that the existence of God is necessary for human to guarantee the certainty of the continuity of one's own existence; because only a God who is good and perfect can overcome the doubter's doubt. Paradoxically, this thesis requires that humans have to doubt first in order to be able to prove God's existence. Jüngel summarizes the logic as follows:

2. Jüngel, *GMW*, 35.
3. Jüngel, *GMW*, 42.
4. Jüngel, *GMW*, 16.
5. Jüngel, *GMW*, 19.
6. Jüngel, *GMW*, 113.

> Without "doubting" (*dubitare*) there is no "I think—I am" (*cogito sum*), without "I think—I am" (*cogito sum*) there is no certainty of a "thinking thing" (*res cogitans*), without a "thinking thing" there are no "modes of cogitation" (*modi cogitationis*) and thus no "ideas," including no idea of God! Without an idea of God there is no proof of God, and without a proof of God there is no certainty of God! Without the certainty of God there is still the self-certainty which was arrived at through doubt, but there is no assurance of this self-certainty beyond the present moment. The self-certainty which I owe to my doubt must therefore be guaranteed through the assurance of the existence of God. God is necessary as the back-up insurance against my own doubt.[7]

Proof for God's existence inevitably starts from the doubt of the thinking ego.

Jüngel then points out that Cartesian thesis of God's necessity for the purpose of assuring the continuity of the certainty of thinking ego eventually leads "to the disintegration of certainty about God."[8] Although the Cartesian model posits God as necessary being, God is eventually relativized by humans because "a perfect God is dependent on the postulate of a less perfect reality—that is, on the self-understanding (or doubting) of man."[9]

In Cartesian thought, which follows the heritage of traditional metaphysics, God's essence is defined as absolutely perfect. God should be "infinite, independent, most intelligent, and most intelligent, and most potent."[10] Therefore, by definition, God should be existed independently. However, according to Cartesian formula of *cogito*, everything including God cannot be conceived to exist unless it is present or experienced in the consciousness of thinking ego. Only the thinking ego itself is present and existing beyond all doubt: "I think, therefore I am." The formula generates an acute contradiction between "the certainty of the essence of God" and "the certainty of the existence of God."[11] Consequently, certainty about God disintegrates.[12]

Jüngel describes this contradiction as an *aporia*. He observes that the contradiction is not immediately apparent because Descartes avoided

---

7. Jüngel, *GMW*, 120.
8. Jüngel, *GMW*, 122.
9. Jüngel, *GMW*, 122.
10. Jüngel, *GMW*, 123.
11. Jüngel, *GMW*, 124.
12. Jüngel, *GMW*, 125.

it by resorting to the philosophical tradition of divine incomprehensibility.[13] However, in the modern era, the traditional metaphysical concept of God has been challenged. Within the dimension of the presupposition of "I think," the existence of the traditional metaphysical God "has become progressively less conceivable and finally unthinkable."[14]

Jüngel then uses Fichte, Feuerbach, and Nietzsche to illustrate the course of this development in modern western thought. Jüngel finds that all three thinkers understand God in traditional metaphysical terms, and in terms of the Cartesian presupposition of "I think." Their thought shows that these two presuppositions inevitably contradict each other and finally leads to the modern impossibility of thinking God.[15] According to Jüngel, Fichte demands God should not be thought at all and asserted it is impossible to think God in order to protect the deity of God.[16] Moreover, Fichte argues that it cannot be stated whether the God who is an infinitely superior being exists or not. The reason is that existence is a concept which is determined by "I think," and the human ego is finite and is not capable to comprehend the infinite.[17] God is inconceivable, and there is no necessary connection between God's essence and his existence.

Along the traditional metaphysical presupposition of God, Feuerbach defines God as the one that which nothing greater can be conceived. He conceives the traditional presupposition of God as "the highest *object* of thought" as "the *highest degree* of the thinking power."[18] From this understanding, he asserts that the idea of God is only a reflection of the intrinsic nature of infinite human reason, and not an objective existence: there is nothing greater than God that can be conceived by the ego. When the ego can magnify itself no further in the thinking process, it thinks of God. Thus, God is the concept that is produced by thought itself, and immanent to thought. It is the boundary concept of thought. It is the thought that cannot be surpassed. In short, "God is a *thought* . . . Thinking is then, so to speak, a creator and God is its noblest creation."[19] According to Jüngel, Feuerbach's assertion further indicates that God as the highest essence and at the same time an independent existence becomes inconceivable for

---

13. Jüngel, *GMW*, 125.

14. Jüngel, *GMW*, 126.

15. As the research interest of this research and limited space, I will not present Jüngel's analysis in details. A very fine work on this topic is: DeHart, *Beyond the Necessary God*, 56–66.

16. Jüngel, *GMW*, 135–37.

17. Jüngel, *GMW*, 140.

18. Jüngel, *GMW*, 145.

19. Jüngel, *GMW*, 146.

modern thought: "the metaphysical concept of God has become inconceivable under the premise of thought which grounds itself in the 'I think.' This thought of God contradicts itself."[20]

Nietzsche is Jüngel's final example. Nietzsche's assertion of God's inconceivability is "the only possible consequence" of the development of the idea of God within the dimension of Cartesian doctrine of "I think."[21] Indeed, for Nietzsche God is not only unthinkable, God has died. Nietzsche posits that God is the conjecture of infinity. But the conjecture of infinity imposes an unnecessary opposition between infinity and finitude. It finally destroys and devalues the finitude of the one who conjectures. But without God the human sees the unendedness of their finitude as the horizon that ever opens before them. Jüngel concludes that "For that reason Zarathustra wants to restrict human conjecturing. For that reason it should not 'reach beyond your creating will.' For that reason it should be restricted to 'the conceivable.'"[22] In other words, God is "an impossible thought which destroys all thought."[23] In short, God is inconceivable. Moreover, human creative will is "a power *capable of transforming everything*" into the humanly conceivable. However, when God is transformed into the humanly conceivable, God ceases to be infinite and thus ceases to be God. If there is a humanly conceivable "god," it is the will to be human superego, the superman. When the creative will creates itself as a will to surpass the finite ego, it is the will to be the human superego.[24] It puts itself to the place which traditionally reserves for God. Therefore, Zarathustra exclaims, "God hath died; now do we desire—the Superman to live."[25]

With the examples of Fichte, Feuerbach, and Nietzsche, Jüngel illustrates the modern *aporia* of the death of God and God's inconceivability as an inevitable outcome of the philosophical development after Descartes. Clearly, the problems are the traditional metaphysical idea of God and Cartesian formula of "I think."[26]

---

20. Jüngel, *GMW*, 151.
21. Jüngel, *GMW*, 151.
22. Jüngel, *GMW*, 147.
23. Jüngel, *GMW*, 152.
24. Jüngel, *GMW*, 148–49.
25. Jüngel, *GMW*, 151.
26. Jüngel, *GMW*, 169.

1.2 Jüngel's Critique of Traditional Metaphysics on the Speakability of God

Jüngel's critique of traditional metaphysical concept of God is not limited to its role in Descartes's *"cogito"* formula. In this sub-section, I will examine Jüngel's criticism of the speakability of God of traditional metaphysics. He finds that traditional metaphysics is in a dead-end. In it, God is unspeakable. If Christian theology wants to continue a responsible talk of God, it should find another way than that of traditional metaphysics for speaking of God. For Jüngel, the heart of the problem is that the traditional metaphysics denies the unavoidability and validity of the anthropomorphism of God talk.

In Jüngel's viewpoint, anthropomorphism is unavoidable in theological discourse because all human talk is implicitly anthropomorphic.[27] He asserts that the critique of anthropomorphism does not really have its roots in the Bible. On the contrary, the incarnation of God's Son as Jesus Christ as well as the narrative of the Old and New Testaments show the unembarrassed anthropomorphism of Christian faith.[28] He finds that it is "in the earliest Greek philosophy that anthropomorphic language is perceived as a cause of offence."[29]

According to Jüngel, the classical theism—the traditional metaphysics—asserts that God "is ineffable and incomprehensible" for its assumption of God's absolute ontological transcendence.[30] If humans want to speak of God, an absolute transcendent and thus mysterious being, it is inevitably "*inauthentic* talk."[31] However, it also asserts that God's existence is self-evident.[32] Then, it faces a dilemma: "how can one express in language and give a name to an existence about which one cannot describe *what* it is?"[33] Traditional metaphysics cannot solve this problem, so it becomes impossible to speak of God.

Thomas Aquinas is an excellent example of the tradition. Jüngel analyzes Aquinas's approach to Divine ineffability and analogy to show the problems. Though Aquinas tries to provide a way to speak of an ineffable God, his

---

27. Jüngel, "Anthropomorphism," 89.
28. Jüngel, *GMW*, 280; Jüngel, "Anthropomorphism," 72.
29. Jüngel, "Anthropomorphism," 73.
30. Jüngel, *GMW*, 233–35.
31. Jüngel, *GMW*, 251.
32. Jüngel, *GMW*, 236.
33. Jüngel, *GMW*, 236. Italics Jüngel's.

attempt is unsuccessful, Jüngel believes, because it cannot really speak of or refer to God's reality. It cannot "corresponding to God."[34]

Aquinas follows the Greek philosophical tradition in asserting that while God's essence is ineffable or unspeakable, the existence of God is self-evident.[35] He suggests that God's essence is the "cause" of an "effect." While we cannot talk about God's essence, the effect of this cause does indeed express God:[36] The "effect" makes us possible to provide material characteristics of the "cause." These characteristics supply the meaning of the "names" used to designate the "cause."[37] Accordingly, "God is brought *to speech* in that he is *named* on the basis of the world contexts which are *recognized* as his effects."[38] Aquinas affirms that, on the one hand, these names "absolutely and affirmatively" speak of God. On the other hand, because they are still captive to created realm, they only can express God imperfectly.[39] "Names" designated to God therefore cannot be understood either *univocally* or *equivocally*. They should be understood *analogically*.[40] Here, we come to Aquinas's doctrine of analogy.

Jüngel suggests that, according to the philosophical tradition, there are two models of analogy of naming: *analogy of proportionality*, and *analogy of attribution*. *Analogy of proportionality* understands analogy to be a *proportion*. It refers to two similar (identical) relations between totally dissimilar things. In this model, an analogy of naming is the transference of a name to a bearer that is actually alien to this name. In the meantime, it affirms that these names have similar or identical relations. In mathematical sense, the proportionality can be expressed as: a:b=c:d. Based on the relational proportionality, one can compare the different names (things) in an analogy with each other within the stable proportional relations of them.[41]

The second model is *analogy of attribution*. In this model, an analogy takes place when one word is used for differing things without making the meaning of the word become completely identical (univocal) or completely different (equivocal). Those different things named by the same word are addressed in a *similar* and thus *analogous* sense. The similarity can be

34. Jüngel, *GMW*, 227: "We call that kind of human talk about God which wants to let him speak himself, 'corresponding to God.' Therefore, talk about God is responsible when it is intention to corresponding to God."
35. See Jüngel's analysis: Jüngel, *GMW*, 232–36, 239.
36. Jüngel, *GMW*, 237.
37. Jüngel, *GMW*, 241.
38. Jüngel, *GMW*, 242. Italics Jüngel's.
39. Jüngel, *GMW*, 244.
40. Jüngel, *GMW*, 273.
41. Jüngel, *GMW*, 267, 270.

conceived because the different things are all related to or proportioned to one identical thing. Each of them is related to this *one common thing* in a different way. The different relations of the different things to the "one thing" justify the varying usages of the same word. Hermeneutically, the one common thing is the "first thing" of those things which it analogizes.[42] In other words, analogy of attribution presupposes "the dependence of different things on one common thing in varying relations."[43] For mediaeval Scholasticism, this hermeneutical dependence has been interpreted as ontological dependence. Analogy of attribution then supposes that its *analogans* ("one who makes the analogy") is the ontic causer of the *analogatum* ("that which is analogized").[44]

Jüngel finds that, though Aquinas ascribed analogous naming of God as analogy of proportion, he incorporated the so-called analogy of attribution into the so-called analogy of proportionality. By this move, Aquinas attempted to assert that God can be expressed analogously by his worldly effects while God's ineffability is maintained.

Aquinas divided analogy into two different kinds according to the proportion between *analogans* and *analogatum*. An analogy can be either a proportion of *many* to *one* or a proportion of *one* to *another*. Aquinas taught only analogous naming of God "according as one thing is proportionate to another" is theological proper.[45] According to Jüngel's reading, the thrust of Aquinas's assertion is his assumption of the "one common thing" as "subsisting in a definite existing thing": the "'one thing' (*unum*) is in a concretely existing being."[46] As the "one thing" is a concrete subsisting, it may carry hermeneutical as well as ontic implication. It may function not only as the first thing in terms of the *order of knowing*, but also of the *order of being*.[47]

As God is posited as the original cause and an ontologically different being with creatures, a valid analogous naming of God is supposed to reflect these ontological arrangements. Aquinas found that, in analogy of *many* to *one*, the "one thing" may not constitutively have ontic priority (as an ontological cause) by itself. A third thing may be ascribed to be the first thing in order of being.[48] This kind of analogy or proportion is not theologically relevant because it puts God on the same rank as creatures: "For God, for

---

42. Jüngel, *GMW*, 269.
43. Jüngel, *GMW*, 270.
44. Jüngel, *GMW*, 272.
45. See Aquinas, *Summa Theologiae*, 1.13.5.
46. Jüngel, *GMW*, 273.
47. Jüngel, *GMW*, 273–74.
48. Jüngel, *GMW*, 273–74.

the sake of his deity, cannot be related to a third thing which would put him hermeneutically in one line with other things."[49]

Aquinas claimed that only a proportion of *one* to *another* can clearly delineate the ontic order between two things named by the same word. In analogous naming of one to another, it has to do with a proportion between one thing and only one other thing. The hermeneutical first thing must subsist in one of the two. One of the two must be ontically prior. Because God must be the first thing ontologically, a legitimate analogous naming of God is as one thing is proportioned to another and not that many to one.[50] The intention of Aquinas's categorization is to guarantee a stable ontic causal relation can be expressed in an analogy.

Clearly, analogy is not causality. For Aquinas, the theological analogy incorporates causality between God and his effects, but it does not operate as a direct expression of causality. Its expression is still analogous. According to Jüngel, Aquinas's actual theological analogy, which according as "the proportion of one to another," is worked with three more propositions. First, God is the *cause* of all perfections, and possesses these perfections in their most original form. Secondly, original possession means that God possesses the perfection in such a way that it is identical with itself. As the perfection exists identically as itself, "having" is equal to "being." God exists as himself: his existence is identical to his existence. God's *having* the perfection in its most original form means that it is equal to *God's being*. Thirdly, the perfections exist in creatures. However, they exist in God in a more excellent way than in creatures, which creatures *cannot comprehend*. Though creatures's perfections are caused by God, creatures only *have* these perfections in lesser degree that appropriate to their created *beings*. They have the perfections *in proportion* to their beings and know them in a way that is appropriate to their beings. In this way, the relation between God and his perfections corresponds proportionately to the relation between human being and their perfections. Therefore, God and creatures are related analogically.[51]

With the concepts of "being," "proportionality," and "causality," Aquinas furnishes a way of speaking of God analogously even while God remains ineffable. However, Jüngel points out that God's unknownness becomes "obtrusive in an unavoidable way" in this account. In Aquinas's doctrine, in which analogy of attribution is incorporated into analogy of proportionality eventually, God's unknownness has to be defined as the

49. Jüngel, *GMW*, 275n50.
50. Jüngel, *GMW*, 274.
51. Jüngel, *GMW*, 275–76.

unknownness of our origin of the world. In this way, God is "an Unknown without which we would not exist."[52] Analogy helps us know about God's relationship to the world. However, "this relationship cannot be taken as a statement about God's being."[53] The final result of the traditional theological usage of analogy is ironically agonistic.

Jüngel points out that the primary concern of traditional metaphysics is to protect God's *ineffability* and *absolute transcendence*. It taught that human language is anthropomorphic. This characteristic is considered as a deficiency for speaking of the transcendent God.[54] Therefore, analogy is assumed to enable human speaking of God while to keep God's ontological difference. Paradoxically, one can only speak of God analogically in *human way*. According to the traditional metaphysical assumption, it is unavoidably "inauthentic" talk. Finally and unfortunately, God is inevitably "inaccessible" to human knowledge.[55]

1.3 Jüngel's Critique of Traditional Metaphysics on Prioritizing Actuality over Possibility

For Jüngel, the traditional metaphysical God is absolute infinite and transcendent. Because of this influence, the contemporary theological *aporia* indeed comes from an intolerance of finitude of human thought and anthropomorphism of human theological language. There is a third reason for the contemporary theological *aporia*: the *priority given to actuality over possibility*. From Aristotle on, Jüngel argues that the priority of actuality over possibility is not simply an ontic precedence of the actual over the possible. Rather, it is the ontological ground of possibility. According to Aristotle, being and actuality are identical. "To be" "can only be said of those things which can also be described as fully realized, as actuality."[56] Something is defined as possible because it is the possible with reference to actuality. The possible is a "not yet" realized actuality. As a "not yet" of actuality, actuality is ontological prior to it. Moreover, Aristotle taught that the possible is always actualized by something which has already been actualized into the same species as it. Actuality is the origin and goal of the possible. Possibility is teleological subordinated to actuality.[57] Jüngel

---

52. Jüngel, *GMW*, 277.
53. Jüngel, *GMW*, 283.
54. Jüngel, *GMW*, 259–60.
55. Jüngel, *GMW*, 247.
56. Jüngel, "The World as Possibility and Actuality," 99.
57. Jüngel, *GMW*, 99–100.

points out that prioritizing actuality equates possibility with "deficiency." Because the primacy of being is assigned to the actual, "the possible had to appear as what actually is impotent."[58]

In Aristotle's account, "actuality" is derived from "act." Actuality is "the act's completion." Because actuality comes from act, there should be a "first" act for the sake of all other actualities. As the origin of other actualities, it should be in the purest form of act. It should be pure actuality without possibility. Actuality without possibility can only be a "permanent now."[59] It should be a unity of act and actualization. Therefore, the first act is the "unmovable first mover." It is a "thinking on thinking" that without any possibility for its thinking object is itself.[60]

Accordingly, traditional metaphysics defines God as "purest act" (*actus purissimus*). God is the "one who has always and already realized himself."[61] In the name of the "permanent now," temporality is qualified as an ontological negative. In this tradition, what is temporal is perishable. Temporal and perishable being is understood to be in a tendency toward nothingness.[62] Temporality and perishability are treated as a threat to being. Conversely, Divine is timelessly imperishable, eternally present, and immutable.

Consequently, as long as traditional metaphysics prevailed, the Christian belief in the crucified God was a scandal. Ironically, as the tradition came to an end, modern philosophy, exemplified by Nietzsche, not only rejected the metaphysical concept of God of absolute transcendence as unthinkable but still rejected the Christian understanding as unbelievable.[63] Jüngel argues that this phenomenon shows how the metaphysical prioritization of actuality over possibility hinders contemporary theological thinking and discourse.

Contemporary talk about the death of God intends to show the absurdity and inconceivability of the metaphysical transcendent God to modern minds. But "God cannot die" is only a presupposition of traditional metaphysics. Jüngel points out that continuing to believe that perishability disproves the concept of God reveals the continuing influence of the metaphysics that prioritizes actuality in modern thought.[64]

58. Jüngel, *GMW*, 214.
59. Jüngel, *GMW*, 212.
60. Jüngel, "The World as Possibility and Actuality," 100.
61. Jüngel, *GMW*, 214.
62. Jüngel, *GMW*, 210–12.
63. Jüngel, *GMW*, 206–7.
64. Jüngel, *GMW*, 203.

Jüngel finds that Nietzsche is ready to praise and justify the perishable. He feels that the crucified God of Christian faith is unbelievable, although he is well aware that the apostle Paul proclaims Christian God is a crucified God. However, he asserts that Paul has *created* a new God. He claims that the crucified God (*deus crucifixus*) of Christian faith must be asserted as the "negation of God" (*dei negatio*). Worshiping a suffering God is "a crime against life." He feels "even less able to believe" in the crucified God of Christian faith, even if his existence can be proven.[65] It shows that Nietzsche praises the perishable only because he wants to justify the perishability of life for its very own vitality. In this aspect, Jüngel argues that though Nietzsche opposes the metaphysical concept of God, he "remained deeply obligated to the traditional metaphysics" of prioritizing actuality.[66] For this reason, Nietzsche's belief in the impossibility of the metaphysical concept of God still does not allow him to find a different understanding of God. He rejects God in favor of the mortal superman.

1.4 Summary and Discussion: The Concern of God-man Distinction and Theological *Aporia*

In summary, for Jüngel, the traditional metaphysics is responsible for the modern impossibility of thinking and speaking God. First, in the Cartesian formula of "I think," the doubt of human ego is the primal source of our awareness of existence. However, because doubt cannot grant an assurance of continuous existence, God—the absolute perfect and transcendent being in traditional metaphysics—is posited as the necessary back-up insurance against my own doubt though he is inconceivable. God is posited as *a guarantee of ultimate security*. However, when human thought progressively came to see itself as self-securing, the metaphysical concept of God, as an absolute transcendent being, finally became an impossible thought for the finite ego. For the sake of the self-securing ego, the metaphysical God should be dead. Consequently, contemporary *aporia* considers God is unthinkable, and therefore *dead* and *meaningless*.

Secondly, the traditional metaphysics teaches that God is *ineffable*, and human language cannot have authentic talk of God for its anthropomorphism. Though it develops the doctrine of analogy as a way to speak of God, it in turn asserts that God is unspeakable in human language.

Thirdly, the traditional metaphysics assumes that actuality is ontological prior to possibility, and God is *pure actuality*. The prioritization of

---

65. Jüngel, *GMW*, 205–6.
66. Jüngel, *GMW*, 207.

actuality over possibility prevents humans perceiving perishability as a good. Consequently, modern thought thinks "the death of God" rules God out while refusing the crucified God in which Christians believe.

The Jüngel's critique is directed to the proper distinction and relation of God and man. He claims that the "difference between God and man . . . is constitutive of the essence of the Christian faith."[67] But the various definitions of deity in traditional metaphysics define God-man distinction inappropriately: they define the distinction between God and human as the *"total differentness"* of God and human.[68] He shows that traditional metaphysics wants to avoid the anthropomorphism which would destroy the distinction between God and human by speaking of God *like* a human. It objects anthropomorphism by dehumanization of God, and insists that no human language is capable of speaking about God. Even analogous talk of God is "inauthentic." Unfortunately, these definitions eventually make God unthinkable, unspeakable, dissolved, meaningless, and dead.

Jüngel points out that these definitions cannot really defend a proper distinction between God and man. The rejection of anthropomorphism only places God in an unspeakable and unthinkable "absolute transcendental realm." When the objective God disappears into that realm, humans project those "transcendental qualities" as their own ideals. Rather than believing in God, humans seek to attain these ideals and put themselves in the place of God. The human can no longer be distinguished from God. In this way, humans also alienate themselves from humanity. The God-man distinction is in fact being frustrated rather than defended. In the same way, the traditional teaching of theological analogy shows its concern to speak of God in human language. However, because it makes opposites of God and man, this human decision forbids us from speaking of God *as* a man. Even though Christian faith believes that God was among humans as the man Jesus whilst remaining very God, traditional metaphysics prevents the development of any thought that follows this event. The distinction of God and human in traditional metaphysics is solely a human projection which prevents the proper distinction of God and humanity.[69]

From this discussion, we can see that the contemporary theological *aporia* is a result of the inappropriate God-man distinction of traditional metaphysics. This makes it humanly impossible to know God. In the next section, I will argue that, for Jüngel, the doctrine of the Trinity, which derives from the event of Christ's death and resurrection, provides the proper

67. Jüngel, *GMW*, 288.
68. Jüngel, *GMW*, 280, 297.
69. Jüngel, *GMW*, 296–97.

understanding of distinction between God and humanity. It asserts that God has happened and spoken to human as humanity's "Other." It opens the possibility of thinking and speaking of God responsibly. In Jüngel's word, it enables our theological discourse to "correspond to God."[70]

In this sense, the doctrine of the Trinity is not only a doctrine of God's reality revealed, but also is a responsible human articulation of God which allows the possibility of human acknowledgment of God as our "Other." When we come to compare Jenson's Trinitarianism with Jüngel's in the section three, I will show that this concern with otherness is the means to revise Jenson's theology.

2. The Doctrine of the Trinity as Jüngel's Solution for Contemporary Theological *Aporia*

This section will examine Jüngel's account of the possibility of thinking God. For Jüngel, the doctrine of the Trinity, as "thinking after" God, opens the possibility of knowing God to modern theology. It indicates that God reveals himself to humans in his word-event. Because God has spoken and happened as the Trinity, humanity may speak and think of God. Humans can think and speak of God through his word in faith. He develops a linguistic ontology to explain that thinking and speaking God through his word in faith is the most proper way for human's participation in God.

The possibility of thinking God, which founded on our faith in the Word of God—the crucified God, leads the question of the relation between faith and God's death. Jüngel argues that if we affirm the ontological primacy of possibility, God's self-determination to become perishable provides us a firm basis for affirming the thinkability of God. After affirming the possibility of thinking God, Jüngel's concepts of analogy and humanity of God will be introduced. From these two concepts, he shows that God can be thought of and spoken of because of his coming. In God's coming to human, God is identified with the crucified man Jesus. However, God remains to be himself in his becoming. Jüngel claims that through God's being-in-becoming a genuine correspondence between God and humanity is established. The concept of correspondence reminds us that God's reality is revealed while human participates in God as God's "other." A communion between God and humans can take place while their distinction is preserved.

---

70. Jüngel, *GMW*, 227.

2.1 Thinking God as "Thinking after"

Jüngel suggests that if we want to overcome the *aporia*—the impossibility of thinking God, we should "learn to think both *God* and *thought* anew."[71] For Jüngel, thought can *think God* anew and truly think God only if it is "being taken along" by God and "thinking after" God.[72] Only when thought follows behind God and traces God's act, it thinks God as the subject of himself rather than as a human conjecture. He insists that thinking after God and with God is not "an arbitrary possibility." Rather, "it is a possibility already determined by the existence of biblical texts and claimed already by faith in God." Christian faith asserts that the Bible is "a history which, beyond the momentary aspect of the 'I think,' implies experiences of God which have happened and are promised."[73] God becomes accessible for humans in and through the man Jesus.[74] Human thought of God is thinking after that event of God which Jesus Christ is. Jüngel argues that the Bible offers us "a possibility" of thinking and speaking God without which contemporary theology faces only an *aporia*:

> The biblical texts are, as fixed processes of tradition which express the event of God's self-disclosure in original objectivity, an irreplaceable reality . . . Thus we have designated the reality of the biblical texts as a possibility which leads theology in its task of thinking God as God, but we have called it only a *possibility*. The reality of the Bible *makes it possible* to think God as God.[75]

The assertion—the "reality of the Bible *makes it possible* to think God as God"—is a direct repudiation of the contemporary *aporia* of impossibility of thinking God. For Jüngel, it is impossible for the thinking self, who thinks in a way that determines and separates God's essence (as absolutely transcendent) and existence solely through its thinking, to think God. In other words, the *aporia* shows that if God is a "conjecture" of thought, the only end

---

71. Jüngel, *GMW*, 154. Italics mine.
72. Jüngel, *GMW*, 159.
73. Jüngel, *GMW*, 154.
74. Jüngel, *GMW*, 154–55. Webster neatly summarizes Jüngel's position: "Jüngel's treatment rests on his very sharp sense of the divergence between the Christocentric understanding of God which he advocates and the divinity of the 'tradition of metaphysical theism' which the atheist rejects . . . For on Jüngel's reading it is precisely these 'theistic' affirmations which the atheist rejects. And so if the incompatibility between 'theism' and a genuinely Christian understanding of God can be demonstrated, the atheist's protest loses much of its cogency as a response to the *Christian* faith." See Webster, *Eberhard Jüngel*, 80.
75. Jüngel, *GMW*, 157. Italics Jüngel's.

is "the death of God"—the impossibility of thinking God. On the contrary, he finds that the evangelical theology teaches that it is possible to know and think of God. The reality of the Bible reveals "God *as the one who speaks*."[76] As God speaks, the thought of God is not a conjecture of the thinking self. God is accessible to the thinking self because God speaks of himself as a self-disclosure.[77] God can be thought by the thinking self because God's self-discourse, that is, when the thought is "addressed" by God:

> When thinking endeavors to think God, then the God who is to be thought has already laid claim on it. What constitutes it as *thinking* is that it cannot reduce itself to a zero point with regard to God, in order then "apart from God" (*remoto deo*) to construct a thought of God. It ... is in fact always and already addressed by God, then it can explicate its condition of being addressed only in a thought of God which thinks God "materially" (*materialiter*) as the *one who speaks out of himself*.[78]

Humans can think and speak of God only if God speaks about himself. Christian theological language is not a human projection or construction. God speaks about himself in human language to human as an *address*. In Jüngel's opinion, addressability is the "true" character of human language. Human language is performed as speech. It is an *"event of addressing and being addressed."*[79] Humans can speak of God when God addresses to them.

2.2 Thinking God through Word in Faith: Jüngel's Theology of Language and God-man Distinction

God's address enables humans to speak and think of God. Jüngel's position is not a repetition of any naïve or uncritical realist or referential conception of theological language.[80] On the contrary, he is developing a linguistic ontology[81] to argue that speaking God is a *possibility* which is realized by God's *address* to human in the *trinitarian narrative* of Jesus Christ.

---

76. Jüngel, *GMW*, 157. Italics Jüngel's.
77. Jüngel, *GMW*, 157.
78. Jüngel, *GMW*, 158. Italics Jüngel's.
79. Jüngel, *GMW*, 161. Italics Jüngel's.
80. It should be noted that in this research the term "uncritical realism" is equivalent to "naïve realism," and "ultra-realism."
81. Jüngel's view on the relation of language and being is influenced by Heidegger, Bultmann, Fuchs, and Ebeling. On this topic one can refer to Zimany, *Vehicle for God*, 9–27.

Jüngel demonstrates the closest relation between being, event, and language. Words can become events in which something happens even to the words themselves.[82] This aligns his position with John L. Austin's speech-act theory: language performs something. Speech constitutes a perlocutionary act.[83] More importantly, for Jüngel language is not only an event; it also functions ontologically. The "being of humanity is constituted and organized by the word."[84] So language is not merely signs used by humans, but rather language is constitutive of human beings. Jüngel identifies two ways in which we are linguistic beings: "Two basic characteristics define our linguistic being. We are both those who are *addressed* and those who *state*. We are both at one and the same time."[85]

2.2.1 *The Human as signifying being*

Human as linguistic being who states indicates human has the power to make signs to represent the reality. Human beings are *signifiers*. The power of making signs in Jüngel's opinion is the power "to *manufacture* the world through the representation of actuality in signs."[86] In the process of reality defining, conceptualizing, and sign assigning, thinking and language are coincident. The power of defining, conceptualizing, and assigning is thus an activity. Moreover, it is a "deed" of "domination": "Changes in the world and changes in ourselves are linguistically determined."[87] Through language and thinking, human beings enumerate, interplay, represent, and determine the information that we grasp of the reality. In this process, language provides a possibility for human to use the world and himself or herself (as a part of the world) in a different way from before. Language, being, and event are closely related.

But speaking about the human as signifier creates has two dangers. On the one hand, a human may uncontrollably exert his or her power of signifying, so there is a danger that he or she will overpower and absorb the world. Consequently, the world itself becomes a completely human manufactured and artificial world.[88] The human absorbs the whole world

---

82. Jüngel, *GMW*, 10.
83. Austin, *How to Do Things with Words*, 109, 118–20.
84. Jüngel, "Humanity in Correspondence to God," 145.
85. Jüngel, "Humanity in Correspondence to God," 145. Italics Jüngel's.
86. Jüngel, "Humanity in Correspondence to God," 146. Italics mine.
87. Jüngel, "Humanity in Correspondence to God," 146–47. See also, Jüngel, *GMW*, 171.
88. Jüngel, "Humanity in Correspondence to God," 149.

into his language and dominates the world as his work. On the other hand, that language is an act of domination that makes us human means that we cannot be human unless actively identify ourselves by constructing our own world. Consequently, we are imprisoned by our connection to our linguistically-determined work.[89]

Jüngel finds that our drive to signify eventually leads to the ambition of the modern human to think of himself as "superman." Moreover, because language as an act of domination binds us to our work, we are dominated and imprisoned by our actuality. When language functions as an act of domination, human persons cannot receive their proper otherness either from their relation with others or from their own relationship with their work. Jüngel argues that the unlimited self-securing thinking ego and the metaphysical priority of actuality, which contribute to an inappropriate God-man distinction, are the cause of the contemporary theological *aporia*. The contemporary crisis is the outcome of the unchecked development of human capacity to signify.[90]

2.2.2 Human as linguistic being who is addressed

The concept of the human being as one who is addressed can help us avoid the danger. Jüngel believes that humanity exists "only as those who are addressed."[91] The human is the being who is addressed because the human is first addressed by God. "We are ourselves as hearers. Only because we can hear are we able to speak, think, act, be human."[92]

The human is constituted by address because language as address includes the being of both speaker and hearer. Language as address is an act of inclusion: the person addresses and the person addressed, are drawn into the word event. Jüngel calls this a perlocutionary-attractive act.[93] In such inclusion, the being of addresser and addressee are united in language:

> The word of address affects not only the consciousness of the person addressed but his whole being . . . Yet, even a word of greeting is really more than just a communication penetrating

---

89. Jüngel, "Humanity in Correspondence to God," 149–50.

90. Jüngel, "Humanity in Correspondence to God," 149–51. Indeed, in Jüngel's description the necessary result of Cartesian thinking ego is not different from that of the result of unlimited human capacity to state. See Jüngel, *GMW*, 179.

91. Jüngel, "Humanity in Correspondence to God," 149.

92. Jüngel, "Humanity in Correspondence to God," 145, 150.

93. Jüngel, *GMW*, 10–11. For example, the invective spoken against a person can repudiates one's being by including the person in its meaning. Jüngel describes this language event "approaches too close" and "penetrates deeply into" the person.

the consciousness. There are acts of speaking through which that which is said is actually ascribed to the person being addressed. Beyond that, there are acts of speaking through which the person addressed is, so to speak, drawn into the spoken word by means of what is said. Language does certainly have the function of uniting people with that which is being talked about, uniting them in such a way that not only through the word something penetrates the person's consciousness (*in cogitationem*), but that the entire person is drawn out of himself in the process.[94]

The unity of being occurs when the addresser's and hearer's being are drawn out of themselves and into the language event. In this sense, language, event, and being are closely related. From this logic, Jüngel claims that "being *occurs* as *history* . . . is constituted . . . by the *Word of God.*"[95]

The ontological function of address not only unites two beings. It also distinguishes the addressee as a concrete other from the rest of the world. In an address, for example in the language of love, the partners do not simply address each other. Rather, they also listen to one another and reply. They understand that they are addressed by one another and thus become specific others to one another.[96] When we are addressed, we are being distinguished as "persons": "To be a person means to be able to be addressed by something over against us, which, in the midst of the indissoluble connection of person and work or person and productivity, makes me distinguishable as a self, an 'I.'"[97] In other words, when we are addressed by someone, our ontological distinctiveness is brought into being. Moreover, because in address we give up to assimilate the world with our power to state, we can "remain faithful to the earth."[98]

In the same way the human being as a history constituted by God's word, acknowledges the distinction between God and world. Indeed, such distinction makes the world actual and does not let it become absorbed into God: "God distinguishes himself from the world. And in that he distinguishes himself from the world, God lets the world be actual . . . [I]n the event of Word, God both distinguishes himself from and relates himself to the world."[99]

---

94. Jüngel, *GMW*, 11–12.
95. Jüngel, "The World as Possibility and Actuality," 113. Italics mine.
96. Jüngel, "Humanity in Correspondence to God," 149.
97. Jüngel, "Humanity in Correspondence to God," 150.
98. Jüngel, "Humanity in Correspondence to God," 149.
99. Jüngel, "The World as Possibility and Actuality," 112–13.

Address therefore preserves the ontological relatedness and distinctiveness of the human being; and saves us from becoming indistinguishable from our signifying. Our being occurs as *history*. However, this history is constituted linguistically by God's address. Proper relation and distinction is vital to Jüngel's linguistic ontology.

2.2.3 *Thinking God through his relational word in faith: Establishing proper distinction and relation of God and human*

With the concept of address, Jüngel does not believe that human speech about God is simply a system of symbols which can be freely interpreted or manipulated. Rather God relates *himself* in his word, and so includes his own being in language. As an address God's word is "an *event* which prohibits the separation of the one who spoke the word from that word":[100]

> If word were only an informative symbol which the speaker can leave behind himself, without continuing to be in relationship with it, then reflection would indeed be a curatorial undertaking . . . God's word is . . . not a relict which goes its own way, distant from and without relationship to God; rather, this word is full of relationship, in every regard it is a "relational word."[101]

The concept of "relational word" is important here. That God's word is *relational* means God addresses us with his being. In the language event of God's address, God approaches us, takes us out of ourselves and carries us along with him. In God's relational word, human and God are ontologically related to and distinct from one another.

Jüngel then says that it is possible for human thought to be taken out of itself and carried along with God only in faith. The emphasis on faith guarantees the distinction between God and man in the process of human thinking of God, and provides a proper ground for human semantic participation in God. His purpose is always to safeguard the proper relation and distinction between God and human.

The human cognitive process thought goes through "a reflexive process." It goes out of itself to the thing which is to be thought and distinguishes between itself and that perceived thing. Then thought relates the perceived thing to the thought itself and formulate concepts. Knowledge is thus a result of a combined comprehension of the thought itself and the object perceived. When it has formulated knowledge, thought returns

---

100. Jüngel, *GMW*, 165. Italics Jüngel's.
101. Jüngel, *GMW*, 164–65.

to itself. For this reason, the thinking ego remains distinct from the objects it perceives. Unfortunately, this process also puts thought in a risk of thinking circularly around itself. Human as a signifying being tends to make its own perceptions and experiences absolute and so finally, becomes enclosed within itself.[102]

Jüngel proposes that if human thinking of God wants to avoid this danger, the thinking ego should "follow after faith." Faith for Jüngel is a *being* defined by God's word as well as a human self-definition:

> Faith is . . . the relation of man who responds to the God who addresses him, a relation which is made possible by the event of the God who speaks and which is existentially called into being . . . [F]aith is not only a being defined by God's word but also and simultaneously a self-definition of man . . . In faith . . . I allow myself to be defined by God for self-definition.[103]

The thinking ego with faith is a *being* that unceasingly goes out of itself. As a determination of the human, faith sets thought free to be taken along by God. It does not allow thought to be enclosed within itself. When God is "thought after" by thinking in faith, God is not a thought of the ego. God's relational word becomes *a being* that takes the thinking ego along with it. Thought, in faith, encounters God's being. Moreover, faith always corresponds to God's word alone. When the thinking ego thinks after God, it has its own experience of God. Thought tends to absolutize its own experience, but faith remains critical of our experience. It always distinguishes God from our experience. When humans think God through God's relational word in faith, the distinction between God and human is firmly maintained.[104]

2.2.4 God's word as God's presence in absence: Addressing word, possibility, faith, and deprivation of security

However, God's word is *relational* does not mean that God is *contained* in his word. Jüngel's assertion of God's word and faith is not a naïve repetition of confessional claims about the Bible or revelation. It does not claim Christians have all truth of God simply because they have Scripture and faith. It is not another uncritical realist and referential conception of theological language, for God's word refers and relates to God's reality. On the contrary, Jüngel's analysis of the linguistic character of God's relational *word* shows

---

102. Jüngel, *GMW*, 167–68.
103. Jüngel, *GMW*, 163–64.
104. Jüngel, *GMW*, 167–68.

that his theology advances beyond the alternatives of uncritical realism and expressivism. He asserts that human thinking and speaking of God in faith is only a "possibility." It does not claim that by itself it secures God. Rather, the *certainty* of faith is a "deprivation of security."[105]

Jüngel emphasizes that God approaches us in his relational word as *word*-event. He agrees with Ebeling that "language does not directly unite the speaker and person or persons to whom he is speaking. The encounter always takes place within the context of a particular matter."[106] Though the biblical texts form an "original objectivity" of the event of God's self-disclosure, "they themselves are to be strictly distinguished from the event by the very fact they talk about it. They do not speak the language of God, but rather our human language." "God, even in these texts, does not disclose himself *directly*."[107] In his relational *word*, God does not abolish his distance with human. Conversely, "the word preserves the apartness of God."[108]

The uncritical realist and expressivist controversy makes the presence and absence of an object in its linguistic sign two uncompromising alternatives. But Jüngel argues that God "*is present in the word as the one who is absent*."[109]

For Jüngel, God's presence as absence is necessary for an authentic human thinking after God. Also, through this concept, he links time, language, and being to formulate an ontological account for the possibility of theology. His argument will be significant for our analysis of Jenson's trinitarian theology because of its insight into the importance of linguistics in our discussion of God's history and temporality; as well as the relation and distinction between God and human.

God can be present as the one who is absent in word because God presents himself to humans in his *addressing* word.[110] Jüngel does not follow the traditional route that understands presence and absence in terms of the referential relationship between word (sign) and the thing signified. He deals with them in terms of the temporal experience of the consciousness of human ego during its interaction with language and reality.

The human is the signifier who is addressed. These two modes of being form two different ontological situations. As the signifier the human who is

---

105. Jüngel, *GMW*, 170.
106. Jüngel, *GMW*, 165.
107. Jüngel, *GMW*, 157. Italics Jüngel's.
108. Jüngel, *GMW*, 157.
109. Jüngel, *GMW*, 169. Italics mine.
110. Jüngel, *GMW*, 170.

present and conscious is in relation with *existing things*. The human is the one who is addressed—an addressee.[111]

The *presence* of an *existing thing* is disclosed to the conscious ego as a "here and now point." Spatially speaking, a present thing always has its specific place or location. It is its "here." The place can change and let the thing be present here or there. Temporally speaking, a present thing is the thing that is present *now* to the conscious ego. To put the spatial and temporal dimensions together, when one says that a thing is present, "one must be able to say that it is now here and only here." Jüngel comes to assert that: the "present of a thing is, therefore, always for a 'now' and restricted to a 'here.' The present thing exists in the *identity* of Here and Now."[112]

The present thing now and here can be *expressed* meaningfully only when the ego consciously relates itself to the present thing. Therefore, it cannot be thought of absent if it is expressed by the ego.[113] Moreover, this expression is done through language. Interestingly, though the ego as a subject is here and now in and of itself, it cannot be distinguished unless it is *there at all*. In this way, the ego "is profoundly determined by what encounters it from outside itself, that which lays claim on it."[114] The distinction between the *there* of the present thing and the *here* of ego can only be experienced if the ego distinguishes or describes the present thing from itself in language. Consequently, the existence or the "being there" of the ego is defined by the word of the present thing: "the ego is always defined by a word which lays claim to it."[115] Again, it shows that human ego is constituted by language. Language, as the power to state and present, is a power that dominates humans.

The presence of *existing things* does not only dominate human linguistically, it also locks the conscious ego in the present. Jüngel finds that the personal presence of human's conscious ego would be reduced to the *identity* of a series of *here and now points* through the *things presented* to it if the ego were only encountered by the presence of existing things: "The state of 'being there' would be, in this mere claim made by an externally present thing, fixed on the unopened, closed identity of the ego–here–now points."[116] In other words, the *presence* of existing things here and now flattens the ego's temporal horizon to a series of heres and nows. Existing things dominate humans

---

111. Jüngel, *GMW*, 170.
112. Jüngel, *GMW*, 171. Italics mine.
113. Jüngel, *GMW*, 172.
114. Jüngel, *GMW*, 171.
115. Jüngel, *GMW*, 171.
116. Jüngel, *GMW*, 171.

linguistically. They lock the conscious ego into a closed identity of here and now. Finally, it makes humans identical to things.

By contrast, as a being who is *addressed*, the presence of the human is fundamentally different from the presence of *existing things*. While the present *things* dominate the conscious ego linguistically, the addressing word approaches the addressed ego in a way that lets the ego come to itself.[117] Therefore, the ego can preserve its own distinctiveness in its relation with addressing word.

More importantly, Jüngel argues that when the conscious ego is in relation with the addressing word, the ego *gains* time. An addressing word is here and now when it addresses the ego. However, it, unlike a present thing, addresses the ego "about something which does not necessarily belong to the identity of ego–now–here."[118] The "something" which is beyond the here and now of the ego provides the ego an "existential distancing." If the "thing" that the addressing word refers the ego to is something *absent*, the ego experiences this existential distancing through something which is "Not–Here–Now." However, in this case, the *absent* "thing" which is "not–here–now" is not nothing. Rather, it is a *being* that addresses the addressed ego through addressing word. As this being is not *here*, the addressed ego is required to relate the *past* and the *future* with its now. Therefore, the ego can experience the temporal-spatial dimension other than here and now through the *presence* in *absence* of the being in addressing word.[119]

For Jüngel, such distancing does not mean the ego loses its consciousness of its presence. On the contrary, this distancing takes place when the addressing word *comes near* to the conscious ego. It enables the ego addressed to differentiate itself from the "ego–here–now point." Thus, it provides the ego with past and future dimensions. When this temporal experience is attained, "the ego's own status of being there is disclosed to it as the present."[120] Jüngel describes the ego that gains its conscious presence *the ego as spirit*. Because the ego as spirit is being addressed by another word and is expected to response, the spirit that can be "present" to the ego itself in temporality is a "living being having word."[121] In other words, *the ego as spirit* is a state of conscious presence which is the result of being addressed. The ego that gains temporality and speech experiences a *spiritual presence*. In spiritual presence, the ego, away from its ego–here–now point, experiences itself and

---

117. Jüngel, *GMW*, 172.
118. Jüngel, *GMW*, 172.
119. Jüngel, *GMW*, 172.
120. Jüngel, *GMW*, 173.
121. Jüngel, *GMW*, 174.

the world anew. *In short, a relational word though is present as the one who is absent; it as an addressing word enables the ego to gain time, to experience anew, and to properly relate with and distinct from the others.*

Through the concept of addressing word, Jüngel crafts a linguistic ontology that integrates being, language, and temporality. In this linguistic ontology, the being or existence is not defined by physical presence. Therefore, God's presence as who is absent in his relational word does not mean God's encounter with human in his word is not true. Rather, as an addressing word, God is a true other to humans who calls human's authentic being into presence. God encounters humans into spiritual presence. This is possible because God is Spirit.[122]

All of Jüngel's maneuvers direct us to this point: humans become authentic, and become different from things, through their relations with other beings in address. If one is open to the address of someone else, one enters into a relation of trust or faith. We return to Jüngel's claim of faith as thinking after or being taken along:

> [M]an is truly human in that he is able to place himself in dependence on someone other than himself... *I am human in that I let someone else be there for me.* That can also be called trust, and with regard to the "someone else" who as God has promised himself to us, we must call this *trust in God*. This is precisely what is meant when we speak of *faith*.[123]

The human is the linguistic being who is addressed and related to others in trust or faith. Faith is being taken along by God's word, and God in his addressing word expresses his most inward being without reservation:[124] "faith is participation in God himself."[125] In faith, we are placed outside ourselves:

> Without a fundamental *extra nos* ("outside ourselves") faith knows of no *deus pro nobis* ("God for us") and certainly no *deus in nobis* ("God in us"). God is only *near* to us in that he distances us from ourselves. As one who distances us from ourselves, God is certainly the one who is farthest away from the man who seeks to exist in and of himself, who seeks to will in and of himself, and thus insists on himself. The converse is simultaneously true: this fundamental "us being outside ourselves" (*nos extra nos esse*) is as such identical with the nearness of God... When

---

122. Jüngel, *GMW*, 174–75.
123. Jüngel, *GMW*, 179–80. Italics Jüngel's.
124. Jüngel, *GMW*, 177.
125. Jüngel, *GMW*, 176.

we, in listening to his word, are outside ourselves, then God is already there for us.[126]

For Jüngel, trust or faith is defined as "certainty which removes security."[127] Because trust requires humans to go out from themselves and be challenged by others, humans cannot have trust without being deprived of their self-attained security. Likewise, human relationship with God, which establishes with trust or faith in God, is "an event of certainty which removes security."[128] The most notable evidence of such deprivation of security in God-man relation is that faith "allows God as the absent one to be present."[129] In faith, humans realize that God, as their other, is distinct from him or herself as long as he or she participates in God through his addressing word. However, the certainty of this participation is not secured by the thinking ego. Rather, the certainty is affirmed through human's relatedness to God in faith. Consequently, humans can think and speak of God in faith even though his existence cannot be grasped as a presented thing by the thinking ego.

In Jüngel's linguistic ontology, words in faith make us possible to think and speak of God. In this sense, language becomes the "more original phenomenon" than thought or consciousness.[130]

2.2.5 *Summary*

In this sub-section, I argue that through the concepts of "relational word" and "faith," Jüngel's assertion is not a naïve repetition of confessional claim of the authority of the Bible and revelation. It does not claim that, with the Bible, Christians have secured all truth of God. Rather, it argues only that the truth of God is a "possibility." Jüngel emphasizes that though the biblical texts form an "original objectivity" of the event of God's self-disclosure, "they themselves are strictly distinguished from the event by the very fact they talk about it. They do not speak the language of God, but rather our human language." "God, even in these texts, does not disclose himself *directly*."[131] God's word "preserves the apartness of God."[132] The most appropriate way

---

126. Jüngel, *GMW*, 182–83. Italics Jüngel's.
127. Jüngel, *GMW*, 196.
128. Jüngel, *GMW*, 196.
129. Jüngel, *GMW*, 182.
130. Jüngel, *GMW*, 300.
131. Jüngel, *GMW*, 157. Italics Jüngel's.
132. Jüngel, *GMW*, 165.

for God to be related to humans, in Jüngel's linguistic ontology, relates to God as an addressing word that present as the one who is absent.

According to the logic of Jüngel's linguistic ontology, the urge for the certainty of God's existence through *representation* (i.e., present thing) of Cartesian philosophical thinking succeeds only in making humans inhuman and enclosed within themselves.[133] But God encounters to humans in *faith*. Faith removes human self-security and establishes the certainty of God's addressing word. Jüngel's argument persistently emphasizes that humans cannot conjecture God. God cannot be human's "thinking thing." Humans can only think of God by means of "thinking after," and he can only be known as a concrete other. This other cannot be known as if he had not spoken. The distinction between God and humans must be assumed, but this difference between God and humans does not mean we are alienated totally from him. Rather, because in his word God addresses humans with his own being, humans may participate in God through faith.

2.3 God's Word Event and the Doctrine of the Trinity

In the first section, I argued that for Jüngel the traditional metaphysics has produced the three problems that have created the contemporary theological *aporia*: (1) the Cartesian metaphysics of the *cogito*; (2) the subordination of possibility to actuality; and (3) the view the anthropomorphism of language makes it theologically deficient. These three problems can be related to an improper understanding of the God-man distinction. I argued that Jüngel's linguistic ontology provides an ontological critique of the metaphysics of the *cogito*, and provides an alternative account of the relation and distinction of God and human. In this sub-section, I will argue that the death and the resurrection of Jesus Christ are Jüngel's answers for the latter two problems. The event of the incarnation and crucifixion of Jesus Christ states that: (1) the humanity of God provides a proper anthropomorphism or analogical language for human God talk; (2) The death and resurrection of the Son show that humans have a new possibility—hope—and are not captive to the power of death. All three contemporary theological problems thus receive an answer. Humans can think and speak of God in faith because God speaks out of himself to humans in the incarnation and death of Jesus Christ.

God's addressing word, and the incarnation and death of Jesus Christ are not three separated events in Jüngel's theology. They are integrated parts

---

133. Jüngel, *GMW*, 177–80.

of the event of God's coming near to humanity.[134] Christian faith proclaims that, because God is love, he identifies himself with the executed Jesus of Nazareth. God himself spoke to humanity in this crucified one. Because God is love, through Jesus's story we also find that God has related and differentiated himself in a threefold way in his unity: Father, Son, and the Spirit.[135] Thus, the death and resurrection of Jesus as God's addressing word to humanity brings us to the doctrine of the Trinity: "The Christian doctrine of the triune God is the epitome of the story of Jesus Christ, because the reality of God's history with man comes to its truth in the differentiation of the one God into the three persons of the Father, the Son, and the Holy Spirit."[136] Finally, we find that the trinitarian theology which asserts that God addresses humanity and thus provides the means for humanity to "thinking after" God, establishes a proper relation and distinction of God and humanity, opens the possibility of knowing God, and serves as a forceful reply to the challenge of contemporary theological *aporia*.

2.3.1 God's death as creative suffering and possibility, and thinkability of God

In the first section of this chapter, I examined Jüngel's view that the subordination of possibility to actuality hinders contemporary theological thought. Traditional metaphysics posits God as an absolutely transcendent being who, because he is immortal, cannot tolerate "God on the Cross." Contemporary talk about the death of God intends to show the absurdity and inconceivability of this metaphysical transcendent God for modern minds. "God cannot die" is a presupposition only of traditional metaphysics. But for Christian theology, God's addressing word is the word of the Cross. Thinking God's unity with mortality is a theological necessity.[137] Jüngel asserts that "'God on the cross' is not only the negation of all arbitrary concepts of God but positively is a God who with his own being confronts the nothingness which is present in all perishability."[138]

Traditional metaphysics is anxious about mortality because it is "a tendency toward nothingness."[139] Jüngel finds that the annihilating power of nothingness is its ontological placeless. This placeless is an absolutely

---

134. Jüngel, *GMW*, 190–91.
135. Jüngel, *GMW*, 368.
136. Jüngel, *GMW*, 344.
137. Jüngel, *GMW*, 199.
138. Jüngel, *GMW*, 210.
139. Jüngel, *GMW*, 211.

THEOLOGY OF POSSIBILITY AND THEOLOGY OF ACTUALITY 219

undefined and empty state, which is like a "negative virulent vacuum," absorbs all being into itself—into nothingness. It annihilates what exists. For Jüngel, nothingness is annihilating because it is totally egocentric:

> Nothingness does not let itself be precisely located . . . It absorbs being until it is full, so to speak, by annihilating what exists. But because it takes being into itself only in the attraction of annihilation, it never has being. *And because it never has being, it must constantly seize hold of being in the act of annihilation.* Because it has nothing, its "egoism" is total, and it wants everything.[140]

Because of the threat of nothingness, mortality is judged a misfortune. In order to avoid this negatively-defined mortality, traditional metaphysics longs for a being that will never pass away. It defines eternity as a "permanent now"—the Now that is timeless, and imperishable. The "permanent now" is *the real and only real.*[141] But as I have argued, Jüngel does not believe the permanent present is a good thing. He argues that "the idea of the 'permanent now' misses the true dignity of time, and along with it the positive character for perishability."[142] The desire for "permanent now," on the one hand, encourages humans to conceive of God as an absolute transcendent being who cannot die, and leads to our contemporary theological *aporia*. On the other hand, as we have also seen, it means that humans are not able to tolerate any real otherness but wish to remain enclosed within themselves.

Jüngel recognizes that perishability leads to nothingness, but he does not believe that mortality is totally negative. The essential goodness of mortality is disclosed as *history*.[143] Perishability is a product of temporality. For temporal beings, even the farthest future will become past—perished.[144] If the past is the end of present being, the perished past leads to nothingness. But Jüngel argues that the past which perishes may not disappear into nothingness. When a being perishes and becomes past, it makes room for what is to follow. There is the possibility that it will be succeeded. The past represents the possibility that new things will come into being. More importantly, this possibility is not cancelled by its realization. It remains realized past and can still be evoked in the future again by the actual. In this sense, possibility links up the past, present, and future of a being. In temporality,

---

140. Jüngel, *GMW*, 219. Italics mine.
141. Jüngel, *GMW*, 211–13.
142. Jüngel, *GMW*, 213.
143. Jüngel, *GMW*, 215.
144. Jüngel, *GMW*, 210.

beings cannot avoid perishability, but perishability can be good because it represents possibility:

> [I]f ... the possibility of the past may be repeated, then what is past remains related to the future as something past ... The past does not have to disappear into nothingness. It does not have to be nothing, does not have to be destroyed. The loss of its reality is not also the loss of its possibility. Even the elementary fact of historical memory contradicts that. "Memory" (*memoria*) preserves the possibility of past reality.[145]

Because perishability represents either the possibility or disintegration into nothingness, it "is the struggle between possibility and nothingness."[146] Jüngel clearly points out that nothingness is called into being by *sin*. It is sin to give nothingness a power of annihilation.[147] For Christian faith, the death and resurrection of Jesus Christ indicates that God exactly involves himself in nothingness and triumphs over it. He finds that in God's death and resurrection, nothingness losses its negative annihilating effect. Nothingness is transformed into the power of creating possibility. God's death and resurrection thus overturns the world's confinement in actuality and overrules the threat of nothingness. In Jüngel's word, it lets "the possible become possible and hands over to perish that which has become impossible."[148] Through death and resurrection, God places nothingness into his own being and creatively redetermines nothingness towards into a new direction. In God's death and resurrection, God redetermines nothingness as *love*. Because God is love, God gives himself for the sake of others. He thus subjects himself immediately to nothingness—death. As love, nothingness is not an annihilating power. It is a power to grant possibilities of being for others:

> Whoever really is for others and seeks to be himself in that, always subjects himself immediately to nothingness. In this self-determination for the sake of others, this peculiar dialectic of being and nonbeing, of life and death, takes place, which as pacified dialectic is called love.[149]

If God is love, God's death and his involvement in nothingness is "the most original self-determination of God."[150] Nothingness is no longer

---

145. Jüngel, *GMW*, 215–16.
146. Jüngel, *GMW*, 217.
147. Jüngel, *Justification*, 112.
148. Jüngel, "The World as Possibility and Actuality," 113.
149. Jüngel, *GMW*, 219–20.
150. Jüngel, *GMW*, 220.

ontological placeless. It is determined by God's self-determination for others. In God's love it is impossible for nothingness to exercise its annihilating power. Moreover, though God's self-determination is his innermost involvement, it is not an inner necessity for God. God determines himself to experience death because of love. Love can never be coerced but exists in freedom. In this sense, freedom is a constitutive moment in love. God's love happens in his freedom, in his self-determination.[151]

God's death is therefore no unthinkable theological *aporia*. Rather it is the event in which God's addressing word comes to humans—the Word becomes flesh. Because God is identified with the man Jesus, Jesus's death and resurrection shows that "God is in and of himself in such a way that he is for man."[152] From this word-event, "God communicates with himself without withholding himself from others."[153] God addresses us with his very own being. Also, in God's death and resurrection, God helps us to come out from the anxiety of annihilating nothingness and grants us new possibilities and freedom. As a ground for new possibility, death is thus not an inadmissible category for God.

In this event God remains a concrete other—a lover—of human being. God's death and resurrection thus helps us escape the egoism of the metaphysics of the "*cogito*," and our desire of present permanence. It establishes a firm relation and otherness between God and the others—human beings—that God loves. For Christians, God is neither *pure actuality* nor *immutable*. Rather he is the one who died for us. In the relation and otherness of God and human, God is thinkable even he involves himself in death.

Finally, with this understanding of God's love, death, and possibility, the world may liberate itself from its uncritical subordination of possibility to actuality or reality (*Wirklichkeit*). It frees us from the nostalgia of uncritical realism in our thinking of God, especially the triune God. From the viewpoint of self-defined human actuality, we demand the Trinity should be verified by our present history, in which God is unthinkable, unspeakable, and non-actual. However, God's word is a promise that makes possibility possible, and a judgment that makes impossibility impossible.[154] Christians discern that it is not actuality but God's word decides what is true and possible; because our "being occurs as history . . . is constituted . . . by the Word of God."[155] We realize that "every step within history has become possible

---

151. Jüngel, *GMW*, 221–22.
152. Jüngel, *GMW*, 221.
153. Jüngel, *GMW*, 220–21.
154. Jüngel, "The World as Possibility and Actuality," 112–13.
155. Jüngel, *GMW*, 113.

(that is, has been made possible by God's word) as a step out of nothingness into history."[156] Nothingness is something "non-actual." God's word converts nothingness into possibility. The historic reality cannot verify God, but God's word makes the actual history become possible:

> God who speaks out of himself assigns to possibility an ontological priority over reality, so that reality stands totally at the service of the possibilities which condition it and which are also conditioned by it. What is impossible for men is *possible* for God according to the judgment of faith (Mark 10:27). And faith participates in the possibilities of God, that faith which by no means leaps over reality but which can be asserted by God (or Jesus) alone against unbelief (Mark 9:23f).[157]

For Christians, "we are concerned with truth (as opposed to actuality)."[158] Jüngel asserts that "truth" is God's love and creative "Yes." It is God's justification and judgment. *In short, "truth" is God's event. Conversely, sin is defined as "untruth," but it is human's reality. It is the reality of human's rejection of God's love.* Therefore, truth for human is an "interruption."[159] One should note that, therefore, there are "in this sense no true theological sentences at all, because truth understood theologically does not permit of measurement by a positivistically understood criterion of truth."[160]

With his reinterpretation of death, nothingness, reality, possibility, and truth, Jüngel's assertion of the priority of possibility gives us another thread by which contemporary theology may grasp the possibility of thinking the triune God.

2.3.2 Proper analogical speech of God and God's word event

Besides the impossibility of thinking God's death, the contemporary theological *aporia* cannot speak of God because it is trapped by the unfortunate mutual opposition of "dogmatic" anthropomorphism and "symbolic" anthropomorphism. The former destroys the distinction between God and humans by speaking of God like a man while the latter defines God and humanity by setting them in opposition and therefore as antagonists.[161]

---

156. Jüngel, *GMW*, 114.
157. Jüngel, *GMW*, 310.
158. Jüngel, "The World as Possibility and Actuality," 110.
159. Jüngel, *Justification*, 81, 103–10; Jüngel, "God—As a Word of Our Language," 40–43.
160. Jüngel, "God—As a Word of Our Language," 39–40.
161. Jüngel indicates that he borrows this categorization of anthropomorphism from Kant. See Jüngel, "Anthropomorphism," 90–91.

The traditional analogy of proportionality, which wants to speak God in human language and accepts a symbolic anthropomorphism, ends in the assertion of the impossibility of speaking of God. Finally, the question of God's speakability reaches deadlock.

Jüngel argues that for the difference between God and humanity, "there can be no responsible talk about God without analogy."[162] In other words, human speech of God must be analogical. The failure of the traditional analogy of proportionality is not its insistence of speaking God analogically but that it finally believes that there is no final connection between God and the world, which makes all theological analogical discourse inauthentic.

This predicament is overcome when Christian theology fully realizes the incarnation as the word event of God's coming to humanity.[163] God's incarnation is the proper analogical speech of God. It is the *analogy of advent*. Unlike the traditional analogy of proportionality, the analogy of advent affirms that God *relates himself* to humans while remaining *different* from us.

In the event of the incarnation, God *relates himself* to humanity because God comes to humans, and speaks to humans, *as a human*: "God is thinkable as one who speaks because and to the extent that he is human in and of himself."[164] God addresses human with his word. God's word is Jesus Christ, *God Incarnate*. He is truly God and truly man. God's word comes close to humans in human words and *so* makes himself knowable. Here we must reiterate Jüngel's linguistic ontology. Speech is not just a voice, but the person themselves. God's speech is not just a voice but the person and the event of that person's arrival. The analogy of advent—the incarnation of God's word—"is in an eminent sense a *language event*."[165] It is God's "arrival-in-language." God's being is in his word-event: God "introduces himself in that he arrives. And this . . . arrival belongs to his very being which he reveals as arriving . . . [It] takes place as an arrival-in-language."[166]

In this language event, God's word is not merely the epistemological device that provides the knowledge of God. It is the event that brings into being the relationship of God with humans. Because God's being in his word takes place in human language, and humans are linguistic beings, the relations that God's word event brings into being are not something external to God or to humanity. Rather, Jesus Christ as God's word is the carrying

---

162. Jüngel, *GMW*, 281.
163. Jüngel, *GMW*, 296–97.
164. Jüngel, *GMW*, 289.
165. Jüngel, *GMW*, 289. Italics Jüngel's.
166. Jüngel, *GMW*, 286.

out of the linguistic being of God and humanity. Jüngel explains how this integration of being, language, and relation takes place:

> God relates to his word not only in a way similar to that in which man relates to his word, but God relates to his word in such a way that he thereby relates to man, and in a very particular way relates to man's relationship to his own word . . . The relations *happen* to the degree that in them—and not only in one of them—God relates to himself. The relations are therefore not external relationships over against the *relata*, but rather the *executions* of language behavior which bring the *relata*, who are entering into relationship to each other, to a new relation which profoundly determines their very being.[167]

In other words, because the relations in God's word event—God's arrival in human language—are ontological as well as linguistic, Jüngel argues that the analogy of advent effectively integrates language, relations (proportions), and beings to form an authentic human speech of God precisely because God *relates himself* to humans in human language.

The word event in which God relates himself to humans is *analogical*. The analogy of advent is not a dogmatic anthropomorphism because the difference between God and human is firmly upheld. Though the gospel requires us to accept the doctrine of the *communicatio idiomatum* (communication of attributes) because God incarnates as Jesus Christ,[168] Scripture shows that we cannot reverse this direction to say human being *is* God. For Jüngel, it is "monstrous" if a human claims that "I am man and God to him (God)": "For nothing is worse for man than for him to cease to be a mere man."[169]

In order to keep the distinction between of God and humanity without falling back into any metaphysical description of their opposition, Jüngel defines their distinction in terms of the *humanity of God* and the *humanity of human being*. It is "the difference of a still greater similarity between God and man in the midst of a great dissimilarity."[170] He asserts that God in the word event of incarnation "carries out his divinity's own humanity, in order to make concrete the difference between his divinity's own humanity and

---

167. Jüngel, *GMW*, 289.

168. Jüngel, *GMW*, 96: "According to his nature God cannot die, but since God and man are united in one person, it is correct to talk about God's death when that man dies who is one thing or one person with God."

169. Jüngel, *GMW*, 334. See also, Jüngel, "Humanity in Correspondence to God," 152.

170. Jüngel, *GMW*, 288.

the humanity of man . . . [T]he mystery of the God who identifies with the man Jesus is the increase of similarity and nearness between God and man which is *more than mere identity* and which reveals the *concrete difference* between God and man."[171] Therefore, human words can speak of God not because they come too close to God, which would make a dogmatic anthropomorphism. But human words speak of God because in revelation "God becomes accessible as God in language."[172]

One question needs to be clarified at this point. How can Jesus's humanity be true humanity if it is different from the humanity of human being? The answer is found in Jüngel's linguistic ontology and doctrine of justification. He believes that the being of humanity as creature is a hearer of God's word. In other words, humans are addressed. "The being of humanity is constituted and organized by the word. We are ourselves as hearers. Only because we can hear we are able to speak, think, act, be human. As hearers we center ourselves upon God's relation to us, in order to correspond to our God."[173] However, because of sin, all humanity is under "a compulsion to relationlessness and dissociation." In sin, human desires "to be like God and to achieve a reckless self-actualization." They are imprisoned in "the urge to subjugate all other relationships to one's relationship with oneself."[174] Jüngel follows Barth in asserting that the "humanity 'of the lineage of Adam' does not constitute true human existence, but rather its mendacity and lostness."[175]

Therefore, there is no true humanity in human being. For Christian faith "the meanings of 'God' and 'humanity' are defined by reference to the person of Jesus Christ,"[176] the *one* man who is crucified and accursed for the sake of *all* humanity. The *being* of Jesus is "the *event* of a selflessness which surpasses all self-relatedness . . . As such, it was the being of a man who corresponded to God, and it was the human parable of the God who is love."[177] Through this man, all humanity that does not correspond to God, is brought into correspondence.[178] The basic feature of Jesus's humanity is "a being in the act of the word of the kingdom of God," in which "a qualitatively new

---

171. Jüngel, *GMW*, 288. Italics Jüngel's.
172. Jüngel, *GMW*, 288.
173. Jüngel, "Humanity in Correspondence to God," 145.
174. Jüngel, *Justification*, 131.
175. Jüngel, "The Royal Man," 134.
176. Jüngel, "Humanity in Correspondence to God," 132. See Jüngel, *GMW*, 341.
177. Jüngel, *GMW*, 358.
178. Jüngel, "Humanity in Correspondence to God," 133.

fellowship with God" is found.[179] However, one should bear in mind that it is *God* identifies *himself* in the *one* man Jesus for the sake of *all* human. Therefore, true humanity is God's humanity in Jesus and not a general quality of human being.[180] In other words, God's humanity is God's event of reconciliation or justification.[181] Because of sin and God's justification, there is a concrete difference between the humanity of human being and God's humanity. It is a difference between sinner and righteous.[182]

The relationship and difference of God and humanity in the event of God's linguistic coming indicate that in the midst of a great dissimilarity there is a still greater similarity between God and man. The coming of God to man is therefore analogical. It compels us to say that "Jesus is the parable of God," and the gospel is the *event* that *corresponds* to God.[183] God's word event enables human speech of God because it *corresponds* to God, and this *correspondence* maintains the *difference* between God and human.

In short, the gospel is the event in which God *speaks* to humans and it is the event in which God *relates himself* to humans. Because of the similarity and dissimilarity between the humanity of God and the humanity of human being in this event, humans know and speak of God through this word event *analogically*. Because of the linguistic nature of the relations between God and human in this event, humanity *relates* to God through this word event analogically.

We should note that human language does not automatically possess the capacity of corresponding to God. Rather, the correspondence comes from God's commitment to carry out his relationship to himself and to world in human language. For human, to "correspond to God is a possibility which comes to language from God."[184] God's speakability is always a possibility for humans and a promise for God. Without God's word-event, language cannot speak of God. One could even say that we cannot speak and think of God through human language outside the context of God's word-event. This discovery frees humans from their obstinacy in looking for a natural referential relationship of human language to God's reality, which is what naïve realism seeks to do. As Jüngel states, in thinking God's relation to human in his word event—incarnation of Jesus, of which it is the

---

179. Jüngel, *GMW*, 353.

180. Jüngel, *GMW*, 299.

181. Jüngel, "Humanity in Correspondence to God," 132–33; Jüngel, *Justification*, 79.

182. Jüngel, *Justification*, 82.

183. Jüngel, *GMW*, 286.

184. Jüngel, *GMW*, 289.

parable of God, "the difference between *signum* and *res significata* ('sign' and 'signified thing')" "is totally inappropriate."[185]

2.3.3 God's word event, knowledge of God, and the doctrine of the Trinity

Humans may speak and know God because of God's word event in an analogy of advent which shows that the relatedness of God and humanity is greater than the difference of God from humanity. Jüngel further argues that it is God's self-relatedness and differentiation of this event requires us to understand God as triune.[186] It is the doctrine of the Trinity enables us to speak God in the midst of the challenge of theological *aporia* of God's death.

God's word event is an event of justification and reconciliation. In this event, God identifies with Jesus the man who is crucified for the sake of all humans, to inaugurate a new relationship with them. Jesus's life and death, because of this identification, is an act of God himself. Moreover, according to Jüngel, to "identify oneself with another, foreign essence implies the capacity to differentiate oneself."[187] Accordingly, in Jesus's death, *God defines himself* when he identifies with Jesus on the one hand; and he *defines the man Jesus as* the Son of God on the other hand.[188] Therefore, God's word event "implies a self-differentiation on God's part."[189] We have to speak of God the Father and God the Son in this event.

In God's word event, God also is Spirit. Jüngel even defines "God as event of the Spirit."[190] He interprets Spirit as "relationship of relationships,"[191] and "mediation."[192]

For Jüngel, God can be considered as event of the Spirit because God is love. God the Father and God the Son are in loving relationship, and it happens in God's word event. In being as love, God relates himself to the man Jesus and his death for the sake for whole humanity.[193] But death cannot be an event for death is pure eventlessness.[194] If death is the final

---

185. Jüngel, *GMW*, 294.
186. Jüngel, *GMW*, 351.
187. Jüngel, *GMW*, 363.
188. Jüngel, *GMW*, 363–64.
189. Jüngel, *GMW*, 363.
190. Jüngel, *GMW*, 374.
191. Jüngel, *GMW*, 374.
192. Jüngel, *GMW*, 388.
193. Jüngel, *GMW*, 329.
194. Jüngel, *GMW*, 363.

ending of Jesus Christ, God the Father and God the Son are eternally separated. It ceases the mutual love between the loving Father and the beloved Son. Also, for sinful humanity the passion story of Jesus Christ can only be a lamentation if death is its conclusion. It results in humanity's desperate loss of relatedness.[195]

According to the New Testament, death cannot be the finale of God's word event. It teaches Jesus's resurrection from the dead rather than a tragic death. Resurrection shows that God's love finally triumphs over death. Because of the resurrection, the loving Father *relates* the beloved Son with the mutual love even in the midst of the separation of death. In love, God the Father and God the Son are united. This love as God's new relationship comes from resurrection. The Bible teaches that resurrection is accomplished in the power of Holy Spirit. One should note that "resurrection from the dead," according to Jüngel, is "the eternally new relationship of God to God," and "ontologically the being of love itself."[196] At the same time, this relationship is the *Holy Spirit*.[197] Thus, he asserts that "the Holy Spirit is a third divine relationship, namely, the relationship between the relationships of the Father and the Son, that is, the relationship of the relationships and thus an eternally new relationship of God to God."[198] In this relationship, God also draws the death of the sinful human into his eternal life so that the human can be saved from the annihilation of the death. The Spirit is the one who establishes "the link between Father and Son in such a way that man is drawn into this love relationship." In that, God is "the *one and living* God."[199]

God's word event of death and resurrection eventually leads us to the doctrine of Trinity. In this event, God is differentiated, related, and united as Father, Son, and Spirit: "[T]he perfected identification of God with the crucified man Jesus is the mutual work of the Father, the Son, and the Holy Spirit . . . Only in this threefold differentiation of the being of God does the statement that God is love become understandable."[200]

In other words, resurrection is understood as an event of establishing or renewing relationship. The relationship incurred in this event is love. The "link" or "relationship" that unites the love of Father and Son is that love which the Spirit is. Jüngel integrates this theological assertion with his linguistic ontology and comes to conclude that "God as event of

195. Jüngel, *GMW*, 328–29.
196. Jüngel, *GMW*, 374.
197. Jüngel, *GMW*, 374.
198. Jüngel, *GMW*, 374.
199. Jüngel, *GMW*, 328.
200. Jüngel, *GMW*, 328–29.

the Spirit." For him, the sinful human is egocentric. Without the Spirit, who establishes relationship, human cannot come out of himself or herself to relate to God. One may recall it is his assertion that an ego, which is addressed by an authentic other, experiences "spiritual presence."[201] For humans, God is known and spoken only because of the Spirit. Because the ego gains its power to speak of God only when the Spirit *comes* to it, the whole process is an event by itself:

> [O]ne can hear and see the eternal word of God only because it was present in the personal union with the man Jesus . . . This identity with the man Jesus which brings God into language is, however, not directly present to every man and to every historical reality, in its historical uniqueness . . . The significance of that event must become an event itself. For, although God has become speakable, addressable, perceivable, and knowable as God in his son, that is not reason alone for us to know, perceive, address, and call him God. We cannot do it without God the Holy Spirit relating to us once more in order to establish himself with us. We do not press through to God; rather, the Holy Spirit presses through to us . . . In the power of the Spirit, man shares himself rather than possessing himself, shares himself with another.[202]

In other words, the death and resurrection of Jesus Christ is the event in which a genuine correspondence between God and human takes place. The Spirit is the event by which God relates the human to himself. Humans may speak and think of God only as they are in the Spirit. In the Spirit, God shares his life, which is love, with us by drawing us to his life.[203] In this sense, for human God *is* the *event* of the Spirit. Because in this event God remains "a being which is coming," God distinguishes himself from humans even while he is relating himself to them.[204]

Finally, it should be noted that the event of the Spirit's coming to human beings takes place linguistically. Jüngel suggests that the Spirit comes to humans and enables humans to correspond to God in form of *narration*: "it is the power of the Holy Spirit in which God's humanity constantly encounters human reason as a story to be told anew . . . man is able to correspond to the humanity of God only be narrating it."[205]

201. See section 2.2.4 of this chapter.
202. Jüngel, *GMW*, 386–87.
203. Jüngel, *GMW*, 389.
204. Jüngel, *GMW*, 304, 388.
205. Jüngel, *GMW*, 304.

In summary, God's word-event is the event of the mutual love of the Trinity which turns out to be God's love to humanity. In this event, God enables the egocentric human to come out of themselves and relates human to him in love. In this loving relationship, God relates and distinguishes himself from humans as a loving other. Only through this word-event, humans can know and speak of God. Human knowledge of God can only be properly understood by the doctrine of the Trinity. Language is prioritized over consciousness or thought in this theological account:

> Certainty of God is not a normal characteristic of the human consciousness, but is rather the event of renewal of all human relationships, including the consciousness, through the fire of love with which God desires to grasp us and in which every person is totally grasped by God. For that to happen, the human *word* is needed which allows the triune God to be expressed in language in that it tells the story of Jesus Christ as God's history with all people.[206]

2.3.4 God's word event as love, and the unity of the immanent and economic Trinity

For Jüngel, God's word-event is the event of God's love through which we discover God is triune. God's word event is his being in becoming, and "a heightening, an expansion, even an overflowing of the divine being."[207] In the New Testament summary: God is love.[208] Then, Jüngel uses his linguistic ontology to assert that a being of love should have both "self-relatedness and selflessness."[209] The being of God as love is an event of "a still greater selflessness within a very great self-relatedness."[210] He argues that the traditional separation of "immanent" and "economic" Trinity is mistaken because it supposes the "immanent" Trinity is God's immutable and absolute self-relatedness in eternity while the "economic" Trinity is God's selfless love of man in temporality. It finally makes self-relatedness and selflessness a paradox,[211] but if God is love, which is self-related and selfless at the same time, we can think of God as "the one who always heightens and expands his own being

---

206. Jüngel, *GMW*, 375–76.
207. Jüngel, *GMW*, 368.
208. Jüngel, *GMW*, 369.
209. Jüngel, *GMW*, 369.
210. Jüngel, *GMW*, 317. See also, 298, 374–75.
211. Jüngel, *GMW*, 369.

in such great self-relatedness still more selfless and *thus* overflowing."[212] He emphasizes that "Love, as the *essence* of something which exists, cannot be separated from its *existence* at all."[213] Accordingly, the "immanent" Trinity *is* the "economic" Trinity and *vice versa*:

> Rahner's principle of the unity of "economic" and "immanent" Trinity is clear if, with biblical discernment, we understand the statement "God is alive," in the sense of "God is love" . . . God is love both in his self-relationship (in trinitarian language, in the distinction and mutual relationship of Father, Son, and Holy Spirit) and in his relationship to the other who is distinct from him, *man*. The inner-divine self-relationship appears as love in God's self-possession which comprises his selflessness. This selflessness enables God freely to step "outside."[214]

In this sense, we can say that the "immanent" Trinity *is* the "economic" Trinity and *vice versa* because God's word-event is "the event of the deity of God."[215] It is God's being in becoming.

Because of this unity, the inner trinitarian relations are not different from the event that they carry out in history. Indeed, these relations are the trinitarian "persons": "The concept of the relations which constitute the essence of God is identical with the trinitarian 'persons,' which as such in their absolute distinctness make up the unsurpassable intensity of their relations, and in their absolute relatedness to each other make up the unsurpassable radicality of this differentiation from each other."[216] For Jüngel, God the Father is "the one who loves out of himself." He is always related to a "beloved one who always receives this love: God the Son."[217] The Holy Spirit is the "eternally new relationship of God to God" or "the constantly new event of love between the Father and the Son."[218] These relations are known through God's word-event and are God's inner relations because God's word-event is God's being in becoming.

However, it should be noted that the "is" in Jüngel's assertion means "the unity" of "immanent" and "economic" Trinity. He claims that theology must retain "the distinction of reason between 'economic' and 'immanent' Trinity" because the formula will be unthinkable if it is "misconstrued

---

212. Jüngel, *GMW*, 369.
213. Jüngel, *GMW*, 371.
214. Jüngel, "The Relationship," 181–82. Italics Jüngel's.
215. Jüngel, *GMW*, 372.
216. Jüngel, *GMW*, 371n9.
217. Jüngel, *GMW*, 371.
218. Jüngel, *GMW*, 374–75.

tautologically."²¹⁹ His proposal depends on this differentiation between God's *inner relations* and *God's relation to the other that is distinct from God—human*. The unity of "immanent" and "economic" Trinity means that the essence of both relationships is love. However, they can be distinguished from each other because the differentiation between God and humanity. We can speak of "economic" Trinity because the Trinity is the event that God *comes* to *the world*. Thus, "God has come to the world and is as such the one who is coming implies a fundamental distinction between God and the world."²²⁰ Therefore, it is the differentiation between God's inner relations and God's relation to the world makes us to discern "the distinction of reason between 'economic' and 'immanent' Trinity."

Again, we can see that, for Jüngel, a proper relation and distinction between God and humans is crucial for Christian theology.

2.4 Summary

Up to this point, we have seen that *language* occupies a vital part in the whole process of human knowledge of God in Jüngel's theology. The human is a *linguistic* being. However, sin makes the human solely a *being who signifies* rather than one who is also *addressed*. In their egocentricity, human beings are unable to think and speak of God. If humans follow the mandate represented by the *cogito*, God can be conceived only as *dead* and *meaningless*.

But humans may think and speak of God if they "think after" God. Thinking after God is possible because God *addresses* to human in human's language. God's address is his *word*-event. *God's word-event is God's being in becoming*. It is not merely a sound or a text but God's relational word which carries his being. In this word-event, God relates himself to humans in his identification with Jesus Christ. In this identification, God proclaims and founds his kingdom in human language. Therefore, human language can *correspond* to God, and speak of God *analogically*. However, sinful humans cannot naturally correspond to God's humanity. Their reason only can think Jesus Christ as a dead man now swallowed by the past. Humans can think and speak of God only when the Spirit comes to them. Humans are enabled to know God's humanity as the present address of God to them when God's humanity is *being told anew* as *narrative* in the power of the Spirit.

In this linguistic ontology, language is not merely a *sign* nor is it a human construction. Rather, one cannot have language unless one *is addressed by another* in language. Therefore, Trinity as a *word*-event implies both

---

219. Jüngel, "The Relationship," 184.
220. Jüngel, *GMW*, 380.

relation and *distinction* between God and human. Relational knowledge of God does not eliminate the distinction between creator and creature. More importantly, rather than remaining within the paradigms of naïve realism and expressivism, Jüngel's linguistic ontology opens up the *possibility* that the *truth* is not limited to human *present reality*. The triumph of possibility over certainty gives contemporary theology its response to atheism. Uncertainty about God's reality in God's linguistic event is not a negative fact for it indicates that God's word event does not coercive human beings. For Jüngel, love ends certainty.

Finally, Jüngel defines God's word-event as a *relational* linguistic event which is *love*. This definition helps him to assert the immanent Trinity is the economic Trinity and *vice versa* because God *is love* as well as *the event of love*. His linguistic ontology leads him to assert that the *persons* of the Trinity indeed are *inner relations* of the Trinity.

In the next section, I will discuss how Jüngel's insights are helpful to Jenson's doctrine of the Trinity.

3. Theological Response to "The Death of God": Jüngel's Possibility of God and Jenson's Actuality of God's Promise

3.1 On the Death of God: How Jenson is Different from Jüngel

In my introduction I showed that right from the beginning of his theological career Jenson has been concerned with the threat of "nihilism"—the triumph of "nothingness," "emptiness," and "hope for nothing"—in contemporary society. He believes that this nihilism makes contemporary society unable to hear the gospel.[221] One of the slogans of this "secular" or "religionless" era is "God is dead."[222]

I argued that the root of the problem in Jenson's view is the concept of divine timeless eternity. Jenson believes that the gospel requires Christians to identify God through a narrative that uses the tense-structure of ordinary language. In this narrative, God is identified as triune. But the Western heritage of Greek philosophy takes western theology in the opposite direction from the gospel narrative.[223] Greek philosophy holds that divine being should

---

221. Jenson, *ST1*, ix, 220.

222. Jenson, *RAI*, 11, 27.

223. Jenson, *TI*, 57; Jenson, "Triune God," 115; Jenson, "The Logic of the Doctrine of the Trinity," 245; Jenson, *ST1*, 20.

be timeless.[224] Eventually, timeless realities are posited as the perfections of temporal realities and all meaning and value are located in timeless being.[225] God is impassible and timeless while the creatures are passible and temporal. The Western Christian doctrine of God since Augustine is an amalgamation of Greek philosophy and Christian gospel.[226] The Christian God is thus posited as a metaphysical entity of the Greek Philosophy.

Jenson believes that timeless metaphysics makes the doctrine of the Trinity abstract and remote from the daily religious practice of believers. It becomes less and less relevant and conceivable.[227] We can even say that "the triune character of God plays no role at all."[228] As I argued in the introduction and chapter 2, Jenson believes that the metaphysical God has effectively been rejected since the Enlightenment.[229] In modern philosophy and theology, Nietzsche's disciples declare the metaphysical "God" dead. Modern theology is no longer able to regard timeless realities as our ultimate ground of existence.

Jenson and Jüngel both believe that the contemporary theological challenge of "the death of God" may be traced back to traditional metaphysics, but I will argue that subtle difference in their approach to the problem leads them to develop their theological proposals in very different ways.

For Jenson, the problem of traditional metaphysics is that it determines that God is timeless, immutable, and impassible. He defines the problem of traditional metaphysics as a problem of doctrine of God. It is the wrong definition and understanding of "God" that leads to the contemporary rejection of Christian faith as irrelevant and dead. Jüngel is also concerned with the problem of divine timelessness, which he regards as the problematic prioritization of actuality over possibility. But this is only one of the threads of Jüngel's critique. I argued above that his main thrust is on the egocentricity of human being and the "alienation" of God and human. He argues that positing God as a totally different being from humanity and the Cartesian formula of "I think" prevents contemporary thought from thinking and speaking about God. He uses his linguistic ontology, which defines humans as the linguistic beings who are addressed by God and by one another, to show that the real problem of traditional metaphysics is an improper relation and distinction of God and human. In his opinion, only the transformation

---

224. Jenson, *TI*, 25; Jenson, "Triune God," 102.
225. Jenson, *TI*, 60; Jenson, "Triune God," 117.
226. Jenson, "The Logic of the Doctrine of the Trinity," 245.
227. Jenson, *TI*, 131; Jenson, "Triune God," 149.
228. Jenson, *GAG*, 96.
229. See Sections 1 and 2 of Introduction, and Section 1 of Chapter 2.

of human egocentricity can alter this situation. In other words, "the death of God" is not only an issue of the doctrine of God, but an anthropology that acknowledges the new possibility that the human may come to hear the address of God and as a result also all his human others.

In chapter 2, I showed Jenson argues that human desire for absolute autonomy has since Enlightenment led to a radically critical attitude to all knowledge and has disallowed any metaphysical speculation of God. For Jenson it is simply the doctrine of God that is the metaphysical problem, so his account of it concentrates on the demise of traditional metaphysics. He limits his concern to the problems caused by the timeless and impassible God.[230] But for Jüngel the metaphysical problem concerns the doctrine of man just as much as the doctrine of God.

Their different understanding of the nature of the problem means that Jüngel and Jenson ultimately have different orientations to their theology.

Jenson develops a trinitarian theology of promise to show the case of God's temporal reality and its significance; while Jüngel develops a trinitarian theology of possibility to show that humans can only know God in proper relation with and distinction from God. Jüngel's theological insight is complementary with Jenson's project, and can help Jenson to avoid some of the difficulties and misunderstandings of his Trinitarianism. The core argument is that language or word in the narrative trinitarian theology should not only be thought as constituting a *real event or history* of God. It should also be thought as constitutes a *real communication*, which constitutes relation and differentiation, between God and God, and God and humans. If the linguistic aspect of narrative Trinitarianism is emphasized, some of the questions identified in this research can receive new solutions.

3.2 God's Temporality and the Actuality of God's Promise

My argument so far is that Jenson's Trinitarianism is premised on actuality. Because he identifies the metaphysical divine timelessness and transcendence as the root of the problem, he urges that "we must look, not to the timeless, but to history" for the final nature of reality.[231] His solution is a "revisionary metaphysics." He believes that it can "free trinitarian doctrine from captivity to antecedent interpretation of deity as timelessness."[232]

---

230. See Section 1 of Chapter 2.
231. Jenson, *A&O*, 17.
232. Jenson, *TI*, 138; Jenson, "Triune God," 154.

We have seen that the material content of Jenson's revisionary metaphysics is gospel narrative. For him, the most important function of the narrative is to *concretely* identify or articulate God's *history* as *promise*.[233] The relationship between narrative, promise, and history is that: Gospel is a story or narrative by itself. In a one sentence summary, "The God of Israel has raised his servant Jesus from the dead."[234] As a story, it is *told* by the Christian community. It is a story of *promise*. It tells its hearers that God's love as his unconditional promise will triumph.[235] However, the gospel as narrative and promise is not merely a *message*. It is a *reality*. It is God's reality and event:[236] "God does not impute a fiction but acknowledges a reality, a reality created by his own love."[237] Because this reality is an unconditional promise to humans, it is an encompassing reality for creatures as well.[238] Finally, because this reality is God's event in temporality, it is God's *history*. In short, the gospel is God's event or history. It is *the actuality of promise*. Jenson emphasizes that this narrative is important to human because it is *actual* and *real*.[239] The thrust of his argument comes in the realization or actualization of God's event and history of promise.

My assertion that actuality occupies a central role in Jenson's thought can also be evidenced by his use of "promise" to describe the gospel narrative. I argued in chapter 3 that Jenson believes that God is a "word-event." It means that "God is the utterance between Jesus and his 'Father,' and us."[240] In other words, it is a communication between God and God, and God and human. When this communication "takes place" and "addresses" us, it is the gospel for us. Jenson points out that the function of language in communication is not merely "information transfer." Rather, "the fundamental question about any utterance is: What does it *do* for the one to whom it is addressed."[241] Then, he suggests that "one thing we can do for each other with words is make promises. The gospel is of this sort."[242] In this sense, the gospel is a word-event of promise. However, the most important part of this word-event

---

233. Jenson states that the characters of the gospel are: "it is specific," "it is a promise," and "it has a history." Jenson, S&P, 3.

234. Jenson, ST1, 4; Jenson, TI, 21; Jenson, "The Triune God," 99.

235. Jenson, S&P, 55, 60.

236. Jenson, S&P, 117.

237. Jenson, AT, 61.

238. Jenson, S&P, 76–77.

239. Jenson, S&P, 49–50.

240. Jenson, S&P, 123.

241. Jenson, S&P, 6. Italics Jenson's.

242. Jenson, S&P, 6.

is the *action* that God's word *promises*. The linguistic aspect of this event is viewed as "a verbal commitment" which incurs action.[243] Therefore, in this framework, language points to action and its actuality. One can even say that it is finally absorbed by actuality. This position indicates that actuality is a crucial issue in Jenson's Trinitarianism.

At this point, we can find that Jenson's assertion is based on his theology of actuality. God must be "identified by and with the particular *plotted sequence of events* that make the narrative of Israel and her Christ"[244] because the evangelical narrative is identical to God's story of promise which is God's self-actuality.

Because of the integration of narrative, reality, and history through the concept of actuality, Jenson claims that the biblical narrative reveals that the triune God is thoroughly temporal: "The specificity of the triune God is not that he is three, but that he occupies each pole of time as a *persona dramatis*; precisely this characterizes Israel's story of God."[245] Thus, Christians identify the triune God by and with biblical narrative is to identify him within *a specific temporal-spatial framework.*

Interpreting the triune reality through a temporal-spatial framework is indeed Jenson's important contribution to contemporary trinitarian theology. In chapter 4, I argued that meaningful human participation in the triune God requires a temporal framework. Also, I argued that Jenson legitimately defends his interpretation of Cappadocian Trinitarianism.

However, Jenson's Trinitarianism, which emphasizes God's actuality in temporality, has its own limitations as well. Jenson's theology of actuality leads him to understand the three divine persons as *identities*. Identity can be traced from one's proper names and identifying description. In this sense, it has its linguistic weight. However, like Jenson's interpretation of the term "promise," God's identities in the gospel narrative *represent* God's temporal acts. Identity is the *temporal actuality* being articulated linguistically. Therefore, he states that one establishes one's own "self-identity" or "personal identity" through acts "of positing oneself in and through time."[246]

In chapter 4, I argued that this heavy reliance of temporal dimension makes Jenson stretch the referential power of language to its limit. The language eventually cannot function as a system of signs for communication.

---

243. Therefore, Jenson argues that the *continuity* of God's *being* "is established in his *words* and *commitments*, by the faithfulness of his *later acts* to *the promises made in his earlier acts.*" Jenson, *TI*, 40. In there, Jenson interchangeably uses the terms "words," and "commitments." Also, "promises" are considered as "acts."

244. Jenson, *ST1*, 60. Italics mine.

245. Jenson, *ST1*, 89.

246. Jenson, *TI*, 110; Jenson, "Triune God," 138–39; Jenson, "Three Identities," 8.

It breaks down or collapses into the arbitrary system of the speaker. This collapse can be seen in Jenson's Christology, in which God's word simultaneously *is* Christ, church, and creatures. The effect of all his theological moves is to make God the final and sole bearer of language. Language is finally an extension of God's own self and is absorbed by God. At this point, the relatedness and distinction between Creator and creatures—the communion of God and human cannot be properly maintained.

Because if language is ontologically identical to God, it blurs the differentiation between the knowledge of God, human speech of God, human's own selfhood, and God's own self. One would suspect that how can we discern our theological discourse from God's own discourse. Though we are supposed to be the addressees of God in Jenson's theology, which indeed is a very good ground for protecting creatures's otherness, we may ask: how can an address be possible if God's language is identical to the whole reality? Because God owns language and reality directly and exclusively by himself, God's encompassing story of promise could be thought of as oppressive to human life.

In chapter 4, I have argued that Jenson's theology of actuality does not finally allow God to be transcendent or free from the dramatic *plot* which is God's unavoidable actuality. Jenson may reply that his theology does allow the freedom of God because the dramatic plot is within God's room. This would suggest that the God outside and inside his room is different, which would contradict Jenson's assertion of the identity of the immanent and economic Trinity. Finally, if God's consciousness is a supreme consciousness that makes his room, it implies the whole process is the manifestation or "unfolding" of his sole-consciousness. Eventually, this interpretation turns Jenson's Trinitarianism modalistic.

3.3. The Theology of Possibility and the Theology of Actuality

I will argue that Jüngel's account can complement Jenson's account of the Trinity. I do not deny Jenson's argument of God's temporal infinity is valid and tenable. I simply suggest that if we follow Jüngel's insights and put greater emphasis on the linguistic and anthropological dimensions, we may enrich and enhance the arguments of Jenson's theology of actuality.

3.3.1 Metaphysics and thinking after

Jenson's Trinitarianism is intended to be a "revisionary metaphysics." It is metaphysical not only because his account *really* depicts God's *reality*;[247] but also because it is an *encompassing depiction* of reality. We should remember that, for Jenson, Christian theology is a "*universal* hermeneutics" or "*universal* grammar" about "an extra-linguistic entity."[248] This "extra-linguistic entity"—God—is an encompassing reality that envelops us.[249]

Jenson certainly intends to articulate God as a *reality* in his revisionary metaphysics. Christian theology will not become a mere speculation or conjecture unless God is objectively *real*.[250] For him, God's reality is God's temporal infinity. Through this assertion, he wants to reply the challenge of modern atheism. Contemporary experience of God's death for Jenson is a problem of the meaning of God and human's life rather than an epistemological problem. Jenson's primary concern is, "Who and which is God?" and "What God is like?"[251] He wants to demonstrate that "God" is not an abstract or empty word. Jenson has articulated a rich *theo-drama* with his Trinitarianism. The God who is vague and meaningless is the metaphysical God. Therefore, Nietzsche's God is the metaphysical God and not Christian God.

However, no one can deny that the phenomenon of God's death is also an epistemological problem. If we think through the contemporary question of God's death from an epistemological perspective, the question "how are we possible to think and speak of God?" is just as important as Jenson's "who and which is God and what God is like?" However, for Jenson, the former question is mistaken. He worries that it implies that the creature "with its capabilities" can know God.[252] He then proposes that "*God is knowable because and only because he is in fact known* . . . God is knowable in that he actually knows himself, in the mutual life of Father, Son, and Spirit, which as personal is mutual acquaintance and understanding. He is then known by us in that this triune life is in its actuality a life with us."[253]

---

247. See Section 3.3 of Introduction.
248. Jenson, *ST1*, 20–21.
249. Jenson, *ST2*, 35.
250. One of the recent attempts to defend the necessity of a Christian realist position in theology is Andrew Moore's work *Realism and Christian Faith*. Indeed, his notes reveal that Jenson's theology is his important theological resource. See Moore, *Realism and Christian Faith*.
251. Jenson, *TI*, xi.
252. Jenson, *ST1*, 224.
253. Jenson, *ST1*, 227–28. Italics mine.

Jenson is right in insisting that we should not let our epistemological concern turn into a quest for natural theology. I agree that God is knowable because his life is open for our participation, but not that the "how" question becomes invalid merely because *God is known*. For Jenson, God is known because God knows himself and he lives with us. However, humans as knowing subject can still legitimately ask: *how* is it possible for us to participate in the actuality of this life that makes our knowledge of God actual? What are the *means and conditions* of this participation? Jenson cannot avoid this question. He suggests that it is through church we converse with the triune God and so we know him in this ecclesial way.[254] This suggestion is certainly important. Humans know God when God converses with us. In linguistic communication, human knowing subjects find God is *objectively* known.

My analysis of Jenson's revisionary metaphysics showed that he makes God's triune reality, language, history, and church finally identical with each other. His metaphysical Trinitarianism posits the encompassment of God's temporal reality to such extent that it is in danger of absorbing everything that is not God into God. God's drama and conversation threatens to become a monologue. The reason for this is that Jenson's theology of *identity* and *person* makes the temporal dimension the sole medium within which we may grasp the reality of God and of humans. The reality constituted within language must be identified by narrative *without regard for its communicative contexts or the limit of language's referential power for present human recipients*. As Jenson's argument progresses, he refers anything he wishes to narrative but he also denies that it refers to anything that he does not wish it to refer to.

Jenson's Trinitarianism is essentially an account of God's own drama from God's perspective and an all-encompassing metaphysical account of temporal reality. It risks blurring the distinction between God and creatures, and weakening God's transcendence and freedom. Like all other encompassing metaphysical depictions of reality, it unavoidably omits some aspects of reality in its account. The limits of Jenson's understanding of language show that his theology does not have much resource to articulate human unbelief and the possibility of belief and his metaphysics does not offer adequate consideration of the present situation of human knowing subjects.

Jüngel's concept of "thinking after" can help us address these weaknesses. Are we speaking of the Christian God when we do metaphysics? Jenson believes we are. For Jüngel, we can speak and think of God not because we have metaphysics but only because we "think after" God. While

---

254. Jenson, *ST1*, 228.

Jenson's theology blurs the distinction between God and creatures, the concept of "thinking after" firmly establishes the mutual objectivity of God and creatures. The concept of "thinking after" locates the contemporary problem of God's death as an epistemological problem. It shows that the question of God's unthinkability comes from the Cartesian *cogito* and asserts that God is unthinkable and that the unthinkability of God is a real human experience. But it suggests that God is unthinkable precisely because humans attempt to think God with their own thinking capacity and from their own perspective even though God is quite different from themselves. For the sinful human, our reality is only our own present here-and-now. But as the specific other to humans, God is only thinkable and speakable when humans are taken along by God. If human thought is taken along with God, it is "thinking after" God. Human unbelief is the result of egocentricity rather than of the invalidity of God-talk.

"Thinking after" is entirely compatible with Jenson's concern with the danger of natural theology. The concept of "thinking after" denies that thinking of God is a natural human capability. We may think of God because, and only because, our thought is taken along by God. In this process, we do not grasp God as a human *reality* or *actuality*, but we think and speak of God in faith because of his presence in absence. Thus, human knowledge of God is the result of that human participation in God's life in which the human is clearly distinctive from God as God's creature.

3.3.2 Word and event: Narrative pattern vs. analogy of advent

Jüngel's Trinitarianism can be a helpful complement to Jenson's revisionary metaphysics in articulation the relation of word and event. The problem of Jenson's attempt is in his understanding of the referential power of language. Jenson attempts to assert the positive relationship between gospel narrative and God's reality. But as his argument proceeds it becomes clear that Jenson cannot articulate all the various functions of language. Church *is* the body of the Son in the perlocutionary act of God's promise, for example. But in the interlocutionary context, the church is consciously distinctive from the triune God's own life. In Jenson's theology, he is unable to make such distinctions in order to delineate these two different contexts. Jenson's two descriptions of "what church *is*" rule each other out: "the church *is* the body of Christ . . . she is constituted a community by the verbal and 'visible' presence *to* her of that same body of Christ."[255] "[T]he church *is* what she *is*, and believers in the church *are* what they *are* . . . The

---

255. Jenson, *ST2*, 168. Italics Jenson's. See also Jenson, *ST1*, 206.

church *is now* the body of Christ only in that within herself she confronts the body of Christ *as an other than herself.*"[256]

A similar problem can be found in Jenson's assertion of narrative pattern. For him, the unincarnate Son "appears as a narrative pattern of Israel's created human story before he can appear as an individual Israelite within that story . . . [The unincarnate Son] is the narrative pattern of *being going to be* born to Mary . . . [He is] a pattern of movement within the event of the Incarnation, the movement to incarnation, as itself a pattern of God's triune life."[257] In my opinion, Jenson wants to state that because the triune life of God is an actuality of loving promise, though the unincarnate Son is not yet a concrete man, as God's Word, he is present in the story as an on-going actuality of God's promise. It is a *fugue* in which patterns repeat through time. This is true, but Jenson suggests that this actuality "as a narrative pattern of Israel's created human story" is at the same time "a pattern of God's triune life." We may not reversely infer that Israel's created human story *is* God's triune life.

Jenson argues that he articulates the distinction between God and creatures with the difference between eternal and contingent community. He states that his assertion cannot be reversed to that Israel's created human story *is* God's triune life: "The triune narrative and the triune community are in contingent fact God's history with a human community actual in that history. We humans belong to the triune history and community only by virtue of this contingency; none of us nor all of us together are one of the Trinity. We belong as those whom the Son brings with himself, whose whole life and intention are the others to whom he is sent and for whom he died."[258] Jesus is the Son who "within creation he is the *creature* as intended by and for God."[259] Then, the problem is that if Jesus the Son is a *creature*, Jenson's argument of divine eternity and creatures's contingency is conflated in this creature. In this case, temporal dimensions of contingency and eternity cannot explain Jenson's position satisfactorily. He needs to find that additional conceptuality by which he can clarify his position here.

God's incarnation is a word-*event*. The one who incarnates is God's word. It is an event of God's being in becoming in which word and event are united. We know God's incarnation through hearing of the gospel, and this gospel is not just information but a promise; we expect the word does depict the divine reality. However, precisely because gospel is an event

---

256. Jenson, *ST2*, 323. Italics mine.
257. Jenson, *ST1*, 141.
258. Jenson, *ST2*, 98. See also Jenson, *ST1*, 226.
259. Jenson, *ST2*, 27–28. Italics mine.

of hearing, it is also a *word*-event. The human addressee of this event needs the means by which to recognize their relation with God, and their distinction from God, when they hear. As the word spoken by God, the gospel needs *a communicating process* by which speaker and hearer are distinguished by each other.

Moreover, when human language is used to speak of God, who is uncreated and different from human, its unavoidable anthropomorphism makes human speech of God analogical. When we speak of God and humans there are similarities and dissimilarities. The doctrine of analogy is a theological response to this linguistic phenomenon. The problem here is that Jenson's theology cannot clearly articulate the anthropomorphic nature of human language. I have shown that Jenson's argument for God's actuality has not found the means to be adequately sensitive. Jenson pushes each doctrine to its very limit. He assumes that language can refer both to a thing and not to that one thing simultaneously and without the need of further qualification. However, such assumption cannot deny the need of clarification.

Jüngel's analogy of advent complements Jenson's theology to show the communicating process of God's word-event, and to clarify the analogical nature of theological discourse. He demonstrates that human speech of God is analogical and positively thinks that analogy helps theology make the God-man distinction clear. He does not follow the traditional concept of analogy to posit God as timeless, impassible, absolutely distanced from human and thus unspeakable: he believes that the traditional approach makes our analogical God-talk inauthentic. However, analogy is unavoidable, so what we need is to discover the possibility of properly theological analogy. It is possible for us to speak of God because God *comes* to be human, and in this becoming, God speaks to human in human's language. He reveals or interprets himself in human's language. God's becoming implies that God becomes and speaks as something other than God. This self-revelation or self-interpretation is thus always analogical. It is an *analogy of advent*.

If we apply Jüngel's analogy of advent to Jenson's theology, we find that on one hand the concept of advent fits Jenson's concern of God's temporal infinity and on the other hand, that it provides a doctrine of analogy to articulate the parameters of the language in order to avoid confusion of meaning in Jenson's theology.

3.3.3 God is love: Emphasizing God's love as both self-related and selfless vs. an actuality of a loving consciousness

Jenson's revisionary metaphysics articulates theology as the actuality of God's promise. As I have analyzed, the content of God's promise is his love. This promise is a decision within the triune conversation or God's consciousness. It is actualized within created time. The main problem of this account is that it may endanger the freedom of God and creatures. Jenson emphasizes the actuality of God's love because he understands the problem of God's death as a problem of nihilism—the meaninglessness of God in modern world. But this emphasis only highlights God's love as event and as unsurpassable decision. It does not reduce our concern for the question of freedom in his theology.

Jenson's understanding of love deepens this concern. Jenson says that "to love is to *give* and to *desire*," which in classical terms are *agape* and *eros*.[260] God's love is not a pure gift but also a desire.[261] Then, he follows Hegel in asserting that these two natures of love inevitably lead to a struggle for domination. The struggle is resolved by the existence of a third party: "What can and sometimes does break you and me out of the mutual struggle for hegemony is someone who objectivizes both of us, in a particular way: who intends us to be lovers of each other."[262] Jenson posits that the Spirit is that third party for God himself.[263] More surprisingly, even when this third party presents, the struggle for domination does not cease: "the third party who intends us to love each other, and rescues us from the I-Thou standoff, has him or herself an interest in our love; and between him or her and either of us this will generate the whole problematic again."[264] If God's love is an eternal struggle for domination and liberation between the persons of God, God cannot be transcendent or free at all.

God's love may also be dominating and oppressive for his creatures if this understanding of love relates to Jenson's notion that "the Spirit . . . is inherently *someone's* spirit, so that he cannot be an autonomous someone."[265] From both interpretations, Jenson needs to revise his understanding of the nature of God's love and its actuality.

Jüngel's theology can provide insights for revising Jenson's proposal. Jüngel affirms that love is both a gift and a desire. In his terms, love is both

---

260. Jenson, *OTH*, 75–76. Italics Jenson's.
261. Jenson, *OTH*, 76–77.
262. Jenson, *OTH*, 82.
263. Jenson, *OTH*, 83.
264. Jenson, *OTH*, 82.
265. Jenson, *ST1*, 121.

selflessness and self-relatedness. The being of God is an event of love. However, it is not an event of eternal struggling for domination. Jüngel does not understand the two natures of love come to conflict with each other in God. Love should not be defined as a conflict. Rather, the being of God is love. It is an event of "a still greater selflessness within a great, and justifiably very great self-relatedness."[266] Love is thus an event of relating others through self-giving. Therefore, love is not a struggle for domination but an event of liberation and freedom. When the lover gives him or herself away to the beloved, the lover and the beloved are in a new relationship. Each of them is related to him or herself anew: "Lovers are always alien to themselves and yet, in coming close to each other, they come close to themselves in a new way."[267] Finally, God's will to love is a will to free.

When love is defined in this way, God is free and transcendent even as he eternally decides to incarnate. Because, love by itself is a self-liberation to step outside of oneself: "The inner-divine self-relationship appears as love in God's self-possession which comprises his selflessness. This selflessness enables God freely to step 'outside.'"[268]

This definition of love is not an abstract concept that invites the timeless metaphysics which Jenson fears. Jüngel asserts that "Love, as the *essence* of something which exists, cannot be separated from its *existence* at all."[269] Accordingly, the "immanent" Trinity *is* the "economic" Trinity and *vice versa*. God's word-event is "the event of the deity of God," which is God's everlasting love.[270] However, the distinction between the immanent and economic Trinity still can be discerned because they are two different sets of relation of love. The Economic Trinity is the loving relation of God with creatures. It is established by God's coming to the world. The immanent Trinity is God's inner-loving relation which is his *perichoresis*.[271] In distinguishing these two sets of relations, the distinction between God and creatures is maintained.

If love is emphasized as an actuality that God determines to achieve without the relational dimension, God's persons may easily become the processes, or means to achieve God's loving consciousness. Under Jüngel's relational understanding of love, God's persons will not be subsumed to a supreme consciousness: "The concept of the relations which constitute

266. Jüngel, *GMW*, 317.
267. Jüngel, *GMW*, 318.
268. Jüngel, "The Relationship," 182.
269. Jüngel, *GMW*, 371.
270. Jüngel, *GMW*, 372.
271. Jüngel, *GMW*, 380.

the essence of God is identical with the trinitarian 'persons,' which as such in their absolute distinctness make up the unsurpassable intensity of their relations, and in their absolute relatedness to each other make up the unsurpassable radicality of this differentiation from each other."[272]

God is love and this love is an event. But this love may not be defined as a struggle for domination and self-actualization. Rather, God's love is an event of "a still greater selflessness within a very great self-relatedness." In being as love, God is free, transcendent, and relational. And in being God's beloved, the creature is free and in relationship with God.

3.3.4 Possibility vs. actuality

Jenson emphasizes the actuality of God's promise because of the threats of timeless metaphysics and modern theological problem of God's death. A theology of actuality is the answer to these threats because Jenson understands the most destructive consequence of them is nihilism—the emptiness and meaninglessness of life. God's actuality as a story of love sets the tenure of the meaning of life. In this actuality, there is no space for vagueness. Only a concrete actuality or reality of God prevents meaningful life regressing into an ambivalent and finally nihilist life.[273] In this sense, Jenson's discernment of the problem of timeless eternity and his proposal for revisionary metaphysics are correct.

Nonetheless, emphasizing God's actuality does not mean that human beings will automatically recognize the meaning of life and the reality of God. This phenomenon implies that the problem of God's death is not only a problem of the concept of God but consequently also a problem of will and of sin. The correction of our perception of God from divine timelessness to temporal infinity does not mean human beings become capable of thinking of God. On the contrary, when we think the whole issue of God's actuality through the problem of sin, the possibility of thinking God for humans is no dangerous door to nihilism, but good news.

Jüngel has a deep recognition of the destructive result of human sin. Because of sin, the egocentric human sticks at their present here-and-now. Humans cannot think the existence and meaning of God with their thinking ego. They cannot comprehend or even hear the gospel. The realism that humans know is only their own present here-and-now. In sin, the final actuality that human has is death—*nihility* or *nothingness*. When God's word-event of love comes to humans, it is the power of the Spirit

---

272. Jüngel, *GMW*, 371n9.
273. Jenson, *ST1*, 54–57; Jenson, *TI*, x–xii.

that enables humans to speak of God in *faith*. In faith, humans can escape imprisonments within their present here-and-now. Consequently, it is *possible* for the human to speak and think after God. In this experience, humans transcend the dichotomy of naïve realism and expressivism. They may be open to the *truth*.

Finally, it should be noted that the theology of possibility is not the opposite of the theology of actuality. Indeed, they are as complementary as two sides of one coin. They speak the characteristics of God's event of love from the human side and from God's side respectively. Jüngel clearly states that theology corresponds to God because of God's commitment to carry out his relationship to himself and to world in human language—God's word-event.[274] God's speakability is always a possibility for humans and a promise for God. Jüngel's theology of possibility continues Jenson's concern with the actuality of God's promise and genuinely addresses the nature of gospel as good news to sinful humans.

4. Summary

Jenson and Jüngel both understand that God is a word-event. Jenson's proposal of God's temporal infinity shows that he emphasizes the eventfulness. But Jenson's over-reliance on the temporal dimension in his articulation of God's word-event is unsatisfactory. Jüngel's Trinitarianism emphasizes on the linguistic aspect of God's event. I have shown that his linguistic ontology, analogy of advent, and prioritizing possibility over actuality can complement Jenson's account of the trinity because they can explicate the relation and distinction between God and creature and the various linguistic contexts of theology with greater sensitivity than Jenson.

Jenson tells us that God is a great *fugue*.[275] Though I do not think it is an adequate one, for Jenson a fugue is a model to describe the life and beauty of God. If the beauty of a fugue is in its contrapuntal accompaniment of voices, it is not just an on-going *movement* of a musical pattern but a call and response of voices. Jüngel's linguistic ontology shows that God's love is his great self-relatedness as still greater self-selflessness towards creatures. Jüngel asserts that "*caritas capax verbi* ('love is capable of the word')."[276] In love, God and creatures are in a relation of call and response. This event of address and response also maintains the distinction of creatures from God. It forms a contrapuntal accompaniment of voices within God's life.

274. Jüngel, *GMW*, 289.
275. Jenson, *ST1*, 236.
276. Jüngel, *GMW*, 298.

We can agree with Jenson that "the end is music."[277] This is so because God's love enables the adoration and praise of creatures. Love is capable of the word.

---

277. Jenson, *ST2*, 369.

Conclusion

ROBERT JENSON INSISTS THAT the Trinity is identified *by and with* the biblical narrative. This study has examined Jenson's view that the biblical narrative is crucial to the doctrine of the Trinity because it denotes God's temporal reality. We have found that Jenson does not give the same weight to the linguistic-communicative aspect of ontology as he does to the temporal aspect of his ontology.

My investigation has found that the prioritization of the temporal aspect of his ontology over the communicative and linguistic aspect in Jenson's Trinitarianism creates problems. I have argued that his system cannot account for both the identity and the distinction of the immanent and economic Trinity, and thus the transcendence and freedom of God, as he hopes. It also fails to formulate the proper relation and distinction of Creator and creatures. When Jenson needs to defend God's triunity through his account of divine temporality, he understands the Trinity as a supreme divine consciousness. This risks becoming modalistic.

Since the Trinity is known and encountered through narrative, it must be a word-event. A word-event is constituted by temporal events within a linguistic communion. The problem of Jenson's Trinitarianism is an overemphasis on temporality (i.e., as word-*event*) at the expense of linguistic-communication (i.e., as *word*-event). Jüngel understands God's word in terms of God's coming, analogy and the theology of possibility. There are three elements needed by Jenson's project. Jüngel understands God's trinitarian reality to humans as an event which is an *analogical advent* of God. It is analogical because God's event is not only a *historical coming* of God to humans, but the coming of the address of God. All created reality exists because it is addressed by God. Likewise, the gospel narrative is not only an account of God's historical event but God's address to humans. Jüngel suggests that as God's word comes to us as an address, it opens a *possibility* for human receivers. In this communicative relationship of God and man, I argue that this allows us to express the proper relation and distinction of God and humans.

I have also argued that Jüngel's theology of the coming of God shows that the identity and distinction of immanent and economic Trinity can be held at the same time as his understanding of the nature of God's love. I have argued that it is his over-reliance on temporality that prevents Jenson from understanding love as Jüngel is able to.

This study is significant because it has shown the importance of understanding God's self-revealing event as an event of *linguistically-modulated communion*. Many studies have followed Barth in demonstrating that the Trinity is a self-revealing subject. We should remember that for Barth the Trinity is not a metaphysical assumption, but an *a posteriori* doctrine that expresses the coming of the Word of God to humans. This study has found that one prominent contemporary theologian, who has followed Barth in understanding God as a self-revealing God, has tended to overlook the communicative complexities of the event of God's self-revelation. Jenson wants to show the meaningfulness of theological discourse and save it from disintegrating into meaninglessness. However, the metaphysics by which he does this finally blurs the distinction between God and humans. As a result, his theological metaphysics loses its revelatory function as humanity is absorbed into the speech of God. Without the conscious balance of linguistic communicative and temporal eventful aspects of God's word-event, Jenson provides a dangerously extreme expression of Barth's theological achievement.

Select Bibliography

Works by Robert W. Jenson

Books

Alpha and Omega: A Study in the Theology of Karl Barth. New York: Nelson and Sons, 1963.
America's Theologian: A Recommendation of Jonathan Edwards. New York: Oxford University Press, 1988.
Essays in Theology of Culture. Grand Rapids: Eerdmans, 1995.
God after God: The God of the Past and the God of the Future, Seen in the Work of Karl Barth. Indianapolis: Bobbs-Merrill, 1969.
The Knowledge of Things Hoped For. New York: Oxford University Press, 1969.
On Thinking the Human: Resolutions of Difficult Notions. Grand Rapids: Eerdmans, 2003.
A Religion against Itself. Richmond: John Knox, 1967.
Story and Promise: A Brief Theology of the Gospel about Jesus. Ramsey: Sigler, 1989.
Systematic Theology, Vol. 1: The Triune God. Oxford: Oxford University Press, 1997.
Systematic Theology, Vol. 2: The Works of God. Oxford: Oxford University Press, 1999.
The Triune Identity: God according to the Gospel. Philadelphia: Fortress, 1982.
Unbaptized God: The Basic Flaw in Ecumenical Theology. Minneapolis: Fortress, 1992.
Visible Words: The Interpretation and Practice of Christian Sacraments. Philadelphia: Fortress, 1978.

Articles

"The Bible and the Trinity." *Pro Ecclesia* 11 (2002) 329–39.
"A Call to Faithfulness." *Dialog* 30 (1991) 90–97.
"Christ as Culture 1: Christ as Polity." *International Journal of Systematic Theology* 5 (2003) 323–29.
"The Church and the Sacrament." In *The Cambridge Companion to Christian Doctrine*, edited by Colin E. Gunton, 207–25. Cambridge: Cambridge University Press, 1997.

"Creator and Creature." *International Journal of Systematic Theology* 4 (2002) 216–21.
"A Dead Issue Revisited." *Lutheran Quarterly* 14 (1962) 53–56.
"Does God Have Time?" In *Essays in Theology of Culture*, 190–201. Grand Rapids: Eerdmans, 1995.
"Epiphany." *Theology Today* 60 (2004) 559.
"The Father, He . . ." In *Speaking the Christian God: The Holy Trinity and the Challenge of Feminism*, edited by Alvin F. Kimel, 95–109. Grand Rapids: Eerdmans, 1992.
"The Futurist Option in Speaking of God." *Lutheran Quarterly* 21 (1969) 17–25.
"The God Question." *Lutheran Forum* 26 (1992) 46–50.
"Hermeneutics and the Life of the Church." In *Reclaiming the Bible for the Church*, edited by Carl E. Braaten and Robert W. Jenson, 89–105. Edinburgh: T. & T. Clark, 1995.
"The Holy Spirit." In *Christian Dogmatics*, vol. 2, edited by Carl. E. Braaten and Robert W. Jenson, 101–78. Philadelphia: Fortress, 1984.
"How the World Lost Its Story." *First Things* 36 (1993) 19–24.
"Jesus in the Trinity." *Pro Ecclesia* 8 (1999) 308–18.
"Karl Barth." In *The Modern Theologians: An Introduction to Christian Theology in the Twentieth Century*, edited by David F. Ford, 21–36. 2nd ed. Oxford: Blackwell, 1997.
"The Kingdom of America's God." In *Essays in Theology of Culture*, 50–66. Grand Rapids: Eerdmans, 1995.
"The Logic of the Doctrine of the Trinity." *Dialog* 26 (1987) 245–49.
"On Becoming Man; Some Aspects." In *Essays in Theology of Culture*, 28–39. Grand Rapids: Eerdmans, 1995.
"On the Problem(s) of Scriptural Authority." *Interpretation* 31 (1977) 237–50.
"Once More into the Breach: The True Historical Jesus." In *Theology in the Service of the Church: Essays in Honor of Thomas W. Gillespie,* edited by Wallace M. Alston, 120–27. Grand Rapids: Eerdmans, 2000.
"Once More: The Jesus of History and the Christ of Faith." *Dialog* 11 (1972) 120–27.
"An Ontology of Freedom in the *De Servo Arbitrio* of Luther." *Modern Theology* 10 (1994) 247–52.
"Religious Pluralism, Christology, and Barth." *Dialog* 20 (1981) 31–38.
"The Religious Power of Scripture." *Scottish Journal of Theology* 52 (1999) 89–105.
"Re-Review: Karl Barth's *The Word of God and the Word of Man*." *The Modern Churchman* 25 (1983) 51–54.
"Response to Watson and Hunsinger." *Scottish Journal of Theology* 55 (2002) 225–32.
"Response." *Union Seminary Quarterly Review* 28 (1972) 31–34.
"Second Thoughts about Theologies of Hope." *Evangelical Quarterly* 72 (2000) 335–46.
"Simplistic Thoughts about the Authority of Scripture." In *All Things New: Essays in Honor of Roy A. Harrisville*, edited by Arland J. Hultgren et al., 181–90. St. Paul: Luther Northwestern Theological Seminary, 1992.
"Thanks to Yeago." *Dialog* 31 (1992) 22–23.
"A Theological Autobiography to Date." *Dialog* 46 (2007) 46–54.
"Three Identities of One Action." *Scottish Journal of Theology* 28 (1975) 1–15.
"The Triune God." In *Christian Dogmatics*, vol. 1, edited by Carl E. Braaten and Robert W. Jenson, 79–192. Philadelphia: Fortress, 1984.
"The Triunity of Truth." In *Essays in Theology of Culture*, 84–94. Grand Rapids: Eerdmans, 1995.

"What Academic Difference Would the Gospel Make?" In *Essays in Theology of Culture*, 76-83. Grand Rapids: Eerdmans, 1995.

"What is the Point of Trinitarian Theology?" In *Trinitarian Theology Today*, edited by Christoph Schwöbel, 31-43. Edinburgh: T. & T. Clark, 1995.

"With No Qualifications: The Christological Maximalism of the Christian East." In *Ancient and Postmodern Christianity: Paleo-Orthodoxy in the 21st Century: Essays in Honor of Thomas C. Oden*, edited by Kenneth Tanner and Christopher A. Hall, 13-22. Downers Grove: InterVarsity, 2002.

With Braaten, Carl E. "Introduction: The Background of Twentieth-Century Theology." In *A Map of Twentieth Century Theology: Readings from Karl Barth to Radical Pluralism*, edited by Carl E. Braaten and Robert W. Jenson, 1-12. Minneapolis: Fortress, 1995.

Other

Albright, John R. "The Story of the Triune God: Time and Eternity in Robert Jenson's Theology." *Christian Scholar's Review* 26 (1996) 36-54.

Alston, William P. *A Realist Conception of Truth*. Ithaca: Cornell University Press, 1996.

Aquinas, Thomas. *Summa Theologica*. Translated by Fathers of the English Dominican Province. Westminster: Christian Classics, 1981.

Audi, Robert, ed. *The Cambridge Dictionary of Philosophy*. Cambridge: Cambridge University Press, 1995.

Austin, J. L. *How to Do Things with Words*. 2nd ed. Cambridge: Harvard University Press, 1975.

Balás, David L. "Eternity and Time in Gregory of Nyssa's *Contra Eunomium*." In *Gregor von Nyssa und Die Philosophie: zweites internationals Kolloqium über Gregor von Nyssa*, edited by Herausgegeben von Heinrich Dörrie et al., 128-53. Leiden: Brill, 1976.

———. ΜΕΤΟΥΣΙΑ ΘΕΟΥ: *Man's Participation in God's Perfections according to Saint Gregory of Nyssa*. Romae: Pontificium Institutum S. Anselmi, 1966.

Balthasar, Hans Urs von. *The Theology of Karl Barth: Exposition and Interpretation*. San Francisco: Ignatius, 1992.

———. *Theo-Drama: Theological Dramatic Theory. Vol. 3: Dramatis Personae: Persons in Christ*. Translated by Graham Harrison. San Francisco: Ignatius, 1992.

Barnes, Michel René. *The Power of God: Δύναμις in Gregory of Nyssa's Trinitarian Theology*. Washington, DC: Catholic University of America Press, 2001.

Barth, Karl. *Church Dogmatics*. 4 vols. Edited by G. W. Bromiley and T. F. Torrance. Edinburgh: T. & T. Clark, 1963-69.

———. *The Epistle to the Romans*. Translated by Edwyn C. Hoskyns. London: Oxford University Press, 1933.

———. *Die Kirchliche Dogmatik*. 4 vols. Zollikon-Zurich: Evangelischer, 1947-1970.

———. *Protestant Theology in the Nineteenth Century: Its Background & History*. Translated by Brian Cozens and John Bowden. London: SCM, 2001.

———. *The Word of God and the Word of Man*. Translated by Douglas Horton. London: Hodder and Stoughton, 1928.

Berkhof, Hendrikus. *Two Hundred Years of Theology: Report of a Personal Journey*. Translated by John Vriend. Grand Rapids: Eerdmans, 1989.

Braaten, Carl E. "Robert William Jenson—A Personal Memoir." In *Trinity, Time, and Church: A Response to the Theology of Robert W. Jenson*, edited by Colin E. Gunton, 1–9. Grand Rapids: Eerdmans, 2000.

Brugarolas, Miguel, ed. *Gregory of Nyssa: Contra Eunomium I: An English Translation with Supporting Studies*. Leiden: Brill, 2018.

Buckley, James J. "Intimacy: The Character of Robert Jenson's Theology." In *Trinity, Time, and Church: A Response to the Theology of Robert W. Jenson*, edited by Colin E. Gunton, 10–22. Grand Rapids: Eerdmans, 2000.

Burkert, Walter. *Greek Religion: Archaic and Classical*. Translated by John Raffan. Oxford: Blackwell, 1985.

Calton, Patricia Marie. *Hegel's Metaphysics of God: The Ontological Proof as the Development of a Trinitarian Divine Ontology*. Aldershot: Ashgate, 2001.

Carnap, Rudolf. *The Logical Syntax of Language*. London: Paul, Trench, Trubner & Co., 1937.

Cary, Philip. Review of *Systematic Theology: Volume 1: The Triune God*, by Robert W. Jenson. *Scottish Journal of Theology* 52 (1999) 133–35.

Chadwick, Henry. *Early Christian Thought and the Classical Tradition: Studies in Justin, Clement and Origen*. Oxford: Oxford University Press, 1984.

Cunningham, David S. *These Three are One: The Practice of Trinitarian Theology*. Oxford: Blackwell, 1998.

Daniélou, Jean. *L'être et le temps chez Grégorie de Nysse*. Leiden: Brill, 1970.

Davies, Oliver. *The Creativity of God: World, Eucharist, Reason*. Cambridge: Cambridge University Press, 2004.

DeHart, Paul J. *Beyond the Necessary God: Trinitarian Faith and Philosophy in the Thought of Eberhard Jüngel*. Atlanta: Scholar, 1999.

Desmond, William. *Hegel's God: A Counterfeit Double?* Aldershot: Ashgate, 2003.

Ebeling, Gerhard. *God and Word*. Translated by James Leitch. Philadelphia: Fortress, 1967.

———. *The Nature of Faith*. Translated by Ronald Gregor Smith. Philadelphia: Fortress, 1961.

———. *Theology and Proclamation: Dialogue with Bultmann*. Translated by John Riches. Philadelphia: Fortress, 1963.

———. *Word and Faith*. Translated by James W. Leitch. Philadelphia: Fortress, 1963.

Edwards, Mark. *Origen against Plato*. Burlington: Ashgate, 2002.

Evans, Craig A. "Jesus's Self-Designation 'The Son of Man' and the Recognition of His Divinity." In *The Trinity: An Interdisciplinary Symposium on the Trinity*, edited by Stephen T. Davis et al., 29–48. Oxford: Oxford University Press, 1999.

Farrow, Douglas, et al. "Robert Jenson's *Systematic Theology*: Three Responses." *International Journal of Systematic Theology* 1 (1999) 89–104.

Frei, Hans W. *The Eclipse of Biblical Narrative: A Study in Eighteenth and Nineteenth Century Hermeneutics*. New Haven: Yale University Press, 1974.

Gilson, Étienne. *God and Philosophy*. New Haven: Yale University Press, 1969.

Grenz, Stanley J. *Rediscovering the Triune God: The Trinity in Contemporary Theology*. Minneapolis: Fortress, 2004.

Guignon, Charles B. "Heidegger, Martin." In *The Cambridge Dictionary of Philosophy*, edited by Robert Audi, 370–73. Cambridge: Cambridge University Press, 1995.

Gunton, Colin E. *Father, Son, and Holy Spirit: Essays Toward a Fully Trinitarian Theology*. London: T. & T. Clark, 2003.

———. *The Promise of Trinitarian Theology.* 2nd ed. Edinburgh: T. & T. Clark, 1997.
Guthrie, W. K. C. *The Greeks and their Gods.* Boston: Beacon, 1955.
Hart, David Bentley. "Mirror of the Infinite: Gregory of Nyssa on the *Vestigia Trinitatis*." In *Re-thinking Gregory of Nyssa*, edited by Sarah Coakley, 111–32. Oxford: Blackwell, 2003.
Hart, Trevor. *Regarding Karl Barth: Toward a Reading of his Theology.* Downers Grove: IVP, 1999.
———. "Revelation." In *The Cambridge Companion to Karl Barth*, edited by John Webster, 37–56. Cambridge: Cambridge University Press, 2000.
Hegel, Georg Wilhelm Friedrich. *Hegel's Logic: Being Part One of the Encyclopedia of the Philosophical Sciences.* 3rd ed. Translated by William Wallace. Oxford: Oxford University Press, 1975.
———. *Hegel's Phenomenology of Spirit.* Translated by A. V. Miller. Oxford: Oxford University Press, 1977.
———. *Hegel's Philosophy of Mind: Being Part Three of the Encyclopedia of the Physical Sciences.* Translated by William Wallace. Oxford: Clarendon, 1971.
———. *Hegel's Science of Logic.* 2 vols. Translated by W. H. Johnson and L. G. Struthers. London: Allen & Unwin, 1951.
———. *Lectures on the Philosophy of Religion.* Vol. 3. Translated by Peter C. Hodgson. Ann Arbor: Scholars, 1979.
Hunsinger, George. *Disruptive Grace: Studies in the Theology of Karl Barth.* Grand Rapids: Eerdmans, 2000.
———. *How to Read Karl Barth: The Shape of His Theology.* New York: Oxford University Press, 1991.
———. "Robert Jenson's *Systematic Theology*: A Review Essay." *Scottish Journal of Theology* 55 (2002) 161–200.
Ive, Jeremy. "Robert W. Jenson's Theology of History." In *Trinity, Time, and Church: A Response to the Theology of Robert W. Jenson*, edited by Colin E. Gunton, 146–57. Grand Rapids: Eerdmans, 2000.
Jüngel, Eberhard. "Anthropomorphism: A Fundamental Problem in Modern Hermeneutics." In *Theological Essays I*, edited by J. B. Webster, 72–94. Edinburgh: T. & T. Clark, 1989.
———. "God—As a Word of Our Language." In *Theology of the Liberating Word*, edited by F. Herzog, 24–45. Nashville: Abingdon, 1971.
———. *God as the Mystery of the World: On the Foundation of the Theology of the Crucified One in the Dispute between Theism and Atheism.* Translated by Darrell L. Guder. Edinburgh: T. & T. Clark, 1983.
———. *God's Being is in Becoming: The Trinitarian Being of God in the Theology of Karl Barth.* Translated by and with a new introduction by John Webster. Edinburgh: T. & T. Clark, 2001.
———. "Humanity in Correspondence to God: Remarks on the Image of God as a Basic Concept in Theological Anthropology." In *Theological Essays I*, edited by J. B. Webster, 124–53. Edinburgh: T. & T. Clark, 1989.
———. *Justification: The Heart of the Christian Faith.* Translated by Jeffrey C. Cayzer and with an introduction by John Webster. Edinburgh: T. & T. Clark, 2001.
———. *Karl Barth: A Theological Legacy.* Translated by Garrett E. Paul. Philadelphia: Westminster, 1986.

———. "Metaphorical Truth. Reflections on the Theological Relevance of Metaphor as a Contribution to the Hermeneutics of Narrative Theology." In *Theological Essays I*, edited by J. B. Webster, 16–71. Edinburgh: T. & T. Clark, 1989.

———. "The Relationship between 'Economic' and 'Immanent' Trinity." *Theology Digest* 24 (1976) 179–84.

———. "The World as Possibility and Actuality. The Ontology of the Doctrine of Justification." In *Theological Essays I*, edited by J. B. Webster, 95–123. Edinburgh: T. & T. Clark, 1989.

Kant, Immanuel. *Critique of Pure Reason*. Translated by Norman Kemp Smith. London: Macmillan, 1973.

———. *Opus Postumum*. Translated by Eckhart Förster and Michael Rosen. Cambridge: Cambridge University Press, 1993.

———. *Religion and Rational Theology*. Translated by A. W. Wood and G. di Giovanni. Cambridge: Cambridge University Press, 1996.

———. *Religion within the Limits of Reason Alone*. Translated by Theodore M. Greene and Hoyt H. Hudson. New York: Harper, 1960.

Kelly, J. N. D. *Early Christian Doctrines*. San Francisco: Harper, 1978.

Knight, Douglas. "Jenson on Time." In *Trinity, Time, and Church: A Response to the Theology of Robert W. Jenson*, edited by Colin E. Gunton, 71–79. Grand Rapids: Eerdmans, 2000.

LaCugna, Catherine M. Review of *The Triune Identity: God according to the Gospel*, by Robert W. Jenson. *Theological Studies* 44 (1983) 135–36.

Leemans, Johan, and Matthieu Cassin, eds. *Gregory of Nyssa Contra Eunomium III: An English Translation with Commentary and Supporting Studies*. Leiden: Brill, 2010.

Mattes, Mark C. "An Analysis and Assessment of Robert Jenson's Systematic Theology." *Lutheran Quaterly* 14 (2000) 463–94.

———. *The Role of Justification in Contemporary Theology*. Grand Rapids: Eerdmans, 2004.

McCormack, Bruce L. *Karl Barth's Critically Realistic Dialectical Theology: Its Genesis and Development 1909–1936*. Oxford: Oxford University Press, 1995.

Meredith, Anthony. "The Divine Simplicity: *Contra Eunomium* 1.223–241." In *El "Contra Eunomium I" En la Produccion Literaria de Gregorio de Nisa*, edited by Lucas F. Mateo-Seco and Juan L. Bastero, 339–51. Pamplona: Ediciones Universidad de Navarra, 1988.

———. *Gregory of Nyssa*. New York: Routledge, 1999.

Molnar, Paul D. *Divine Freedom and the Doctrine of the Immanent Trinity: In Dialogue with Karl Barth and Contemporary Theology*. London: T. & T. Clark, 2002.

Moltmann, Jürgen. *The Trinity and the Kingdom of God: The Doctrine of God*. Translated by Margaret Kohl. Minneapolis: Fortress, 1993.

Moore, Andrew. *Realism and Christian Faith: God, Grammar, and Meaning*. Cambridge: Cambridge University Press, 2003.

Mühlenberg, Ekkehard. *Die Unendlichkeit Gottes bei Gregor von Nyssa*. Göttingen: Vanderhoeck & Ruprecht, 1966.

Norris, Richard A. *God and World in Early Christian Theology*. New York: Seabury, 1965.

Ochs, Peter. "A Jewish Reading of *Trinity, Time and the Church: A Response to the Theology of Robert W. Jenson*." *Modern Theology* 19 (2003) 419–27.

Otis, Brooks. "Gregory of Nyssa and the Cappadocian Conception of Time." In *Studia Patristica*, vol. 14, edited by Elizabeth A. Livingstone, 327–57. Papers presented to the Sixth International Conference on Patristic Studies held in Oxford 1971. Berlin: Akademie-Verlag, 1976.

Pannenberg, Wolfhart. "Eternity, Time, and the Trinitarian God." In *Trinity, Time, and Church: A Response to the Theology of Robert W. Jenson*, edited by Colin E. Gunton, 62–70. Grand Rapids: Eerdmans, 2000.

———. *Jesus—God and Man*. Translated by Lewis L. Wilkins and Duane A. Priebe. London: SCM, 1968.

———. "A Trinitarian Synthesis." *First Things* 103 (2000) 49–53.

Peters, Ted. *GOD as Trinity: Relationality and Temporality in Divine Life*. Louisville: Westminster/John Knox, 1993.

Powell, Samuel M. *The Trinity in German Thought*. Cambridge: Cambridge University Press, 2001.

Prestige, G. L. *God in Patristic Thought*. London: SPCK, 1952.

Rauser, Randal. "*Logos* and *Logoi Ensarkos*: Christology and a Problem of Perception." *International Journal of Systematic Theology* 5 (2003) 133–46.

Ricoeur, Paul. "The Function of Fiction in Shaping Reality." *Man and World* 12 (1979) 123–41.

———. "On Interpretation." In *Philosophy in France Today*, edited by Alan Montefiore, 175–97. Cambridge: Cambridge University Press, 1983.

———. *Oneself as Another*. Translated by Kathleen Blamey. Chicago: University of Chicago Press, 1992.

———. *Time and Narrative*. 3 vols. Translated by Kathleen McLaughlin and David Pellauer. Chicago: University of Chicago Press, 1984–88.

Ritschl, Albrecht B. *The Christian Doctrine of Justification and Reconciliation*. Vol. 3. Edited by H. R. Mackintosh and A. B. Macaulay. Edinburgh: T. & T. Clark, 1902.

———. "Instruction in the Christian Religion." In *Three Essays: Theology and Metaphysics: Prolegomena to the History of Pietism*, translated by Philip Hefner, 219–92. Philadelphia: Fortress, 1972.

Roberts, R. H. "Barth's Doctrine of Time: Its Nature and Implications." In *Karl Barth—Studies of his Theological Methods*, edited by S. W. Sykes, 88–146. Oxford: Clarendon, 1979.

Schleiermacher, F. D. E. *The Christian Faith*. Edited by H. R. Mackintosh and J. S. Stewart. Edinburgh: T. & T. Clark, 1928.

Schlitt, Dale M. *Hegel's Trinitarian Claim: A Critical Reflection*. Leiden: Brill, 1984.

———. "The Whole Truth: Hegel's Reconceptualization of Trinity." *The Owl of Minerva* 15 (1984) 169–82.

Schwöbel, Christoph. "Introduction: The Renaissance of Trinitarian Theology: Reasons, Problems and Tasks." In *Trinitarian Theology Today: Essays on Divine Being and Act*, edited by Christoph Schwöbel, 1–30. Edinburgh: T. & T. Clark, 1995.

Seitz, C. R. "Handing over the Name: Christian Reflection on the Divine Name YHWH." In *Trinity, Time, and Church: A Response to the Theology of Robert W. Jenson*, edited by Colin E. Gunton, 23–41. Grand Rapids: Eerdmans, 2000.

Shea, William M. Review of *The Triune Identity: God according to the Gospel*, by Robert W. Jenson. *Journal of the American Academy of Religion* 54 (1986) 178–79.

Steiner, George. *Real Presences*. London: Faber and Faber, 1989.

Taylor, Charles. *Hegel*. Cambridge: Cambridge University Press, 1975.

Thiselton, Anthony C. *The Two Horizons: New Testament Hermeneutics and Philosophical Description with Special Reference to Heidegger, Bultmann, Gadamer, and Wittgenstein*. Grand Rapids: Eerdmans, 1980.

Thompson, John. "Jüngel on Barth." In *The Possibilities of Theology: Studies in the Theology of Eberhard Jüngel in his Sixtieth Year*, edited by John Webster, 143–89. Edinburgh: T. & T. Clark, 1994.

Torrance, Alan J. *Persons in Communion: Trinitarian Description and Human Participation with Special Reference to Volume One of Karl Barth's Church Dogmatics*. Edinburgh: T. & T. Clark, 1996.

———. "The Trinity." In *The Cambridge Companion to Karl Barth*, edited by John Webster, 72–91. Cambridge: Cambridge University Press, 2000.

Torrance, T. F. *Divine Meaning: Studies in Patristic Hermeneutics*. Edinburgh: T. & T. Clark, 1995.

———. *Reality and Evangelical Theology*. Philadelphia: Westminster, 1982.

Vanhoozer, Kevin J. *Biblical Narrative in the Philosophy of Paul Ricoeur: A Study in Hermeneutics and Theology*. Cambridge: Cambridge University Press, 1990.

———. *The Drama of Doctrine: A Canonical Linguistic Approach to Christian Theology*. Louisville: Westminster, 2005.

Waldrop, Charles T. *Karl Barth's Christology: Its Basic Alexandrian Character*. Berlin: de Gruyter, 1984.

Ward, Graham. *Barth, Derrida and the Language of Theology*. Cambridge: Cambridge University Press, 1995.

Watson, Francis. "'America's Theologian': An Appreciation of Robert Jenson's Systematic Theology, with Some Remarks about the Bible." *Scottish Journal of Theology* 55 (2002) 201–23.

Webster, John B. *Eberhard Jüngel: An Introduction to His Theology*. Cambridge: Cambridge University Press, 1986.

———. *Holy Scripture: A Dogmatic Sketch*. Cambridge: Cambridge University Press, 2003.

———. "Justification, Analogy, and Action. Passivity and Activity in Jüngel's Anthropology." In *The Possibilities of Theology: Studies in the Theology of Eberhard Jüngel in his Sixtieth Year*, edited by John Webster, 106–42. Edinburgh: T. & T. Clark, 1994.

———. "Systematic Theology after Barth: Jüngel, Jenson, and Gunton." In *The Modern Theologians: An Introduction to Christian Theology since 1918*, edited by David F. Ford with Rachel Muers, 249–64. 3rd ed. Oxford: Blackwell, 2005.

Welch, Claude. *The Trinity in Contemporary Theology*. London, SCM, 1953.

Yeago, David S. "Catholicity, Nihilism, and the God of the Gospel: Reflections on the Theology of Robert W. Jenson." *Dialog* 31 (1992) 18–23.

Zimany, Roland Daniel. *Vehicle for God: The Metaphorical Theology of Eberhard Jüngel*. Macon: Mercer University Press, 1994.

Zizioulas, John D. *Being as Communion: Studies in Personhood and the Church*. Crestwood: St. Vladimir's Seminary Press, 1985.

Zuckmayer, Carl. *A Late Friendship: The Letters of Karl Barth and Carl Zuckmayer*. Translated by Geoffrey W. Bromiley. Grand Rapids: Eerdmans, 1982.

Subject Index

actuality 38, 123, 146, 156–58, 185n128, 191–92, 200–203, 207–8, 209n95, 209n99, 217–18, 220–22, 234–47
Alexandrian Christology 25–26, 149
analogy 2, 37–38, 42, 60, 76–80, 88, 96–102, 114, 116, 126, 154, 159, 166, 175, 177–79, 188–89, 196–200, 202–4, 217, 223–24, 226–27, 232, 243, 247, 249
anthropomorphism 192, 196, 200, 202–3, 217, 222–25, 243
aporia 30, 190–93, 195, 200, 202–3, 205, 208, 217–19, 221–22, 227
Aquinas, Thomas 47, 90, 96–100, 121n22, 196–99
Augustine, Saint 6–7, 30, 76, 130n62, 145n122, 147, 234
availability 128, 173, 180

Barth, Karl 1, 3n10, 7, 13–14, 18, 23–27, 36n211, 37–38, 53, 58–60, 61n6–8, 62–80, 114n157, 151, 159–62, 164–73, 175–76, 180, 188, 191, 225, 250
Barnes, Michael R. 132n67, 133n68–72, 134
being 2, 6–7, 11, 14–17, 19–20, 22–27, 32, 34–36, 41–42, 47, 56–58, 60, 63, 65, 67–68, 72–76, 78–80, 84, 87–89, 91–93, 97–100, 102, 108, 113–14, 118–21, 124n37, 125–32, 134–39, 144, 146n126, 149–50, 153–54, 156–57, 158n172, 159–72, 175–80, 184–91, 193–94, 196, 198–221, 223–34, 237, 242, 245–46
becoming 38, 48, 54, 58, 63n18, 82, 91–92n55, 116, 134, 145, 155, 158–60, 162–66, 169, 172, 175–76, 179, 186–88, 190–91, 204, 210, 230–32, 242–43, 249
body 152–54, 165, 169–73, 179–81, 241–42

Cappadocian fathers 7–8, 38, 117, 119–26, 128–29, 134–36, 139, 144, 237
Church, the 4–6, 8–9, 19, 21–22, 34, 39–40, 50–51, 56, 61, 66–67, 70, 73–74, 83, 85–86, 90, 105n113, 114n158, 120, 135, 137, 152–54, 156, 165, 169–75, 179–81, 191, 238, 240–42
cogito 192–93, 196, 217, 221, 232, 241
communication 9, 11, 22, 26–27, 29, 36–38, 61, 79–80, 82, 86, 113, 115, 117–18, 124, 148–51, 161, 183, 208, 221, 224, 235–37, 240, 243, 249–50
communion 2, 27n159, 38, 72, 75, 79–80, 118, 129, 150, 160, 186–87, 204, 238, 249–50

SUBJECT INDEX

consciousness 11, 17, 18n98, 19, 52n86, 70, 88, 142, 144–48, 150–51, 155–58, 181–88, 193, 208–9, 212, 214, 216, 230, 238, 244–45, 249
conversation 109, 138, 144, 146n126, 148–51, 153–54, 166, 174, 191, 240, 244
creation 15, 18, 35–36, 54, 71, 76, 91n55, 93, 113, 129–130n60, 130n62, 133, 148, 151–53, 155, 165, 170–71, 185, 187, 194, 242

Descartes, Rene 192–93, 195–96
drama 8, 12–13, 37, 39, 56–58, 67, 70, 84–86, 102–4, 107, 112, 114n157, 115–16, 122–23, 136–37, 140, 156–57, 165n42, 237–40

economic trinity 2, 8, 11, 18, 38, 58, 117, 132, 136, 157, 230–33, 238, 245, 249–50
Ebeling, Gerhard 13, 28–29, 108–9, 206n81, 212
Edwards, Jonathan 66, 91–92n55, 142n110, 151
Enlightenment, the 5, 7, 13–14, 16, 22, 60–66, 70, 73–78, 105, 159, 234–35
eschatology 45, 99–100
eucharist 169, 173
event 3–4, 8, 9n55, 10–13, 21, 23–25, 27–31, 34, 36, 38–40, 42, 47–50, 52–59, 62, 68–69, 72–77, 79–80, 87, 103–5, 107–8, 110–11, 113, 115, 116n165, 118, 121, 124–25, 130–31, 134–36, 143n116, 144, 146–49, 151–52, 154, 157, 161–67, 169, 174–80, 183–84, 188, 191, 203, 205–12, 216–18, 221–23, 225–33, 235–37, 241–47, 249–50
existence, 4, 15–16, 26, 35, 55, 64–65, 71–73, 76, 92–95, 97–99, 104, 106–9, 112, 124, 132, 136, 138–39, 150, 152, 184, 192–94, 196–97, 199, 202, 205, 213, 215–17, 225, 231, 234, 244–46
experience 6, 12, 15, 17, 20, 28, 30, 32, 39, 41, 51, 57, 65, 67, 69, 73, 76, 83, 85–86, 88, 94–95, 102–4, 107, 109–110, 131–32, 134, 145, 148–50, 152–53, 155, 177, 183, 186, 191–93, 205, 211–15, 221, 229, 239, 241, 247

Fichte, Johann Gottlieb 194–95
Frei, Hans W. 21–22, 51n76
futurity 6, 28, 30, 32, 41, 42n18, 43–51, 53–54, 57, 60, 63, 77–78, 80, 89, 107–111, 113, 122, 124n37, 127–30, 132, 153–54, 156–57, 165, 214, 219–20

God, being of 125, 144, 163–64, 178
God, death of 3, 7, 9, 11, 18, 38, 40, 44–47, 49–50, 55–57, 67–68, 75, 82, 89, 94, 103–4, 124n37, 133, 160, 176, 190–92, 195, 201, 203–4, 206, 217–18, 220–22, 224n168, 227–29, 234–35, 239, 241, 244, 246
God, the Father 5–8, 19, 22, 24, 27, 39–41, 44, 46–51, 54, 58, 60, 74–75, 78–79, 84–86, 89–93, 118–23, 125–26, 129, 131–32, 134–46, 149–51, 155–57, 161–64, 167, 176, 187n133–136, 188n137–138, 218, 227–28, 231, 236, 239
God, the Son 6, 8, 20–21, 24, 27, 34, 40–41, 44–46, 48–49, 51, 57–58, 60, 71, 74–75, 79, 83–86, 89, 92–94, 118–23, 125–26, 129, 131–46, 149–51, 153, 155–57, 161–64, 167, 176, 184, 196, 217–18, 227–29, 231, 239, 241–42
God, the Spirit 5–6, 8, 11, 16–20, 24, 27, 34, 40–41, 47–49, 51, 58, 60, 62, 65–66, 68, 74–75, 78, 83–86, 91–92n55, 93–94, 105, 119–23, 125–26, 129, 131, 133–46, 149–51, 155–57, 161–64, 167, 173, 176, 184–85, 187n133–36, 188,

SUBJECT INDEX

214–15, 218, 227–29, 231–32, 239, 244, 246
God, the Trinity 1–2, 4–5, 7–11, 13–16, 18, 19n110, 20–22, 23n127, 24–25, 27, 38, 48–52, 57–60, 62, 66–67, 73–75, 78, 83n4, 85–86, 90, 117–20, 122–24, 128–29, 132, 135–37, 139–43, 145, 149, 157, 158n172, 159–66, 168, 170, 175–76, 183–84, 190, 203–4, 217–18, 221, 227–28, 230–34, 238, 242, 245, 247, 249–50
God talk 2, 16, 27, 77, 196, 217, 241, 243
gospel 3, 4n19, 5–8, 10, 41, 45, 47–52, 56–58, 60–62, 64–65, 68, 70, 75, 82, 84–86, 89, 94–95, 110–13, 116n165, 117–19, 121–22, 135–37, 142, 148–50, 152–53, 171, 173–74, 191, 224, 226, 233–34, 236–37, 241–43, 246–47, 249
Gunton, Colin 20n117, 187, 188

Hart, David Bentley 130–32
Hart, Trevor 23n127, 27
Hegel, G. W. F. 16–18, 33n202, 64, 73, 115, 145n122, 154, 184, 186, 191, 244
hermeneutics 10–11, 51n78, 101, 104, 105n113, 114n158, 239
historicism 36
history 2, 4, 9, 12, 14–15, 18–19, 21–22, 29, 31–33, 36, 41, 45–46, 52–53, 57, 65, 67, 69–72, 75–77, 82, 86–87, 91, 94–96, 100, 105–13, 115, 121–22, 129, 146, 148, 151, 155–57, 159, 164, 169n63, 179–81, 183–86, 188, 191, 205, 209–210, 212, 218–19, 221–22, 230–31, 235–37, 240, 242
hope 3, 12, 40, 44–46, 55, 63, 66, 75, 111, 124, 129–130n60, 131–32, 134, 142–43, 217, 233, 249
human 2, 4, 9n53, 11, 15–16, 18–20, 22, 24–27, 30, 32, 34–35, 37–38, 42–44, 47, 56, 58, 61–68, 70, 72–73, 75–76, 78–80, 84–85, 87–88, 91, 93–95, 97, 99, 101, 106–110, 112, 115–18, 120, 130–32, 134, 136, 139, 148–50, 155, 159–62, 164–72, 174–88, 190–96, 197n34, 199–200, 202–19, 221–30, 232–43, 246–47, 249–50
Hunsinger, George 23n127, 36, 114n157, 158n172
Hypostasis 56n104, 78, 119–24, 128–29, 136–40

idealism 11, 18, 25, 115n161, 144
identity 2, 5–6, 8–10, 12–14, 19, 21–24, 30–34, 36–43, 44n38, 46–58, 60, 74–76, 82–84, 86, 89, 92, 94, 98, 108, 112–14, 117, 119–26, 128–29, 131n64, 134–49, 151–55, 157, 161–62, 165–66, 172–74, 178, 180–81, 184, 197–200, 204, 207–8, 213–15, 218, 221, 225–29, 231–33, 235–38, 240, 246, 249–50
imagination 18, 31, 172
immanent trinity 2, 11, 18, 58, 117, 132, 136, 230–33, 245
infinity 36, 58, 117, 120, 126–35, 144, 146, 155, 195, 238–39, 243, 246–47

Jesus Christ 4, 12, 18–21, 24–26, 35, 59, 65, 67–68, 71–76, 79, 84–85, 94–96, 100, 102–4, 107, 109, 116n165, 148–50, 161, 163–64, 168, 171–72, 176, 179–81, 183–85, 191, 196, 205–6, 217–18, 220, 223–25, 228–30, 232
justification 2, 12, 33n202, 34–35, 53, 159n1, 220n147, 222, 225–27

Kant, Immanuel 1, 14–16, 18–20, 61, 222n161

language 3, 5, 9, 12–13, 26–29, 31, 37–38, 58, 77, 79–80, 82–83, 85–86, 88–92, 94–105, 108–117, 122, 131, 148, 153, 158, 162, 177–78, 182–86, 188, 191–92, 196, 200, 202–3, 206–13, 215–17, 222n159–160, 223–26, 229–33, 235–38, 240–41, 243, 247

SUBJECT INDEX

love 17, 20, 44–49, 52, 54–55, 57, 71, 75, 101, 132, 146, 149, 156–57, 209, 218, 220–22, 225, 227–33, 236, 244–48, 250
Luther, Martin 33–35, 46n53
Lutheran 14, 33–35, 160, 187

Mattes, Mark C. 33n202, 34, 35n208, 36n212, 37
Maximus Confessor 149
McCormack, Bruce 23n127, 27n159, 27n162, 78–80, 114, 169n63
metaphor 26, 41, 159, 165, 170, 173, 177n99, 187–88
modalism 48, 132, 135, 138, 141, 144, 156, 158
Molnar, Paul 36
Moltmann, Jürgen 1, 14
Mühlenberg, Ekkehard 129–30

Narrative 2, 5–6, 8–9, 11–14, 16, 21–22, 24, 29–37, 39–43, 47, 49–52, 53n91, 54, 56–58, 60, 74–76, 78, 82, 84–86, 94, 100, 102–5, 107, 110, 113–14, 116–17, 119, 121–24, 129, 135–38, 140, 142, 148, 152, 154, 156–57, 159, 165, 174–75, 183–86, 191, 196, 206, 229, 232–33, 235–37, 240–42, 249
Nietzsche, Friedrich 7, 194–95, 201–2, 234, 239
nihilism 3–4, 35, 63, 103, 160, 191, 233, 244, 246
nothingness 3, 63, 201, 218–22, 233, 246

objectivity 18, 147, 167–73, 175, 205, 212, 216, 241
ontic 34, 59, 130, 165, 171, 182–83, 186, 198–200
ontological 6, 8, 11, 15–16, 20, 22, 29, 33–34, 60, 65, 73, 75, 82n1, 86, 91–94, 96–99, 101–2, 107, 110, 112–13, 123–24, 128–30, 145, 147, 154, 165, 170, 173, 181–82, 184, 186, 190, 196, 198–201, 204, 207, 209–10, 212, 217–18, 221, 224, 228, 238

ontology 16, 34, 38, 58, 65, 96, 117, 182n115, 186n132, 190–91, 204, 206, 210, 215–17, 223, 225, 228, 230, 232–34, 247, 249
Origen 90–96, 100, 145n122

person 1, 7–9, 14–17, 19–20, 22, 27n159, 29, 32, 34–35, 38, 40–42, 46, 48, 56–58, 62, 71–73, 80, 85, 93, 95, 108, 113–14, 115n161, 116n165, 117, 121n22, 122–25, 128–29, 133n68, 136–52, 154–58, 165–67, 169, 171–74, 177, 186, 208–9, 212–13, 218, 223, 224n168, 225, 229, 230–31, 233, 237, 239–40, 244–46
possibility 2, 24–25, 32, 38, 46–47, 63–64, 68, 78, 80, 91–92, 105–6, 123, 131, 149, 152, 161, 185n128, 190–92, 200–207, 209n95, 209n99, 212, 216–22, 226, 233–35, 240, 243, 246–47, 249–50
postmodern 3, 37, 142, 159
presence 20, 26, 45, 55, 91, 108–9, 150, 152–54, 165, 169, 171–72, 180, 182n117, 191, 211, 212–15, 229, 241
promise 5, 10, 13, 20n117, 32, 37–39, 43–47, 50–52, 54–57, 75, 110–11, 113, 124, 146, 148, 154, 156–58, 173–74, 179, 191, 205, 215, 221, 226, 235–38, 241–42, 244, 246–47

realism 9, 11n63, 13, 25, 45n46, 82, 112, 114–15, 191, 206n80, 212, 221, 226, 233, 239n250, 246–47
reality 2, 4, 9–12, 14, 16, 18–34, 37–39, 46, 52, 54–55, 58–61, 65–75, 77–82, 86, 88–97, 99–104, 107–13, 114n156, 115, 117–18, 122–24, 128n49, 134–40, 144–48, 152–60, 163–66, 168, 170–74, 180, 182, 186, 193, 197, 204–7, 211–12, 218, 220–22, 226, 229, 233, 235–42, 246, 249

relation 4, 8, 12–15, 19, 21–23, 25, 27, 29, 32, 34–35, 37–39, 41, 48–50, 56n104, 57, 60, 65, 68–70, 72, 77–86, 98–99, 101–3, 106, 108–9, 113, 116n165, 120–22, 128–31, 135–36, 138–40, 144–46, 149–50, 153, 155, 159, 161, 163–65, 169, 175–79, 181–82, 185, 187–88, 190, 192, 197–99, 203–4, 206n81, 207–8, 210–18, 221, 223–26, 231–35, 241, 243, 245–47, 249–50
revisionary metaphysics 2, 8–13, 34, 53n91, 117, 120, 125, 135, 235–36, 239–41, 244, 246
Ricoeur, Paul 13–14, 30–33, 124
Ritschl, Albrecht 18, 20
Roberts, Richard 26

Schleiermacher, F. D. E. 1, 7n43, 14, 18–19, 63–64
selflessness 225, 230–31, 245–47
self-relatedness 93, 176, 225, 227, 230–31, 245–47
space 11n63, 12–13, 15, 27, 38, 43–44, 46, 69, 80, 85–86, 126, 129–30n60, 147–53, 155, 158–59, 164–65, 170, 175, 182, 194n15, 246
story 8, 13, 30, 32, 37, 39, 41, 49–52, 54–58, 73, 75, 77, 80, 85–86, 88, 102–5, 107–13, 115, 124, 140, 146, 148, 152, 157, 185, 191, 218, 228–30, 236–38, 242, 246
subjectivity 7

temporal 2, 6, 8, 11, 28–30, 32, 36–38, 41, 43, 48–49, 52, 55–56, 58, 60, 67–69, 73, 75–78, 80–81, 87–91, 91–92n55, 93, 95, 98, 100, 103–5, 108–110, 117–18, 121, 124, 126–32, 134–36, 140–41, 144, 146–47, 153, 155–59, 178–79, 185, 188–89, 191, 201, 212–15, 219, 230, 234–40, 242–43, 246–47, 249–50

thinking after 161, 204–5, 212, 215, 217–18, 232, 239–41
time 3–6, 8, 11n63, 13, 15, 21–23, 26, 28, 30–33, 36–38, 40–41, 43–44, 47–50, 53–56, 60, 64, 67–72, 76–78, 80, 82, 87–93, 99, 101, 103–5, 108–9, 111–15, 117–19, 122–25, 127–37, 140–41, 143–44, 147, 150–53, 155–58, 164–65, 167, 169, 172–73, 175–77, 179–80, 185–86, 194, 207, 212, 214–15, 219, 228, 230, 237, 242, 244, 250
timeless 2, 4, 6–8, 11, 14–16, 36, 53n89, 54, 59–61, 65, 70, 72–73, 75–80, 82, 87–93, 96, 100, 119, 122–23, 127, 129, 134–35, 145–46, 150, 153–54, 156, 178–79, 191, 201, 219, 233–35, 243, 245–46
Torrance, Alan 24, 27n159, 79, 80n98
Torrance, Thomas F. 82n1, 114, 116n165
traditional metaphysics 8, 73, 83, 91, 97, 99, 101, 160, 178, 190–96, 200–203, 217–19, 234–35

Vanhoozer, Kevin 12n69, 32n197, 114n17, 115n162–163, 116n165

Waldrop, Charles 25–27
Ward, Graham 26
Watson, Francis 37n224, 42n21, 86n25–26
Webster, John B. 3, 22, 36, 159n1, 160n3, 160n5, 161, 205n74
Welch, Claude 1, 20, 22n126
Wolfhart Pannenberg 3, 36
word-event 2, 10–11, 13, 23, 25–29, 38, 101, 108–13, 115, 117–18, 150, 153, 159–60, 175, 178–79, 183, 188–90, 204, 212, 221, 223, 226, 230–33, 236, 242–43, 245–47, 249–50

Yeago, David 4n19, 11–12, 36n212

Zizioulas, John 128, 129n54

www.ingramcontent.com/pod-product-compliance
Lightning Source LLC
Chambersburg PA
CBHW071247230426
43668CB00011B/1625